women : poetry : migration [an anthology]

women:
poetry:
migration

AN ANTHOLOGY

edited by
Jane Joritz-Nakagawa

Copyright © 2017
ISBN-13: 978-0-9883891-6-8

Acknowledgments:
Cover Design: Jeremy Luke
Artwork: Steve Seidenberg *www.sjseidenberg.com*

theenk Books
107 Washington Street
Palmyra, New York 14522

To order: *http://theenkBooks.com*
Email: theenkbooks@twc.com

Exile (to echo Edmond Jabès) is a fundamental condition of poetry. These 50 poets make diaspora home ground. They are the lightning rods of a non-national poetry of "between" that pushes against nativism through sheer aesthetic exuberance and necessity of innovation.

– **Charles Bernstein**

Women : Poetry : Migration is a superb, refreshing anthology. As nationalism and the rigidity of territorial and linguistic boundaries, under challenge, erode, this anthology of poetry by women provides a wide-ranging and innovative look at this migratory time in the writing of poetry. Migratory in terms of place and the changing nature of location, undergoing challenge and redefinition in terms of gender identity, and in transit as a polylingual consciousness and multilingual ways of writing become more and more evident. My congratulations to the editor for her vision, imagination, and persistence, and to the women who have contributed such remarkable writing to the anthology.

– **Hank Lazer**

Jane Joritz-Nakagawa has undertaken a remarkable editorial task in bringing together avant-garde women poets who are also migrants. If, as Susan Suleiman wrote, the avant-garde woman poet is doubly marginalised, then these poets are in a triple lock of marginalisation. Yet, as the anthology demonstrates, this can be a source of strength and transformation, which gives them a centrality, not only in their own lives, but in the cultural development of their adopted country. Indeed, some of these poets have played a crucial role in shaking up mainstream poetics.

– **Frances Presley**

"On google earth I write down my name," writes Ania Walwicz in this ecstatic anthology, *Women : Poetry : Migration*. With sharp eye and ear, Jane Joritz-Nakagawa has gathered arresting, often experimental, poetry by women living outside the lands of their birth. These are poems where the "trans" – translation; transculture; transformation – inhabits the unsettling language of identity and location, with multiplicity, cosmopolitanism and the "push and pull" (Bella Li) of writing desire. Every page offers shifts of imagery or perspective as witness to embodiment, alterity, and hybridities of language. In the plural worlds of the poets, we hear how border crossing constructs a life (Fawzia Afzal-Khan) and "utopianism" always "goes wrong" (Donna Stonecipher).

– **Anne Elvey**

"Where am I going? I am getting there." Amanda Ngoho Reavey's words might serve as a motto for this wide-ranging, transnational anthology, which gathers 50 women poets who live in countries other than the ones in which they were born. This premise is the spark for an explosion of aesthetic experimentation that both maps and crosses boundaries of gender and nation. From the shuttling between Japan and Canada, Vietnam and Australia, or Zimbabwe and the United States, the authors gathered here elucidate a poetics formed in process.

– Timothy Yu

My response to this collection is subjective, as I was once someone who lived and wrote for a while outside of my native land. In *Women : Poetry : Migration*, I could relive the excitement of pleasurable dislocation I felt some of the time I lived abroad. For instance, I liked experimenting or "deconsecrating" one language with another language to "make it clearer" (Jody Pou) and discovering through writing "what I don't know" (Tsitsi Jaji). That said, this collection is open to any reader who is engaged by thoughtful, sensual, humorous and political ideas. In her essay in this anthology, Rosmarie Waldrop concludes, "If the poem works . . . it will set off vibrations in the reader, an experience with language – with the way it defines us as human beings." I certainly felt the reverberation of language(s) as I read the poems and essays in this collection. It's up to us as readers what we do next.

– Deborah Richards

This anthology edited by Jane Joritz-Nakagawa is more than a poetic fact. It is a political fact because it presents to the public poets displaced from their countries and in conflict with their cultures. Perhaps this is the definition of poetry: art in conflict with languages and origins. Jane Joritz-Nakagawa offers to the reader double exiles: the exile of the tongue and the full "exile" of the female voice in patriarchal societies. Joritz-Nakagawa, in the words of the Brazilian modernist poet Oswald de Andrade, reinstitutes the "matriarchy of Pindorama." It is a work of breadth and rigor, which deserves all attention and applause. As contributor Safaa Fathy states: "I write about what I lost." Migrating is at the center of being a poet; this anthology also answers the question of what poetry is. And maybe this is what we ultimately gain from Joritz-Nakagawa's anthology.

– Régis Bonvicino

CONTENTS

INTRODUCTION / x
ADEENA KARASICK / 1
AMANDA NGOHO REAVEY / 8
ANDREA BRADY / 13
ANGELA CARR / 19
ANIA WALWICZ / 25
ANNE TARDOS / 28
BARBARA BECK / 34
BELLA LI / 38
CARRIE ETTER / 43
CECILIA VICUÑA / 49
CHRIS TYSH / 55
CIA RINNE / 61
CRISTINA RIVERA GARZA / 67
DONNA STONECIPHER / 73
ÉIREANN LORSUNG / 78
ZHANG ER / 83
FAWZIA AFZAL-KHAN / 89
HAZEL SMITH / 100
IVY ALVAREZ / 105
JANE JORITZ-NAKAGAWA / 109
JANE LEWTY / 115
JENNIFER K. DICK / 122
JENNIFER KRONOVET / 129
JI YOON LEE / 134
JODY POU / 139
LARESSA DICKEY / 147

LEA GOLDBERG / 153

LEE ANN BROWN / 157

LISA SAMUELS / 163

M. NOURBESE PHILIP / 168

MAIRÉAD BYRNE / 174

MARCELA SULAK / 179

MEGAN M. GARR / 187

MICHELLE NAKA PIERCE / 193

MỘNG-LAN / 200

NANCY GAFFIELD / 208

NATHANAËL / 215

NORMA COLE / 220

PATRICIA DEBNEY / 226

WANG PING / 231

RACHEL TZVIA BACK / 247

ROSMARIE WALDROP / 251

RULA JURDI / 256

SAFAA FATHY / 262

SASCHA AURORA AKHTAR / 268

SHARMILA COHEN / 275

SHEIDA MOHAMADI / 281

SUN YUNG SHIN / 289

TSITSI JAJI / 295

YUKO OTOMO / 301

NOTES ON TRANSLATIONS / 307

CONTRIBUTOR BIODATA / 309

ACKNOWLEDGEMENTS / 322

NOTES / 325

INTRODUCTION ───────────────

women : poetry : migration [an anthology]

After having lived in Japan for quite some years (almost half my life) though born in the U.S., as a poet who uses a different language for her poetry than for most of her daily life, as somebody who feels both part of the local mainstream and not part of the mainstream, over time I came to become intensely curious about other women poets living in countries other than that of their birth -- women poets moreso than men poets due to feeling outside the mainstream as a woman (in a male-dominated society/world), not just as a person who grew up elsewhere and has a foreign passport and whose primary daily language is her second versus first language. How does a woman's knowledge of more than one language and culture affect her and her poetry? was something I wanted to investigate further by finding and reading poetry by other women for whom this is the case. What kind of eclecticism, richness or complexity might occur for those of us whose lives and work encompasses more than one culture? Of course I am using "culture" in a certain sense, although its use nowadays is broad and also rightfully includes such things as gender, sexual orientation, living with disability, age, income level, possession of a home, and other factors and characteristics too numerous to list here.

Be that as it may, I began work on this anthology in the summer of 2015 by contacting female poets whose work could be called innovative / experimental / avant-garde / adventurous and who were or would be (at the time of submitting her work) living in a country other than that of her birth (as I wished to exclude repatriates). In fact I didn't know or think I knew many poets who fit these criteria. There are many more of us out there of course than I initially was aware of, and this book only represents a small sampling. I hope that the work of more poets not collected here might be included in future volumes. I'm grateful to the many poets who introduced other poets to me for this anthology. I know that there are yet more poets I'll continue to find out about. Most of the poems in this anthology are written in English by poets for whom this is a first language. There are exceptions, however; for some poets English is a second language and some works are in English translation; of fifty poets forty-nine of us are still living. While not a world poetry anthology, but, rather, a migrant one, an attempt was made to find an interesting cross-section of work by many poets from a variety of regions. But we do not represent all migrant poets of course. And in the end, our work only represents itself.

I felt and feel there is a need for an anthology of poetry exclusively by women like this one for many reasons related to both gender and multiculturalism. Despite progress, there is of course lingering inequality in our world for women including sometimes a devaluing of our work products and ignorance about what we think and feel and how we wish to live (things unique to each woman of course although at the same time somewhat broadly generalizable under patriarchy). There is a clear need for more understanding of the cross-cultural type overall, including a need to strive to address the inequality of minorities including minority poets, even in or especially in "nations of immigrants" like my native U.S. as well as a country like Japan where I live now where non-Japanese comprise less than 2% of the total population, or elsewhere. I feel concerned about what seems to be an unfortunate emphasis on regionalism which even affects many poetry anthologies. There have been in recent years for example many excellent English language poetry anthologies devoted exclusively to poetry in the U.S., or in the U.K., or other countries, or of poets belonging to specific ethnic groups in specific countries, or related to ecopoetry in specific countries, or LGBTQ poets in specific countries, or women poets of specific regions and so on. Why the regional focus? The country we were born in is not something we choose and geographical boundaries were created by others. Although many of the contributors to this anthology are either living in or are originally from the U.S., a country with a large foreign-born population, all are certainly not.

Peter Caws (1994) has written: "every 'first' or 'native' culture . . . is not something one has freely chosen or worked to acquire" and thus "the development of an authentic identity . . . require[s] the transcendence of one's culture of origin" (p.371-372). Luce Irigaray has proclaimed: "Women cannot be self-assured without language and systems of representation being transformed, because these are appropriate to men's subjectivity" (1993 p. 96). Julia Kristeva has asserted "all identities are unstable: the identity of linguistic signs, the identity of meaning and, as a result, the identity of the speaker" (1994, p 110) whereas Dani Cavallaro explained: "the notion of a conscious and unified self is imaginary . . ." noting that this insight "is relevant to contemporary feminism because it stresses there are no given identities and that there is therefore nothing sacred or immutable about . . . patriarchal definitions of woman" (2003, p. 78).

Although keenly aware of my own gender as marked, as other, as non-mainstream under patriarchy, while starting to draft the introduction to this book I heard and am now still hearing on the television news repeatedly stories about a "migrant crisis" in Europe, fearful reactions of rightwing politicians and citizens concerning the inflow of migrants into various countries, talk of the erection of new boundaries and border patrols to keep out migrants, both legal and illegal, violence and protests against migrants, and presidential candidates in various countries using xenophobia as political platforms. Clearly, more public xenophilia might be a good thing.

Yet many of us here will be considered (by others and ourselves) relatively or even highly privileged persons as we may have secured the essentials for physical survival and much more, and many of us left our home countries voluntarily without undue duress. A large number of people worldwide including many migrants of course live in poverty, in war zones, experience hunger, disease, violence, slavery, incarceration, are homeless.... Many of the migrants we learn about via mass media are homeless, poor, and in danger. And of course while women and minorities may take the brunt of the world's poverty and sexual violence the world's problems obviously affect us all.

An American professor of Islamic studies recently appeared on a BBC program broadcast here in Japan, summarizing statistics concerning rising Islamophobia in my native post-9-11 U.S. Recently I hear less in the news about rape of women on buses in India. I've just recently seen documentaries about honor killings, child sexual abuse, rape of boys believed linked to gender segregation in their societies and a social notion of female "purity", and Western college campus rape of women, among other gender-related atrocities, as well as a news story about fifty people being killed by a gunman at an LGBT bar in the U.S.; another gunman intending to kill LGBT persons elsewhere was arrested before he had the chance to carry it out. While we may try to brush off these kinds of incidents as perpetuated by people "unlike ourselves," that doesn't seem to be the case. Many of us as well as our friends and relatives have been victims of similar kinds of actions. Some even surmise that in many parts of the world xenophobia and misogyny could be on the rise, perhaps in conjunction with globalized economies creating more losers in the game called capitalism.

To offer some hope perhaps, in *Strangers to Ourselves* (1991), Julia Kristeva wrote of "our [human] disturbing otherness" but stated: "by recognizing our uncanny strangeness we shall neither suffer from it nor enjoy it from the outside. The foreigner is within me, hence we are all foreigners. If I am a foreigner, there are no foreigners" (p. 192). As a poet attempting to write an introduction to a poetry anthology of migrant women's work, I am also thinking of language itself as foreign. Japanese poet Kora Rumiko said in an interview that she " . . . felt even as a child that language was not mine, that I existed outside the language that surrounded me, like a foreigner . . . (in

Buckley, 1997, p. 104). Here she is discussing her first language, Japanese, not a second or third one.

How do I write an introduction like this? I'm trying to explain why and how this book was created, and/or what the book's premise is. But I don't think there is one premise. And I think each poet's work here of course should be looked at individually. The introduction thus far is only or mostly my thinking, not the thinking of all fifty of us. Even so, part of me wants to go back further, even to talk about my childhood in a suburb called South Holland where I donned wooden shoes and Dutch dress and danced in the annual tulip festival with the other children, even though none of us were in fact Dutch, where I came to long to live in a more multicultural place than my white middle class suburb, long before moving to Japan.

In a Japanese resort town called Kiyosato, not far from my current home in the mountainous section of a small farming village in central Japan, was (it closed in the fall of 2015) a very small modern art museum that specialized in Fluxus art. A few years ago there I picked up a pamphlet about American sculptor Richard Nonas which includes an anecdote describing Nonas noticing he could make art by having pieces of wood communicate with each other by putting them in proximity. This interested me because poets do this with words as their objects, and at the time I was thinking that was what I was doing as a poet, making words, phrases and occasionally sentences communicate with each other in the context of a poem. I wonder what kind of dialogue occurs for the reader by reading poems by women doing innovative work in countries other than that of their birth in proximity with each other within this anthology. Do interesting themes or concepts such as displacement, indeterminacy and/or rupture surface? Are complexities associated with our identities apparent? In what ways do the or some poems reflect or reference more than one language or culture? Once again, by culture these days we refer not only to geographical regions of course but also gender, shared sociopolitical outlook, language background, skin color, sexual orientation, (not) living with disabilities, ethnicities, religious beliefs and other factors and identities, life circumstances, and attributes, unique to each person but at the same time creating potential circumstances for establishing or maintaining human connection.

Kristeva (1991 p. 110) conflates Machiavellism with patriotism. Catherine Belsey (2002), following the work of Lyotard, has noted: "The avant-garde is not just a matter of style. Because it poses questions, it undermines all certainties, including the certainty that you possess the truth—and are entitled to kill people in its name" (chapter 5, Kindle version, n.p.).

In this volume, Marcella Sulak comments in her essay titled MY POETRY I BELIEVE IS LOCATED. IT IS I WHO IS NOT "It feels as if the etymological root Locute should be related to Locate, because what you are allowed to say, what you think to say, depends a great deal on where you are and who you are talking to and who else is listening (i.e. why you are talking)." Angela Carr writes "I am interested in the possibility of bilocation, that is the possibility to be both here and there simultaneously, or to be here in there and away from there at once." Fawzia Afzal Khan explains that her poetry "sits astride, explores and emerges from the border crossings that make up my life." Ivy Alvarez comments that being uprooted "gives me the advantage of the outsider, one who looks in, is never comfortable, always questions, observes, records." Michelle Naka Pierce writes of "a transitional space, occupying a position at, or on both sides of, a boundary or threshold." Mong-Lan states: "I write what I witness, what I feel and think, bridging cultures, bridging understanding between the sexes and human beings. To make people drunk with words, yet also make people sober" while Sharmila Cohen states that her "work is preoccupied with the spaces between language and cultures, the places where one thing can't necessarily be transposed into another context and still look the same." Rosmarie Waldrop comments "The fact that I am a woman clearly shapes my writing, but does not determine it exclusively. The writer, male or female, is only one partner in the process of writing. Language, in its full range, is the other." Donna Stonecipher writes: "In my poems I am interested in exploring travel and and how it touches on ethics, privilege, and aesthetics. I've long been intrigued by what I call "voluntary exiles," people who without economic or political imperative choose to live in a country in which they were not born and/or are not citizens. The trivium of love, job, fellowship does not apply to these seekers. What are they looking for? Why do they willingly give up the support system of family, citizenship, native tongue, a known culture, for the unknown?" Éireanne Lorsung states: "I associate home more and more with the feeling of safety, and safety more and more with an abolition of borders, prisons, and surveillance. And finally, I'd like to quote Jennifer Kronovet: "In writing, I try to remain foreign to myself, to my tongue, to keep my way of seeing from settling over what it doesn't match, from levelling the territory."

Selections from fifty poets' work plus short accompanying essays follow. While reading these poems and essays, I hope readers may make their own connections and draw if they wish their own conclusions -- "building something new with the existing blocks" [Sharmila Cohen, in this volume].

Many of the works here might be described as difficult or complex, requiring patience or re-readings, thinking and empathy, imagination and resourcefulness -- the sorts of skills useful, we could say, in refiguring others, in crossing borders of various types.

Jane Joritz-Nakagawa
Nagano and Shizuoka, Japan

References

Belsey, C. 2002. *Poststructuralism*. Oxford: Oxford University Press.

Buckley, S. (ed/trans) 1993. *Broken silence: voices of Japanese feminism*. Berkeley: University of California Press.

Cavallaro, D . 2003. *French feminist theory*. London: Continuum.

Caws, P. 1994. Identity: cultural, transcultural, and multicultural. In D. T. Goldberg, *Multiculturalism: a critical reader*. Oxford: Blackwell, pp. 371-372.

Irigaray, L. 1993. *Je tu, nous: towards a culture of difference*. Trans. A. Martin. London: Routledge.

Kristeva, J. 1991. *Strangers to ourselves*. Trans. L. S. Roudiez. New York: Columbia University Press.

THANK YOUS

In addition to the contributing poets, I'd like to thank the following people for providing advice, encouragement, and information helpful for this anthology:

Charles Bernstein
Mei-mei Berssenbrugge
Chana Bloch
Pam Brown
Ken Edwards
Tony Frazer
Jen Hofer
Paul Hoover
Brenda Iijima
Jeremy Luke
Hank Lazer
Harryette Mullen
Aldon Lynn Nielsen
Lauri Ramey
Lisa Robertson
Judy Roitman
Susan Schultz
Steven Seidenberg
Eric Selland
Steve Tills

I'm sure there are others to whom I am indebted who I have failed to name. For that I sincerely apologize and hope to make future amends!

ADEENA KARASICK

from *Salomé: Woman of Valor*

Song of Salomé

Drape me with wild
rampage, wrought
mementos, re-chérched embers:
we will be riddled in juicy entrées,
we will remember the aching logos
like fragrant trysts
indices of iffy hysteria

I am a bricolage but cadenced.
Oh yes, a draughter of rused asylum
as the tenets of catered radar
as the torqued courtiers of silly men

*

How fancy
you are, rhizome,
disguised as love

How fickle
like phonemic fairies
of jouissance
woven gatherer

How grand
our bet of levity
our grafters of cinders
our engines of deceit

*

And what shadowed abyss
of taut turns is riddled by the flux
      of campy anon

And what breathy mambo
of moaning nomads
is frothing in the foolscape of
your wet roulette?
What sluiced verity
What twangy biases
What cooing lurks in the sashay of racy traces

Dear preponderance,
the mounting inertia
of flailing labors
bedside
like chaperoned tenets

                *

I have parsed thee, oh my love,
to a symphony of hollers
in the flurry of riot

Come with me
My livre
Come away

For the langue whet with mouthy repasts
terrains of slang blurred slinging
in the penned err of puffy affect
furtive inertia nourishing debris and fine
gowned figura and rendered gaps
gowned and trendy, vagrant

                *

Come myth me
my livre
campy mélée

*

Come, crooked surplus
Succumb, let me harness you

Your viscous lacquer of weighted eros
Your bountiful brooding

like a chimera
of mounting salience
In the curve
of the raucous
In the shadowed fancy
of ranty contretemps

My beloved saunters as a cluster
of confers in the
zippers of giddy engines

*

How fine
your artifice, my labyrinth
your aisles of meandering thirst
growing utopias
of martyred homily.

Your lair –
as brackish as giddy
swindles of sloped polis.

Your tracings –
A flickering of shapely
frames, dramas
of twitched myths, wild fielder!

Your ellipses –
like woven treads
groomed slick

A glom of plummy grammés –
your fiery hiding
through hewed veils.

*

How phantomatic
you are my livery,
map of perfumed affects

I have coveted / oh my love, a
tympany of hors-text
A paste of wild parses.
Poesis of sweet disorder

***

JuSt dAnCe, DanCe foR Me dAnCe
FOr RHyThM IS a DAnCeR,

a PRiVaTe DaNcEr, RAin DaNcEr moOnDaNCe,
sALOmé yOu ArE tHe DaNcInG QuEeN
DAnCe nOw SAlOmÉ COmE
dNnCiNg In tHe nJgHt oF thE dAnCiNg fLaMe DaNcinG
oN tHe CeiLiNg, iN tHe DArK, JuSt pUt On YoUr red sHoeS aNd dAnCe

'caUsE yOu WerE mAde for DaNciNg, DaNCiNg IN tHe STreEet
iN tHe mOoNlIgHt, sALoME dO YOu WaAnNa daNcE NoW

iN a laNd oF a 1000 DaNceS, MUsiC boX DAnCeR,
dANcE mE tO tHe EnD oF LoVe,

DaNCe oN gLAasS, oN a VoLcaNO daNcE wiTh mE
aNd doN't foRgeT to daNcE, daNcE tHe NiGhT aWay
JuSt DanCe litTLe SiSteR, TiNy DaAnCer aNd
SAvE tHe Last DaNcE fOr mE

***

Salomé, I have purloined riddles like rooms riffing with revery wrested screams of gilded debt, torqued like the ballyhoo of fluid numena, billowing singes sensors, the solace of shawled myth, Salomé I will bestow it upon you shower you with the carousel of saucy insouciance strewn elixir; and I will give it all to you excess upon excess angles of undulance, kinships of crystal caverns quarries of fluted treasure, measures menageries fashioned from the luxurious garments of stretched letters

*

And as shadows scream masked
in the fury of decay
yes i will yes say yes i *will* dance
an au courant bon vivant vampy-amped
nymphy symphony
an uproarious emporium
of morbid dysphoria

i *will* dance

nested with buttered languing, a festive tempest of flitting iterates glistening through, a slippery ellipsis, lexical elixir, archived in feverish torrents parsed in the spectres of a purring circus

la corPSe d'accord encore de la corpse succor d'accord courting ma coeur la corpse succor ma coeur encore. Encore. Encore. Encore. Encore. D'accord

HEADEROGLOSSIA

*And if the origin of "martyr" (martur) is witness
no one bears witness for the witness
who witnesses the witness
blind witness –*

These selections are from *Salomé: Woman of Valor* the libretto for a multi-media performance / spoken word opera I have been working on, that revisions the apocryphal narrative, historically perverted by patriarchy and prejudice.

I have always been fascinated by the myth of Salomé as a Jewish woman who's been violently misrepresented through history. compulsively drawn into a world of conflicting histories, myths, legends and became passionately dedicated to creating a work where Salomé was not repeatedly victimized, scapegoated and silenced, but opened a space of female empowerment.

Traversing through Conceptual homophonic translations of both Strauss and Wilde monologues, midrashic interpretations, Kabbalistic infusions, and a Conceptualist re-working of the Song of Songs (now Song of Salomé), drenched with semi(o)tic desire, Salomé is re-contextualized, made new.

The term "Woman of Valor" (in Hebrew, *Eshet Chayil*) comes from Proverbs 31. The text is originally a 22 verse Hebrew acrostic, each verse beginning with a different Hebrew letter and is usually sung on the eve of Shabbat by a husband to his wife, praising her as a valiant woman, mother and partner. According to Aggadic Midrashim (the interpretation of the non-legal portions of the Torah), the poem was originally composed by Abraham as a eulogy for his wife Sarah. Kabbalistically read, the poem is a reference to the *Shekhinah* (The Female indwelling, divine Presence), the soulmate of the Jewish nation, and also understood as a song to the Shabbas Queen and Torah itself. But, throughout history, as Salome has been deemed a seductress and "murderess" to attribute the term valor to her, is wildly ironic. However upon closer investigation, the term "valor" cross linguistically references *voir. vouloir*. And if *voir* (Fr) is *to see* (re-see), *vouloir* (Fr) is *to want*, I am interested in ways Salomé becomes an embodiment of courage, bravery, daring and desire – which is explored through fragmentation, stuttering, ranting, intrusion, adaptation, homage, parricide, intertextual spectrality, hypertextual palimpsest, echoes, assemblage, grafts and inversions.

And if from the ancient Greek, *Orcheomai* means to both "dance" and to "play". And if in French *joue* as in *jouissance,* is about playing and coming, Between the dance of veils and the "dance of the intellect" where "the play's the thing" and "subjectivity is always-coming," I am committed to a playful dance of language where Salomic texts erupt as a joue/ jewey ārche *oh my!* of contemporaneous desire.

AMANDA NGOHO REAVEY

from *Marilyn*

It started with walking. But I wonder if most things start with walking.

Walking. Towards red.   The catalyst.

Fear.

Not finding red. Instead. Abyss. Abysmal. A bay. A bahay. A bahay kubo. In Cebuano, this means "house-cube." It is a house-on-stilts. My friend's uncle won't leave the bamboo house-on-stilts.

Where am I going? I am getting there.

In the jungle there is a foreboding that surrounds a sentence. It lactates. It drowns.

They say that by the time a child is one year old her brain has been wired to know and understand only the phonemes of the language that surrounds her.

I spent eight years in speech therapy learning how English letters and words should be formed in my mouth. Hollow. The tip of the tongue placed behind the back of the top teeth. Bared. Legs – I mean, lips – spread.

A slight vibration as the air pushes out. Unlike Tagalog, the 'S' is voiceless. Like the /s/ in 'self.' Or 'citizen.' But what if you have something to say and can't understand an English tongue?

A barefoot girl in a black dress twirls in the moonshine.

Will English never be mine?

Last night I cried myself to sleep. Dreamt I was barefoot on red soil. Climbing a balete tree. Someone called my name: Marilyn. A tin roof and no windows. To keep the cool inside. Humidity out. Humility. Tropical architecture is tricky.

In 2011, I returned to the Philippines. Took a 14-hour ferry from Cebu to Iloilo, then a 15-minute pumpboat to Guimaras. Where they are famous for their mangos. They trade them. Below a
20-foot cross that lights up at night.

This man. I picked him up in a basement bar. Fervent with theatre lights. He wants to know more about this relationship. To place. To place something. To find place. To find self in place. To self. To identity. To water. To family. To mangos.

Yes, I desire to know more too.

I hate mangos.

Meeeennngggooooohhhh. That is how my friend says it. She is a writer from Cebu. Met her for the first time while living in Italy, having won a scholarship to study fine arts on the outskirts of Pistoia. And later, in Greece. On a beautiful island called Paros. Five hours by ferry from Athens. Reminds me of Manila. Gritty.

In Athens, we dance with transients in Monasteraki. We bum cigarettes. And Mythos, a kind of beer. Children hold out an empty palm and a yellow rose. They ask: *Tha thélate na agorásete éna louloúdi*? Would you like to buy a flower? It is late, but they are not allowed to go home until the roses are sold. We cannot afford to pay them.

Malakas. The first Greek word I learned. It means 'bastard.'
But in Tagalog it means 'one who is strong.'

The children fall asleep in our laps.

ESSAY

From the perspective of a transnational, transracial adoptee, I explore liminal spaces and that which cannot be said. I'm interested in the very real yet not concrete space within the borderline. In other words, *not* the edge of something, but in fact the space contained *within* the edge itself: names, identities, race, countries, language, politics, economics, (mis)memory and family.

I am particularly interested in institutions (orphanages, foster care, immigration system, etc.), their effects on child development including dissociation, and healing through the re-discovery of ancestral language. Each fragment (sentence) reminds me of tesserae, the small tiles or pieces of glass used in making a mosaic. How they make up one's narrative. How the weaving of these fragments also represents *basahan*. In Tagalog, this means "tattered rag" or a piece of waste. However, in other translations, it means "the person being read to," its Malay root word is *basa* meaning "language," and in my ancestral language, bikol-naga, *basahan* is the written script. I think often of how language is connected to perspective, understanding and transformation. It has the ability to re-member the body and to reconcile contradictions, or at least, it gives us a space in which to hold them.

But if you have lost that language and are thus, left only with the body? How do you articulate this disenfranchised grief? And, perhaps more important, how do you find a language you can live in?

ANDREA BRADY

from *THE BLUE SPLIT COMPARTMENTS*

OPENED

It sits on smooth parquet, reflecting
scarlet upward   boxy the gorge the manufactured
throat, square, edged in crimson and breathing
coppers green into sickness but for the feather
duster of the Djibouti zero-
hour cleaner. The sides press
neither outward nor inward   reliably
dry, independent of scrutiny
but not uninviting. The void is ample
because it is finite, the stub bottoms out
bleeding out verbs and stroking the senses.
The manufacturer is part of a trend
famously to kick off illusion; sanctity
not guaranteed if used as combiner.

                             Some days
the daughter of All Saints is seduced
by a jewel-like ladder. Curiosity
is legendarily lethal, zeroing
in on a pulverised motor
made new as a smooth metal surface.
This is the kill box, frozen into sculpture
at a value of some $10m.
And who hover over it are tempted to wonder

where the 'art' went or where the 'work' went
looking for their circus face in the bottom,
or the secret of its underside, where it makes contact
with the gallery floor,
but it says nothing other than 'construction'. It really is
like swatting flies; we can do it forever
easily and you feel nothing.

ACTIVATED

It is 30' by 30'. Being a busy goddes and gredie to loke,
you will see small scout teams, roaming the compartment,
eluded by Object Kojak. Their major role
is to sanitize the field. A cleaned box
hovers over stone screed, acquiring
everything that goes straight up, which includes
  the disturbed earth shows up
as a dark heat
signature, brown bread, now a little toasty.

                This is the common reference system
                in a state of activation. You experience it as a box
                pressing both outward and inward,
                facilitating integration of our joint fires
                (about which lessons have been learned
                in our previous engagements) sanctity
                is a problem of the genre we cannot guarantee
                safety or legitimate adventure

Flaming up through the gorge it kicks off,
constructing a square of throats, wrapped up
   illusions into crimson edges and breath
     by contract   cleaners are not
outward, not inward, dry and scrutinised
#########radio static##########
by strict processes. The void is not ours
to sample because it is infinite not cleared
for release the disposition
matrix blanks out distinctions, the party
is held every Tuesday, boxes tied up
in green night-vision
pastures smiled on by a black god
It's not science fiction. It's what we do every day.

FROZEN

Floating on gold and red and green life-savers,
our standard bearer in the conduct of drowning.
Count her parting and fixate on method:
one arm in front of the other, frog-legs,
eyes fogged with chalcedony, thrashing matrix
of purely tactical relationality. That lady
is carrying a kid, huh? Maybe. No. No. Uh, yeah.
The baby, I think on the right. Yeah. Yeah. The middle.
Yeah. Right there in the crosshairs.

   The punchline is *whose* 4-year-old gets killed.
Three men in a boat, four cigarettes, axes,
sinking is a moral problem; lighting up
is comedy.   She kicks off
    as hard as she can but her three
relations are pulling her down, they gasp
only one life jacket she must tear
off the biggest for the smallest
to have any chance and trust her
ability to float upwards, or choose one
who cannot spell 'lavitate' or one who gets
an erection in the shower knows nothing
of the drain on I, for one, wish
    to put the myths to bed, geed up
after a target storyboard and designer song,
bunks sheltered by the distinctive clamshells,
drily responding, watched from a com-
partment where teenage gamers are bent
on squirt for bonuses.

CLOSED

What happens in Vegas stays in
                      Menwith Hill stays in
                      Chabelley stays   in Shamsi
                      in Miranshah,   in pieces
      of my family all over the road hop-
scotch of blue squares, a keypad

shape smart players choose the roughest
stones because they stick good,
tissue dropped with a spangled hair clip. It was later on,
through a couple more missions, that the dreams started
        piqued by Object Stiltskin

when you had an 18-year-old daughter
that was a dream and that dream was killed
        jumping from square to square

So an easier word is bugsplat her eight
face   restored by an artist
in 90' x 60' vinyl, and laid
over the blinded
field, a shell in her printed hand:
'Maybe put a photo of Sasha and Malia there',
though the bugs do go splash indefinitely
inside them is rich green

        And goes out in camo and spins the wheel
        futile for gold   and goes out to collect from math club
        has a lead foot   presses the accelerator
        picks up some stuff from 7-11
        drives the freeway shimmering in trademarks.

No suggestion of going to *live* there.

The heritage carving knife and fork
are brought out. They lie cased in blue velvet.
        We need them to get chalk on their cleats,
pop the tins, slice the thigh at its thickest part, does it
run clear and oily or tinged as the half-
time show defibrillates its icon. He can run
but he'll just die tired.

FROZEN

Count the snaps, the tongues, tables, window
envelopes, polling cards, count the pops, likes, glasses,
ledgers, toy trains, stubs, bubbles, poops, sparrows,

the teeth, donuts, cells, forevers, flags, fillets, swims, count
the orgasms, fender-benders, tunes, potatoes,
get-togethers, last nerves, adverts, count the toes
the nevers, count the statements
necessary to construct one American
poem: what they know has come by observation of themselves,
         they have found within them one,
         highly, delicate and sensitive specimen of human nature
         such as can be read off without much study.

      that life is radiant
means it can be captured
      that the dash is still a human
statistical trace from kerb
      to coffee shop, factory, school and market

even if the nozzle at the centre
      of the QR code won't stop spinning it is ours
target, downtown, those nations of laws
         of prediction for worker behaviour

           the worker's movement choreographed as light
     like zenana our movement
desultory and bewildered we run from the factories
      wander drunk into the archive, suppliers
of a weaponisable pattern of life,
charts of temperaments

and seed the clouds
      to make a film barrier for *plein soleil*
showers us with liquid metal
fruits and golden
sections

ESSAY

The Blue Split Compartments is a work in progress, continuing my experiments with the verse essay form. It seeks to infiltrate the schizoid space of the drone: simultaneously close (operators regularly claim that they are 18 inches from the battlefield, i.e. the distance from eye to high-resolution screen on which they can literally watch blood run cold, and this coupled with their boring obsession fabricates an abusive intimacy with their 'objects') and far (7,500 miles or more from the air-conditioned loungers outside Las Vegas to the target), drone warfare is the epitome of imperialist violence which traduces traditional state boundaries while maintaining the aggressor in a regal separation from danger. Apparently all of our movements, glibly squandered, are being harvested for a massive 'pattern of life' archive. This can be mined for evidence of irregularities, which under the right conditions (Waziristan not Paris) might trigger a signature strike. Destruction will retrofit your life as combat.

In particular I was moved by Gregoire Chamayou's account of the killbox, a mobile three-dimensional zone of aggression which can be open, activated, frozen and closed, and which could be as large as a territory or as small as your body. In the poem I replicate the structure of the killbox formally, reinforcing the militant tendencies of the avant-garde through allusions to Donald Judd's sculptures, and invading the false relations of intimacy and separation by cannibalising mediatised reports on casualties. Again I understand the jargon of the military to be a display of poetic ideology: 'bugsplats' buzz under the feet of Marvell's mower. I have chosen this set of poems to represent my relationship to the US where I was born, and the UK where I find myself living.

ANGELA CARR

Other Signs

The first impression a name makes is as a motif,
the talon or claw of an animal.

Its sex is civilized in the bureaucratic form.

The name is easily replaced, or it is the unattainable extreme of any designation.

The name is a property of invention. Imperial, it is indifferent to heat and cold.

The name in its powdered state presents us with an opportunity to share instant refreshments in a waiting room surrounded by magnificent flowers.

The name is a trace of placation in the hierarchy of desires. It slips between choice and another's indication of belonging. A door, any name rotates on the axis of identity.

A lack of name would mean to have no place.

A name is any number of cities. The wind drives its enactment.

A name is any number of exits.

The maximum strength of any geometric pattern depends on a balance of tension vectors.

Then I will cease to address you by name.
This name is like the dyed wool of living sheep.
A row is formed first by making the stitches meet,
second by making them touch along their length, partly or completely.

The names form a chain, back and forth
fasten, tie, tack
they draw attention to embodiment of patterns.

We formed the borderline between the name and its debt.
The name owed everything to the chain.
Monochrome was our error.
The fastening of ecstasy stripped of its colour.
Credit was rapidly forming fresh public opinion.
What is said about glass and its hardness can also be said about currency.

The name is distributed against a monotonous background of vibrating colour.

I could name the exquisite principle that sustains diversity.
This "I" names the level opposition between extremes.
I is as much a name as an archive. A situation rightly unaided – velvet.

There were rules with fine vents impervious to representation.

There were remarks as wrong as their identities.
The name was an exception.
Its design, something hanging down,
mediating a contrast between head and ground.

This is the gravity of your name when the sun enters your constellation.

This is how absolute formal beauty serves every technical purpose.

I was beckoned by the place name into credit.
What we guard is what can be credited to us.
Now the cells are insisting on a certain process.

ESSAY

I am interested in the possibility of bilocation, that is the possibility to be both here and there, simultaneously, or to be here *in* there and *away from* there at once. Fairly recently, this phenomenon was by necessity manifested on in reality when I was living in both Montréal and New York at once; other times, bilocation can happen on the dream plane when the psyche is restless and free. There is also the fact of overlapping and distinct communities (some not overlapping) and the different languages that inform my writing: of Montréal, of Québec, of Canada, of the United States, of New York City. And in terms of literary influences, to commence with a lesbian feminism that has francophone roots or a postmodern feminism of high rises and rhizomatic underground passages: the fact of being positioned on the outside surface of this one and that other, on the threshold of more than one community simultaneously. I am interested in the way that the past and the present persist softly and fiercely in dictionaries. In intertextual and multingual writing practices, where the punctuation mark is the eye of the storm. I am also concerned with the pace of the city, which always resists slowing down, insists on its velocity. Velocity that liberates the mind if only by imposing neutrality in a form of speed that refuses corrective intervention, like the one-hour constraint Fragonard used to paint each of the portraits in the *Figures de Fantaisie*.

Translation and transformation, impossible sublimation. Translating poetry has taught me much about writing poetry. Even though translation appears to oppose the one to the other, the source to the so-called target language and thereby to insist that one comes before and one after, a poem in fact is always a mixture, either before or after its reality is thus unfolded, re-enacted, re-commenced. Translation is not the realization of a second text but a literalization of the common fact of writing *between* that is poetry. It reminds us of the fragility of our realities, of their mutability, but also asks us to question: to what and who do we listen? The future text is a wide, temporarily vacated avenue, an extended question mark.

ANIA WALWICZ

earth
on google earth I write down my name wroclawska 3 ulica wroclawska street view now swidnica poland in 1963 I go in now descend a cloud from a cloud like a cloud I fly over now 52 years to my house just the same same house but worn out zoom in and zoom out vine gone and done did damage damaged worn in into office block of flats divided by divide now divvy up flats a block of flats now this is where born where is same town as red baron prussia von richtofen says kaput now where am I now in another town and layer and layer on another level inside a box a magic box and lantern inside the castle of the king of the ants now inside abandoned abandoned hospital and school and palace ceiling falls down where is memory now I return to me where I was where I am now just a little ghost hat with pompon pink hat red hat now how old am I I don't know tell me how old and where in a tunnel of time and place under world now and where I can't stop looking now under world over lord where god is cathedral now leaves a snow pen for me to write on white makes small snow falls snow queen returns this is where I was and am and am where am I now a loss a loss lost object of albert loos what building comes up corner school where it's bigger now park park exactly like I remember in winter where no snow falls and where I was with my sled red gloves all little lonely lone riding bicycles little little trike a bike a toy a little toy my bear mister bear comes to my station swidnica schweidnitz another town and another town on top of a town show pictures and paintings and slide slides on street on top of another and staying same in prison town in aspic set in jelly now set in glass a bubble says this is where it is little red point map now I zoom out I zoom in again and again ho right now I hold a mouse a white mouse it tells me where the grey cat is where ferdyduke is where everything is now and will be and was and is all time collides with me in the cinema kino now nova in faraday street and lygon street in melbourne dark town of my dreams in winter a picture in 1920 before me and after me little people cross roads and cross roads their picture in old photos and and black and white colour now postcards of swidnica bank and park with lake a lake with bridge that I don't remember at all but it is here and was there and the postcard of the prussian city with same lake and ratusz rathaus rat comes out in adolf hitler platz now called rynek marketplace all painted up paint me up my face old lady now with pompon hats and money from eu from euroes from somewhere else from denmark where the map shifts but I get it back to cinema cinema gdynia now closed I can't enter this or enter I can't come in now it's all boarded up but I can get into this I can get in here bright red photos of the cinema falls to pieces now

tynk plaster falling falls on seats like ice where I sit with my father on sunday picture at twelve exactly at twelve I cry if I am sad now I cry now red cinema and gold closed now closed they keep a little town just how it was exactly how it is now I come in zoom turn and turn left now up first of may street and river bystrzyca I come back now station station peron train steam trains now diesel youtube takes me to Wroclaw Breslau and I come back to me now cheap travel safe travel missed times of 52 years in the palace abandon palace abandon russian barracks that left little stickers on walls and medecines they go away in youtubes waving flowers waving flowers the river upside down in russia murmansk that is a town in hrubieszow selling herring my grandfather dances with my beard who am I now the cinema gdynia in a youtube unfolds unrolls through swing doors and green tiles brown tiles my memory makes it grey but is red now bright red chairs and red walls and carpets all lights blaze now the screen is empty and closed behind gold curtains valhalla cinema in northcote and richmond the paris opera they copy me here build theatre and theatre in a theatre build me a bank man with a hammer in park I remember bronze but he is marble now I twist this upside down what I

ESSAY

The "earth" text is an exercise in autobiography. This year in teaching, 2015, I referred to a childhood memory of the statue of Mercury – my first mythological reference. I recalled walking in my childhood town, the site of my childhood, which I had not revisited since 1963.

The seemingly frozen image stayed with me ever since. The messenger of the gods, the flying statue on the roof of a building in Swidnica, Poland, is still there on google earth images. I looked it up out of curiosity and then the flood of memory as the whole town unfolded, together with the house where I was born, intact and still there as it was in the past. Eerily nothing had changed in the small town – more flats and factories – but basically just the same, though the satellite images are from 2013, two years ago.

I began to revisit the old sites with very mixed feelings of unearthing the past that remains in the dreams and memories that format my life. Memory is a reconstruction and construct; all at once and each time I look at the town and travel within it, I am filled with a morbid fascination of digging up a grave where the corpse of the past is buried.

At the moment I am writing "horse," a psychodramatic reading of a fairytale – with a commentary on the process of psychoanalysis. In this context, my memory of the town is both artifice and invention, both the seat of trauma and an adjacent and fictitious scenario that I invent here.

My work deals with fragmentation, abstraction, collage, montage and notation/enactment of inner states of feeling/being. I construct a real and artificial diary. I surprise myself.

ANNE TARDOS

from *UXUDO*

Efnogla 1

Efnogla, skin on grass, multiplicatering delta veinard.
Durchschnittlich windy—je ne me le plastic wrap.
Eigentlich.
Ja chasch tänkke!
     Penses-tu.
          We eat your parents.

Efnogla 2

(We eat your parents.)
Somebody screams mondván schreien szigorú
Esténként pistula eighty-nine facets.
Mon âme, das Rad, mon ami,
Zwingli came to a sweeter blank.

Efnogla 3

(Sweeter blank)
Glick-glick armature en voiture shano-glick.
Elképzelhetetlen problems and sentiments.
Arachnid juicy-fruit Klebestoff.
Only the self can know.
Ötvenen got on the bandwagon

Volga.

Ami Minden from CAT LICKED THE GARLIC

Ami minden quand un yes or no je le said viens am liebsten hätte ich dich du süßes de ez nem baj das weisst du me a favor hogy innen se faire croire tous less birds als die Wälder langsam verschwinden. Minden verschwinden, mind your step and woolf. Verschwinden de nem innen—je vois de void in front of mich—je sens, als ich érzem qu'on aille, aille, de vágy a fejem, csak éppen (eben sagte ich wie die Wälder verschwinden). I can repeat it as a credo so it sinks into our cerveaux und wird embedded there, mint egy teória mathematique, "d'enchâssement" die Verankerungstheorie in der Mathematik, hogy legalább . . .

Some of Them from THE DIK-DIK'S SOLITUDE

Some of them restent en anglais.
Some of them then die wenigen
petit pois go jouer. Them then die
vielen grossen állati nagy Imre.
Sway this way, petit pois des bois.

Then, je partition my own (mon)
petit cheval, c'est égal, go. Play Go.
Go and play Noh. Playdough. Whoa.

This way and ainsi our ancestors
formed ce qu'on appelle die Sprache.

Itt Pedig Hunting, Nine 122 from NINE

Itt pedig egyik hóvihar a másik után seemingly normale.
Ding brother binging feminini thé flavian venez donc rêvez.
Sentimentali thé avant garde vani thé voici the voice.
Le chapeau de la forme all about equipping poetry.
You must know what I mean männlich durván cluelessly.
Application très compliqué vaguely vapeur divisibili thé nyilván evidenced.
The selfishness of offering période artistique facing abstaction action.
Heartily herzlich epicentric épicure Salvatore di Benedetto charming man.
Downfall de nous les artistes not given to hunting.

Ziglio While (Compendium), Nine 126 from NINE

Ziglio lusty mannequin gooey saliva shiva tzim-tzim tchebaba.
Voulez-vous German hegemony gazebo sex appeal lingering armor.
Tchebaba society self knowledge through doglike valor readily belittled.
Zinger je je zinger je: mich dich Villa nicht.
Djibouti laptop polyrhythmic stevedore imagination for example people die.
Roquefort sabotage of randomized juvenile popcorn scapular Kodiak high-
    jack.
Bolondok djenny all is bakada sinecure vampiric lending fee.
Zygote stimulate bingo frenzy—Middle East wannabe head dress.
Ixum bexum predilexum, question: is this worth my while.

ESSAY: ON MY MULTI-, PLURI-, POLY- OR NEOLINGUAL WRITING

I considered including the term "monolingual" to that list, since I am gradually moving from amalgamating multiple languages to more English-centered* texts over the years—having moved from one linguistic center to another, following the fluidity of my life.

I grew up in four languages, with French being my cradle tongue. When I was five, we left France for Hungary, where my father was from. I was 12 when we moved to Austria, where my mother was from. At 21, I moved to New York, where I am from.

I adapted, by necessity, to each new language and consequently to each culture, and became aware of the relation between language and thought, and between language and non-linguistic behaviour. I noticed using different gestures, having different opinions and find even the pitch of my speaking voice to vary according to which language I speak.

In the above poems there is no discernible subject, no topic, no direct pointing or reporting. These poems are not interpretive. Whatever meaning emerges from these syntactically wide-open texts tends to be as much of a surprise to the writer as to the reader.

As a poet, what interests me is the integration of various languages, incorporating them into each other, letting them converse among themselves, as I construct an art-language by freely allowing in linguistic and syntactic incongruities. Even in my monolingual writing, I pay as much attention to sound, cadence, rhythm, and form, as to meaning.

My current, more English-centered writing could not be what it is, had I not written multilingually for so many years. These days, I continue to explore multilingualism, but from a different, more translingual perspective, while I continue to operate between languages, and observe their effect on thought and imagination.

---

*English-centered, as in "soft-centered chocolate or a computer-centered industry."

BARBARA BECK

edge conditions

the green wedge of unknowns marked
        actionable (given margins
                where axing is done)
      various mocks the more usual
            busy noises
frayed (from running late)
            if she could get them
past the dark agenda only
                one pie-slice keeps
    the money coming
        clean (out of mingled source)
talk false-color images poleward
                for instance causal
      (ghosted thought regime
                having the power to lay waste)

*

quick scare up some business she hears a rushing sound
      keener windier than transmutation
            led to a distant cloud of protoplasm
      definitely toward
           old bastard theories (a force like
              ten thousand takeovers)
           multiply chances
wearing her several
      hats tight cultural moue
      (must be recognizable by attributes) define
           the cross-hatched zone of face
      (at risk) any light
              not swallowed up

*

absolutely ragged
viridian sap emeraude spinach mantis Hooker's
      jungle
        (hue close to evergreen
                as to be almost black)
watches her language
          for recapitulation
      straight line never to return the low
            wedgings (in the narrows of size and time)
                nor flimsy precise
from above (wing shadow moving over)
tit for tat termed *epic*
      enzyme cascade and other attempts
      stop-gap she says imagine
          a slow scramble
              the dirty work there

                *

                economic in nature
    matter-energy transfer processes
                  always
        slipping through her fingers (at least
    two different accelerations and
        glow episodes) in situ
    by eating pizza
raise your hands those who want
mystically a forest floor equivalent
      without any irritable reaching after fact & reason
that inventories (rounded off)
            take to pieces

                *

    whose job it is
maps obstacle patterns around each will (formatted
           Fate sex functional constructs tied
      into bundles with the higher taxa)
poorly demonstrate her show sliding
               to the gummy part
      supply-side coagulum
                    this birthright that
                          huddle
      activate the next factor by entrapment
baby fat of the land but individually diminishing
            rewards any day now (weather
                         moves and dwells)

heat island

of studied objects the hottest
buildings
      with that ritual in mind (until intrusion
      cooks it)
             I know where I am maybe
twice a year reradiates carefully
(colorful twilights clear into
             relative place) his office
    self's parsimony
(would prefer not to think until cooler)
             typically shooing
      approach from
                    the empty quarter
but misses by a thoughtlet
                  (in the wake of one
          high-inclination
body) oh so bossy a gradient (till
      he finds delay
           at the core)

middle

get only one chance
        (amid jollification)
                simultaneous with hierarchy
                        vibrations oddly
hybrid (his brain colonized)
        modes of possibility whenever the talk
                is of (others)
        value of the variable
                      interference
goes directly into *same is true here*
        saying *well put together* for no good reason
(first amidase then bombshell)
                as if anyone were asking
        (a little welcome quiz)
and he stood among elbows
        trying to control in the desired
                direction after it was
                      already said

ESSAY

Writing poetry is a way of exploring the world and ourselves in it. Once we have tapped into language, whole networks of elusive connections open up, sometimes expanding slowly, sometimes proceeding by leaps and bounds. Most often for me, the poem accretes words gradually when I am working my way through an idea, and it makes jumps when a sound draws it in a new direction. Currently I've become very interested in the interactions between work and the environment, which can be interpreted as society, climate, or the physicality of place. Another recent focus has been the humble preposition, the often overlooked function word. It catches both eye and ear, for short units such as *up, to* or *in* can lead to a wealth of material possibilities.

I still remember the excitement of first coming across an anthology of Language poetry. Later influences were Alice Notley, especially hearing her read. Then came the work of Cole Swensen, Mary Jo Bang and Ann Lauterbach. I consider myself very lucky to be living in Paris, where opportunities for hearing poetry are many and varied!

BELLA LI

io sono l'amore

MILAN

Edo arrived with a girl, and it was generally agreed that she was, yes, very beautiful and, yes, very rich, though there was little to see but for The ice at the window (it was December, it was Christmas), The silver soup tureen. With the family arranged, just so, around the table, facing The severe portrait, The piano, The paintings—with The table arranged so as to face the frozen tableau of family photographs. Here they sat, at the elegant dining table Where all happy families go. *Sei bella signora*. Beautiful, yes, and so richly panelled in oak. They discussed the weather, its elegance. Tomorrow, Up the steps of the cathedral on a sunny day, trams rattling past, cloudless, unseen, except for an ascending speck, seen from the ground by a faithful observer. The one whose eye followed faithfully from below, tracking up The steps, steps and spires.

SOME MONTHS LATER

In the hard sunshine of March she appears as A woman more beautiful than you. Carving the vegetables, drinking the wine At lunch, with a reservation for three, seated between tasteful linens the women. In Russia, we are told, many years ago the daughter of an art dealer is visited by an apparition—*dalla Russia con amore*. Young and alone, but Answering dutifully as one does a vision Deserving of a fame all her own. Emma, or Anna, wandering forgotten among the famous pictures, all that fine colour and light becoming, through inverted glass and often and in many years afterwards the passage of centuries, Wives of men.

SAN REMO

Time on the farm Above the hills above San Remo. That soft haze of hills. Wearing a Sweet orange dress, to many and good effect. The young rake. The young chef in his garden, raking, hoeing, harvesting sweet peas out of season. Basking in the forgotten sun Overlooking Sanremo, Moscow, *Antonio, Antonio, dove sei* on the hills looking over And so on, and so on, and then—"Time passes, darling. Things change." At the villa, below successive and diminishing tree lines Doors sliding. A handsome boy with a closed smile, noose around his neck, leans across. Seeing, with great severity, The contract, thin and suave on the kitchen table, the pointed ring finger.

LONDON

Far away, many miles distant, against The pool of blue. The Count writes left-handed across the card: *Aspetta, ascolta*. His faithful ally watching from the steps The book (hidden) in the closet. A fall, the lovely head, black water gently bruising the marbled edge. All this fine Venetian marble, block upon block upon people in black and Rain darkening the cemetery statues. Like ink We find in The brilliant conservatory—*la famiglia* arranged as statues before the final act, brief and contained. When the moment arrives, in the cool of the afternoon, She appears, tailored slacks and Hand on heart in the antechamber. In Russia beneath the clocks among the crowd, red bag in hand, empty compartment thin, rattling to its destination. Centuries Ascending from the platform Finding in the last brief flood of light The open track the door A shallow cave. To arrive to find Light on, glimmering on, water.

The Memory Machine Elena Obieta

> *The automaton outlasts time, the worst of plagues, the water that wears down stones.*

I. THE MEETING

There is a very old tradition of automatons in the Black Forest. Through the ages—in the shooting galleries, the cheap bars, the lottery booths—they meet by chance, they meet in silence. A body is a body, but only voices are capable of love. The first law of desire is, always, to remain still. The first law is always lost in motion, replicating blindly and without cease. The story begins in 1956, in a small town in the province of Buenos Aires. But in the sixteenth century there are reports of bodies moving silent through the trees; impervious to frost, immune to disease. They meet by chance, without voice. Desire remains, when understood finally, completely, a compulsion to be still. In the forest they killed them like sparrows—running, hooded.

II. THE MUSEUM

Beneath the museum the series of hotel rooms was reproduced in successive halls. The grand suites of the Majestic, the Málaga, the Colón; the lobbies, the lottery booths, the cheap bars. Galleries and pavilions extending for miles without end, voices at the end of telephone lines. When a man loses his wife, he builds a machine. A machine exhibited as a vessel of loss—the second law of desire, more immutable than the first—an automaton has no past; it does not mourn, but returns. In the province of Buenos Aires, in 1956, the story begins—in a small town completely destroyed by the war. It is dark, the sirens are retreating, the facades blink, blink and fade. Counting, in silence, the end of days. Last towns like hills in the distance.

III. MECHANICAL BIRDS

The story begins in a small town in the province of Buenos Aires. The year is 1956. A woman—we will call her Elena—dies. A woman emerges, blinking, from the *hospital general* with no name, an alibi, a view of the plains. There is a scene at the hospital, in which the theatre lights dim, the doctors lay down their instruments. It is the beginning, it is remembered, of something else, though there is no alibi of which to speak. In the morning they begin again: theatre, lights, instruments. The doctors blinking, the small town provincial, the absent woman. In absence we will call her Elena; we will speak of the plains viewed through an eclipse, its duration, the darkest night of the year remembered as 1956. It will play, this scene, though in different forms, countless times—white birds changing colours as they fly. Sometimes a man and a woman are lovers. Sometimes they speak, in unison, in love on the shore. But he has left, he has departed. Elena, he has departed and will not return.

IV. ON SHORE

In that time you could see the ocean from the small window in the kitchen—*el hermoso océano, las ondas lentas*. And the stove, above the oven, was the only light at dusk. In that house, by a nameless sea, I was alone; I was an endless succession of rooms, surrounded by lanterns, armed men. In the dusk I awoke and was gone. He has departed, he has gone and I am: hospitals, pavilions, rooms. There is an old tradition, there are laws; there is a necessary habit of names, a window; there is a stove and it is the only. But here the night has not yet arrived: we are on the shore, in the kitchen at dusk. We are, by the light of the stove, on the shore beyond which something else—in a small town, in the province of Buenos Aires, in 1956—begins.

La ténébreuse

"Remember," he said, "the landscape changes three times." The door to the left. The door to the right. At this hour, one discloses the garden—trees thick, roses overripe (in the arbour we see the outline of what appears to be a kite—or knife—). The other opens into the shuttered chamber at the top of the stairs. We will call this "the apothecary's" lair. Against the wall a wooden chest heavy, loaded with charms. Locked drawers. The rows of empty beds, neatly made; in sequence they are—"before, during and after." Recall that from the ceiling—one dim bulb eye. Aged starch. Formaldehyde. Before, during and

"At the ball," he says, "the masks are subtle, but proliferating." (Outside, planets.) In the Château de Compiègne, the room composed of shattered glass. Scenery of nature, steady eye. Harpsichord: proceed. Remember—each step, like each room, is /not like/ the last. Closer, discreet. Remember the day of flight—running backwards through the petrified forest. Old notebooks strewn along the floor; diaries in a familiar hand, though distinct and [in]complete. Locked drawers. There are two in the forest. There is one, running (two), and there are none. Closer to—the light refracts, the phonograph plays on. [*The dance continues as before, during*]

A brief interlude, having arrived at "the last door." Interior: curtains in apricot or figured linen (with yellow, rose, mauve or green). Above the mantel—rows of mounted heads: stag, bear, hawk. We will call this picture "lost in the woods." With brocade. We will recall the interior—eyes glazed and fixed on what arrives petrified, moving. From left to right and. Left to right against the wall. From the ceiling the sound the telephone ringing. A copy softly of a copy softly stepping, backwards through the frame.

ESSAY: ON POETRY AND DESIRE

Recently, for a period of about a year, I lost all interest in poetry—reading it, writing it, thinking about it. I was a third of the way into a PhD in creative writing, which involves precisely reading, writing and thinking about poetry, so this was problematic. In that year, I became obsessed with film photography. I acquired numerous second-hand cameras, taught myself the basics of exposure and focal length, formats and film speeds, and walked around taking photographs of everything—empty basketball courts, chairs, the sea. I read very little—words seemed to have lost their ability to speak, to invent, to move—and my own work seemed only to repeat the same scenes, the same words, the same ideas, like terrible figures in recurring dreams.

It wasn't until the beginning of the following year, when I taught a subject on poetry and poetics, that my interest revived. At some point during the semester, I remember thinking, 'Yes, this matters', although attempts to spell out exactly why and how seem to miss or undersell or simplify the point. A statement of poetics can only ever be a snapshot of a moment in time: I could say that at this moment I am interested in the prose poem form, in absences, syntactical slippages, in the play between genres, foreign languages. But all this can be seen in the poems themselves.

What seems less obvious, and perhaps occupies a longer moment of thought, is this: the writing of poetry is contingent upon desire. It is an activity, a state, a mood, that can be moved both toward and away from. Some poets—most famously Arthur Rimbaud and Laura Riding Jackson—did not count themselves as such all their lives. Others, like Valéry, spent decades in silence. To write poetry, to write at all, is perhaps to recognise that one day you may cease to do so—that one day the desire may disappear and never return. And that the very precariousness of this desire, the unpredictability of its push and pull, is entirely necessary.

CARRIE ETTER

Notes for A

from *Grief's Alphabet*

Alchemy: how to translate agony into
An ague had her
Advice be fucked
It advanced quickly, a week between
Arlington Drive, 1974 to 2011, a quarter-acre corner lot overrun
   with crabgrass and dandelions come summer
Allotment as in an assumption about justice—
   i.e. since Dad died early—
Arthritis in her knees and fingers, the ache of winter
A as in the teacher's apple, her aspiration
Always, I thought. Always.

Body

from *Grief's Alphabet*

A body, prostrate   above the duvet, its teal floral

the street's whir of tires, clank of a truck and rumble

which is to say, a species of silence   sound become peripheral, aloof

the windows closing out, closing in   October or November's crisp

the body still, eyes open   a soundless, resounding *no*

*

after the disbelief, her bones grew soft   the spine pliable

onto, across the floor   not as though they melted but

like rubber, a curl and bouncing unfurl   whip-snap of sob and shriek

after a day of curving roads   through the Devon green

after the riverside restaurant, the summer wine   a reflexive, mundane call

a post-procedure check-in   changing her

bones   at the molecular level   soft, as in askew

*

O leaky body   such water   such flood, mucus and

mascara she'd forgotten   her charred cheeks in the mirror
she hesitated to wash   the natural tattoo

and so stared long to memorize   or memorialize

charred, as though she could flick at it and her face would
                                          crumble

*

the daily waking to   mourning

the white ceiling's plateau   so unlike childhood's white ceiling

its peaks and ridges, a topographical map

patterns, images   but here: nothing

nothing and nothing and nothing   to rise to

the body become stone, the breath   reluctant

*

And after years?   the body's subtler flux

amid the elements: an hour aflame   or drenched

weighty as mineral   deep in earth   or almost

transparent, nearly air   thin linen pinned to string

adrift or aloft   depending on

Future Interlude

Where are you? Normal, Illinois

What do you see? Cornfield upon cornfield splayed, flattened by tornado

What do you see? Stunted stalks, palest soil under a heavy sun

What do you see? Soybeans submerged in water

What do you see? Tomorrow

What do you seek? Our great-grandfathers' ghosts: we'd have a word

Conservation

based on "Updating the Illinois Wildlife Action Plan: Using a vulnerability assessment to inform conservation priorities"

along the Mackinaw
                plant trees and more trees

      to shade, to cool
                    smallmouth bass

                          southern redbelly, blacknose dace

and head northwest   to the sand prairies

  make them safe   and the ornate box turtle   thrives

now to find rocky outcrops   nurture oak openings

  for the slender glass lizard   timber rattlesnakes

and last *(never last)*   and here *(and here, and here)*

  the wetlands: common moorhens

  king rails   marsh wrens:

                                so they live

ESSAY: ESSAY AT POETRY

As a poet growing up in Normal, Illinois, I always felt an outlier, an alive and engaged participant in a reality that only partially overlapped with others'. As a young adult among the poets of Los Angeles and later Orange County, California, I found more community with the acquaintance of many more poets, yet still felt alone in my practice, that my pursuit in words was quite different from that of others I knew. This sense of difference became more profound as I shunned linear autobiographical narrative to evoke more accurately, as I saw it, my sense of reality, the life of my consciousness.

On moving to England in 2001, I became an outlier both in my nationality and my vocation, yet in becoming friends with poet Claire Crowther in 2002, I finally found someone else who shared similar goals in the writing of poetry with whom I could discuss relevant matters regularly. Living in Britain and reading its poetries also gave me a much more precise sense of my own approach, such that I began to find it a little, just a little easier to create the style and quality of writing to which I aspired.

The four poems here derive from two manuscripts in progress. In *Grief's Alphabet*, I strive to use language to express my grief over my wonderful mother's death, and it seems that means going back to the letters, to language's constituent parts. The latter two poems come from *The Weather in Normal*, a manuscript bringing together family, weather, climate change, and home, which for me is Normal, Illinois and the state of Illinois more generally.

CECILIA VICUÑA

I am the evidence of the loss

The mother of breath is my tongue
A city made of tongues
Breathing death into life
Life into death

* * *

What of Mem?

The mammal memory in m?
Latin memoria,
         me morí?

To remember sorrowfully,
To mourn
         M
The cosmic M other who guards
The well of wisdom?

* * *

Word and Thread (Variation)

A little bit of thread
A little bit of thread
A little bit of thread
A little bit of thre-e-e-e-e-e-e-e-ad
The thread is broken [defeated]!
Joined [united] with the sea [Motherfucker]
The thread is broken
Who is going to come
You are always threading
The thread most broken [It is the most shattered]
That overcomes [vanquishes] [victorious]

Most broken [most worn out]
Most broken [most worn out]
Most discarded than anything
More discarded than nothing
Discarded disjoined
More discarded than all discards
Sutra Sutra that is discarded [weakened] [dejection]
Sutra, that's a sacred text
It also means thread.
Tantra, tantra, tantra, [chanta] you are messing about
Tantra messing about
That also means thread
The I Ching the I Ching
Of Tao Te Ching
Also thread
What are you thinking
Another thread
Until when you are going to be
In this question
Of thread, thread, thread?

Transcript of performance of *Palabra e Hilo/Word & Thread*, at the World of Poetry Reading, Biblios, New York, 1998

* * *

Para ir al pasado elevar el atrás (chant)

La poesía es la vida de la vida
… la velocidad de los astros contra la infractora de nuestros pensamientos…
el tiempo en la hebra, el tiempo estaba en la hebra y….. estaba en sus pensamientos
dános esta vida
para que estar en esta vida sabiendo que es tan corta
… "En el nombre sea" dice mi madre, yes, al plantar, "en el nombre de dios y la virgen" dice yes, en las semillas, el donde y el cuando es todo,
su habilidad depende de su habitación
… traicionando su propia transición (chant)

* * *

Este poema es para alguien que me dijo "yo tengo un poema sobre una vocal" le dije "muéstramelo!" ella me dijo "no no, no sé donde está lo perdí." Este es el poema que ella perdió y yo encontré en mi futuro.

Una vocal, quién es?
Formándose en voz perdiente de son, un sonido rajar, esperanar…
Un resequido en pleno en tu paladar
El paga la luz con temblando en solar, Estaba por ser… antes de ser al alma intacta ensotea empalada Incitada y bordear…
La voz de un vocal durmiendo en pasando… silvando, tornando.. en pasar, llamándolo estoy la voz en durmiente
La voz inhalando el rumor el ínsito paso … fragante despido, instante y no son
Mi ser de sonido es el único mar.

Transcript of a live performance misheard at Barnard College,
New York, 1997

                * * *

Justice

"Justice" began as a ritual form, an exchange.

O así lo veía mi corazón embelesado en la con templación,
the temple of consciousnes
        the fulcrum of change.

To carry back is to relate.
Language and love,
Milk del translate,
        a grammar contained in amma.

A flowing of milk
    from tit to tongue
                la leche manando,
la lengua y el trans.
        Una grammatica fluía de la mama a la gramma.
The music of am
        "el amor que congrega"

                              dice el guaraní
Migrar y migrar y llegar al interior del estar.

We are only exiled from the inner estar.

> *"Love in the genes, if it fails*
> *We will produce no sane man again"*
>   George Oppen
> (Excerpt of Alba Saliva)

* * *

Well & Come (The Immigrant)

>   The *in me granting me life*

Vulva, wel, *wolw-a*, volver
covering womb
valley surrounded by hills
welik helix, spiral, comienzo del mundo
oulos, woolly curly
begin
a deep hole
rise to the surface
ready to flow
        source
        source
source
rise or surge
from the inner source
wel come!
received with pleasure
cuman
desirable
wilcume
venire
varuna, seer, wise one
willa, well, desire
receive or accept gladly

well-up
voluptas
well & come
the healing of sorrow
you will see
a desire
to welcome
the other
into coming
a being
in yes
sí.

Notes for a performance at the AMNH American Museum of Natural History, New York, 2008

ANOTACIÓN

> "La poesía es la anotación de una respuesta."
> José Lezama Lima

Ví que volvía siempre a los poemas centrados en una fugacidad, buscando en ellos el fundamento de una otredad, un modo de ser en la lengua al interior de la lengua, una sintaxis com *unal*. El choque del *com* y el *ún*. Ahí está la semilla de nuestro hablar, su *di* sonancia total. No la negación del individuo, si no su doble realización.

La lengua es una forma iluminada.

El sonido de la luz germina al ser deseado, des cubierto y *con* vocado. Sólo falta afinar la atención. El có-digo de la lengua es su gozar. Las cuerdas vocales gozan al ser tocadas. La lengua sueña la *con* vivencia y la hermandad: un lenguaje po-ético fundado en el intercambio y la equidad, el recíproco dialogar.

El poder imaginal del re *cor*dar vuelve siempre a la unión, la música de la *com* posición.

El imán del gen es una futura posibilidad, el "regreso" a una sociedad humana donde "todos son semejantes y se *con* sideran personas," decía Darcy Ribeiro.

Hoy, la revolución sería imaginar la vida y no la destrucción. Que la humanidad actuara como un solo ser buscando su *con* tinuidad, no su final.

Elena Poniatowska dijo: "Immigrants are the future, if the world has a future".

The poem is the migrant, changing the heart of the earth.

El hallazgo del paraíso co-incidirá con el hallazgo de un lenguaje.

> "Even the humble word brush *gives off a scratch of light.*"
> C.D.Wright

Buenos Aires, Noviembre 2003 /New York January 2016

CHRIS TYSH

from *Ravished* [1]

XI. Scaffolding dawn

Sentenced to repeat itself
the train for Town Beach

would be empty at this hour
in its vertical

descent toward the sea
no mother to call Lol

mon petit chou
widely spaced trees

frame an open
canopy we glide by

like wooden horses
mounted on a carousel

---

1 Source text: Marguerite Duras. *Le Ravissement de Lol V. Stein*. Paris: Editions Gallimard, 1964.

I trace her name
on a window pane

as we approach
the sea resort

in the whining noise
of engine brakes

From here on I enter
Lola's memory vault

petrified wood
and fossil logs

we toss onto
layered rock

Arm in arm
man and wife

"You're now part of this trip
they kept me from"

"How silly," she adds,
"a thousand years have passed

and I'd recognize it at once"
With its milky white skin

frosty garlands and angels
cupolas and balustrades

the municipal casino
surrenders its arms

at the stroke of noon
It is not without magic

even if padlocked shut
and forsaken by gamblers

Lol sneaks a look
in every door   flushed

hair slightly damp
at the temples as if

stepping out of
the surf   a girl

from before
We start to laugh

past vitrines
holding tiaras and gowns

"Can I help you?" a little man
in black asks

A tiny peek, I explain
would do, you see

in our youth we came
here to dance

The ballroom appears
like a huge cruise ship

when its ten chandeliers
light up at once Lol cries out

I tap the man: a single switch
and darkness all around us

As if she were guiding my hand
to pen a letter I follow every curve

remember a curtained lounge
bordered by green plants

a blonde is roaring
with laughter   a mother screams

On the tracing paper of my mind
events overlap and condense

before the lovers descend
a scaffolding dawn

"Has it been long?" the custodian
wants to know

"Ten years," Lola replies
We are spared his recollection

A quick "I'm sorry" and we head out
into the vast tract of daylight

ESSAY

Ravished is the closing section of a three-book project, entitled *Hotel des Archives*, consisting of verse recastings from the French novels of Beckett, Genet and Duras. It is a deterritorialized type of literary translation I've been calling "transcreation." Taking the French prose of *Le Ravissement de Lol V. Stein*, Marguerite Duras' 1964 novel about female voyeurism, as a point of departure, I operate a double shift: one of language and genre. Consonant with postmodernism's practice of appropriation and détournement, this tactical move away from ground and origin directs me to writing as a site, passage or arcade, where the lyric opens up to the endless traffic of signs. Ultimately, transcreation signals to both the first text and its after-life, the graft that lives on under a new set of linguistic and formal conditions. This regeneration is a participatory, dialogic communication beyond continents, languages and temporalities. Duras' admittedly always-already poetic narrative is carried into prosody as a mode of expression, that without entirely losing the novel's diegetic arc, travels along its border and yet always retains the libidinal shadow which haunts her lines.

CIA RINNE

excerpts from *l'usage du mot*

sent a letter

\#
a brief brief

\#
you lack three things:

o ...
o ...
o ...

(three letters each)

\#
n, oui
(ennui)

\#
et si je et si je et si je et si je (exigé)

\#
sei T
p/age no.

\#
write a text.now,
take out all lies.

\#
voici le résumé:

    ( )

les derniers insectuels

\#
l'insecte vocalivore
(selon henri chopin)

lnsct vclvr

il ferait
m de moi
ch - un suisse du moi allemand
y - une connexion du moi espagnol
et - il ferait disparaître complètement le moi anglais

    ( )

vl`.
mrc, rvr.

\#
ea, oui
 a, oui
    oui
     ui
      i

\#
hear: i am
here i am

\#
i : america
i am erica

\#
human involution

(évolution
et, vos solutions?)

human beings are not the same
human beings are not insane
human beings are not to blame

continue.

\#
impossibilities
i'm possibilities

\#
intention
in tension

\#
langue longue lange lingua lunga llengua larga.

#
love poem

one)

i io yo eu ja ich je
i io yo eu ja ich je
i io yo eu ja ich je

unarticu
two)
      late

#
mon amou (heu) reux
mon amou (heu) reuse
was so im heu passieren kann.

#
mon amou (mal/heu) reux
mon amou (mal/heu) reuse
was auch mal im heu passieren kann.

#
a B
a bee
(un bébé!)
abeille
abuela
a, ¡vuela!
(abu, éla!)

\#
17 questions
(eine frage des charakters)

caractéristi/¿qué?
misanthropi/¿qué?
philosophi/¿qué?
hédonisti/¿qué?
sympathi/¿qué?
hystéri/¿qué?
grotes/¿qué?
exoti/¿qué?
pani/¿qué?
blo/¿qué?
ni/¿qué?
o/¿qué?
/¿qué?
¿qué?
qué?
ué?
é?
?

ESSAY: THE USE OF WORDS

All texts, visual, conceptual, and sound pieces and publications of mine so far for me do belong to a single writing project that I call *zaroum*. The pieces are mainly composed in English, German, and French, which is not the result of a conscious choice really. It is much rather so that as a non-native speaker of two of these languages, the words are free of many associations that are built in for native speakers, not too familiar, and thus open for discoveries.

If there is one concern in my work, it is to reduce the form to the minimum necessary in order to visualize a thought or idea. Tomas Schmit put it like this: "What you can say with a sculpture you do not need to build as architecture, what you can do with a drawing you do not need to search in image, and what you can clear up on a piece of paper does not need to become a huge drawing; and what you can make up in your mind does not even need any piece of paper." This is something I can definitely relate to. In general, I try to keep a certain simplicity or minimalism both in writing and in visual expression, as well as in realizing the final object. This minimizing of means is also intended as a countermovement against today's massive flood of information and waste of material; my ideal would probably be a continual reduction towards almost nothing.

CRISTINA RIVERA GARZA

ABOUT TO SOMETHING

I. CONJURING

There was something human in all that.

Someone walked or dragged along the undergrowth and stopped, every now and then, to take a breath.

With time, it would be clear that the person who walked or dragged along was a man.

It is at all possible that the first image was a bird's
                                                    dream.

The undergrowth is a terrified accumulation of carnivorous plants and thorns and violent sky-blue humidity, and foliage.

Painters recommend the use of cadmium and natural sienna to get the most intense greens, and certain combinations of cobalt with very dark cadmium, burnt sienna or warm orange to get alternative shades of green.

Waking up is like looking at a clearing through the undergrowth where a woman rests with her eyes closed.

In the poem "Sleeping Beauty," José Carlos Becerra writes: "And we laughed a little bit awkwardly, a bit ashamed at our own creation, like the children we had killed, those two through which we went through to get to this beautiful and hesitant gaze of today."

At the center of everything lies, naturally, murder.

Death is never a vacillation.

I looked for the first time at the paintings of the series *Briar Rose*, by Edward Burne-Jones, at a small museum on a Caribbean island. It was a very sunny day.

How many dreams are there in a one-hundred-year-long dream?

Children, this is clear to all, are often murdered by adults.

"Together the two of us, about to seize mystery, about to be invaded by nakedness and all its extensions, about to see how the princess who had been sleeping for centuries opened her eyes, about to witness how the young traveler found the door of the enchanted castle, about to see the possibility of the existence of such a castle, about to give life to the spell, and in such a way about to conjure it, about to touch the cape, the sword and the mere possibility of a royal lineage, about to only, about to something."

And when you look back and see their destroyed, surgically dismembered bodies, do you feel something?

The hand of a child, trembling.

Duchamp's green camera is still a mystery to me.

Waking up is one of the most difficult moments of the day.

Guilt is, at times, an emotion.

In order to get a very shiny green, painters recommend
                                                the use of viridian.

Large-format paintings make us believe for a moment that we can jump into them without any difficulty.

In the Briar Wood, right in front of the five sleeping soldiers, I thought: "In my will burns a dark bird, words have suddenly acquired the weight of unknown facts, they now have the greenish air of the statues."

Briar Rose is a version of Sleeping Beauty, originally written by the Grimm brothers.

There is always something morbid in dreaming.

Does the child know that he is about to faint under the sharp edge of a furious sword?

I do not know what the girl knows.
It is an exaggeration to describe a front yard as an "undergrowth."
But, I insist, when you look back and you are able to see their faces, still burning, and their thin bodies spread with geometric rigor on the green, humid ground, do you feel something?

When pronouncing the words "undergrowth" and "spell," the speaker may have the impression he is talking about the same thing.

Feeling is a very large green.

In the Garden Court, right in front of the six sleeping women, heads on bent arms, all of them languid on wooden tables, peaceful, I thought: "Perhaps we will never know if we were palpated by the kind of life we never managed to know."

Few things are more terrible than being witnesses of the death of children.

Palpating. Appalling. Palatal. Pupil.

And inside the Council Chamber, right there, in front of the king of fallen shoulders, walking through thorns and still fabrics, I said: "I do not know who we are anymore either, José Carlos."

The only thing even more terrible than being witnesses of the death of children is treading very slowly on their light bones.

Often looking at the sky is useless.

It is at all possible that the image of a man and a woman treading very slowly on light bones is also the hallucination of a bird.

Do you feel something?

And when dreaming arrives, right before closing one's own eyes but after the will disappears.
There is a line right here.

Often, there is, in dreams that last one hundred years, something human and something malignant, something like that green with much cobalt, something like that red, thick and broken.

II. BE NOT TERRIFIED

Marisela Escobedo, in memoriam

a.
Something ought to be understood. The way we look at the sky, for example. The way we look at our hand´s palms and the way we advance tentatively. At times it is necessary to touch a wall and, at times, it is necessary to scratch a wall. Pain in fingertips. Under fingernails. The knuckles´ lock. The wall exists because of the echo, which feels it. The wall is your against what. This is as far as they go, right? What we do, in fact, is falling apart, and then, if possible, we fall apart again. Reading is a way of prostrating oneself.

b.
Speaking and crawling are often the same. Which means: we touch the floor with our bare hands, advancing tentatively. Which is not, like walking, a movement healthy and articulated and vertical. Which is to go back in time, encroaching over childhood or irrationality. Stammering. Stumbling. Which means to break apart, get it. To say: here. To say: it hurts here. To repeat it. Which means I won´t get up. Which is this asking that they come back alive, crawling or walking. Talking. You win. Get it. To fall to one´s knees is an event, cosmic in nature.

c.
The one who prays kneels down. The one who begs. The one who insists: bring them back alive. The one who murmurs that they find their way back home, that they hear me, that they not be terrified. The one who moves his lips so softly so sweetly so silently. The opposite of confession is the offering. The contrary to this fingernail.

d.
The one who continues praying through the body, under the sheltering vault, within the ceasing. Look for genuflection, reverence, adoration. Look out for fear. Feel it. Feel the terror. Something ought to be understood. Look at the empty hands, for example. Feel the weight of the body not there. Scratching is a way of growling with fingers. To shiver. To wound. A wall is also a thing made out of night dew.

e.
The one who asks or the ones who ask. Those who get together to clutch each other´s hands and pray. Begging is an infinite action. The mother who

sees through her daughter's veil. The sister, who awaits. An uncle or cousin is taking his leave. A spectral circle. We will have to unearth a door in the middle of here. A doorknob in the margin of a rectangle. A diminutive key. A sewer. The hand, trusting. The step, you take the step.

f.
Breaking apart is breaking apart again. Always. Repetition as echo, or the shadow of an echo or the stain left by the shadow of this echo. I lit 435 candles yesterday. Consuming is a way of producing time. This is the wax I use to mold your neck, your mouth, your hair.

g.
Something ought to be understood or something ought to be seen or something must definitely collapse over something else. Faith is a matter of walls or the blind. The one who whispers: bring them back alive. Bring them back. The one who turns the key. The one who asks: is somebody out there?

ESSAY

We write with others. Always. We borrow and we let go; we take, we give, we forsake; we intervene; we, above all, disappropriate, which is another way of saying: we give back, we honor the roots of our constant give-and-take; we name the names, and the lack of names. A plural practice from the start, writing connects, subverts, provokes, disrupts. Writing is the opposite of loneliness. In times of the increasing, spectacular violence of processes of contemporary capitalist accumulation—as they are painfully obvious right now in my country, Mexico—writing might as well contribute to the general geology evoked by Villalobos-Ruminott in his article "The corpse's ages: dictatorship, war, disappearance": "its task is not to organize bones and corpses as if in an archive, but to unearth the secrets of accumulation and to make possible the question about justice." For, as in soil itself, collective experience and collective memory dwells in the language that writing interrogates.

DONNA STONECIPHER

from *Model City*

Model City [1]

It was like slowly becoming aware one winter that there are new buildings going up all over your city, and then realizing that every single one of them is a hotel.

*

It was like thinking about all those empty rooms at night, all those empty rooms being built to hold an absence, as you lie in your bed at night, unable to sleep.

*

It was like the feeling of falling through the 'o' in 'hotel' as you almost fall asleep in your own bed, the bed that you own, caught at the last minute by ownership, the ownership of your wide-awake self.

*

It was like giving in to your ownership of yourself and going to the window, looking out at all the softly illuminated versions of the word 'hotel' announcing their shifting absences all over the city.

Model City [2]

It was like reading in the newspaper one morning that the city's building minister has placed a moratorium on the construction of new hotels, and feeling yourself flooded with relief.

*

It was like only at that moment realizing how the proliferation of new hotels has filled your own head with vacancies, how each new hotel has added 50, 100, 200 emptinesses to a proliferation of emptinesses.

*

It was like suddenly thinking about the emptinesses in yourself: your body with its cells, your heart with its chambers. There were already too many emptinesses.

*

It was like feeling your cells and chambers flooded with relief, though you sense that the moratorium may have come too late, that the city with all its hotels may have already slid irrevocably into vacancy.

Model City [3]

It was like taking the train across a border between two countries with disparate languages, one built like a fortress and one slinky as a river, and thinking about how orderly languages are, keeping within their borders.

*

It was like anticipating how the station-names will change abruptly from words stout as fortresses to words slinky as rivers right after the border, as if each language lived in a world untroubled by the existence of the other.

*

It was like crossing the border and trying to feel it underneath the train, to feel this instance of division, of order, of force, of fate. But the border was an abstraction ordering other abstractions, like stout and slinky languages.

*

It was like noticing the train has stopped at the border and seeing a woman outside with the wrong passport apprehended by police — and remembering the luxury of forgetting the brute ordering force of abstractions.

Model City [4]

It was like taking a taxi one night through the streets of your adopted city to get home to your rented apartment, and passing new hotel after new hotel in every neighborhood.

*

It was like seeing the word HOTEL echoing through the city and feeling the urge to take off your clothes in the taxi, and then to see how much if any of your skin you can take off, to get down to some thing you own.

*

It was like wanting to take off everything, clothes, skin, down to the heart working inside your body, and thinking about how our bodies are hotels for guests we may know but have never seen.

*

It was like arriving home and entering your rented apartment like the hotel guest that you are at heart, knowing that you own nothing, not even the vacant body you offer to your loved one.

Model City [5]

It was like feeling very uncertain one afternoon outside a non-model city, like that feeling of uncertainty one gets while riding in an elevator that opens on both sides.

*

It was like riding in an elevator feeling very uncertain, wanting the elevator to open on one side only, and to know what side before the door opens, to know that one side of the elevator is pure interior.

*

It was like thinking about the windows in the houses of the non-model city, with their ogive shapes and faulty latches, as two-way openings rendering interior life utterly porous, interior-less.

*

It was like standing inside an elevator outside a non-model city one afternoon, disturbed by the excess of apertures and openings, points of access and multiple entries — by the triumph of flow.

ESSAY

In my poems I am interested in exploring travel and and how it touches on ethics, privilege, and aesthetics. I've long been intrigued by what I call "voluntary exiles," people who without economic or political imperative choose to live in a country in which they were not born and/or are not citizens. The trivium of love, job, fellowship does not apply to these seekers. What are they looking for? Why do they willingly give up the support system of family, citizenship, native tongue, a known culture, for the unknown?

When I spent the summer in Berlin in 2002, I could hardly believe my luck. I had found an amazing city abandoned to artists. Rents were low, and a poet could live in the very center. No one was too worried about money. It was uncrowded, unhurried, green, flat, safe, and full of interesting people. I met East Germans, who changed my world-view. There were impromptu beer gardens in empty lots. The streets were lined with charming shops and cafés full of overstuffed green velvet couches rescued from an earlier era. There were "free stores," where you could bring things and take things. There was the Weinerei, where you paid what you could for the wine. There was a gentle idealism and sense of fairness and the feeling that everybody had time.

The fall of the Berlin Wall had brought with it a euphoria. The Cold War was over; Berlin became capital of Germany; there were vast swathes in the middle of that capital ripe for utopian architectural ideas. Former death strips and no man's lands would now serve as fertile ground for enlightenment in glass and stone. Everyone predicted a boom, which never happened, and never happened, and never happened,—until, after the financial crisis of 2008, it happened. Global capital discovered Berlin's cheap real estate. The city, anxious to fill its empty coffers, accelerated selling off city land to developers who unfailingly built either luxury condominiums or hotels. Long-term tenants in desirable areas found themselves squeezed out.

There is utopian thinking behind every model city. I am interested in how this utopianism goes wrong, how all utopianisms eventually go wrong. I am interested in the alienating experience of seeing the city as a series of commodities, composed not just of people but of their dwellings and temporary dwellings, dwellings that are as much commodities as they are homes.

ÉIREANN LORSUNG

When I say fathers I imagine the picture of my gentle father with his brother (dead now) and his mother (also dead) and his father, laughing, no one looking at the camera and no one noticing the photographer, who must be a friend or maybe my uncle on my mother's side, and who is in the room but invisible, and who for us has handed down these bodies as they once were, and outside the room the crush of history goes on

Is there such a thing as just an iceberg?

Our neighbors are students, maybe 20 years old. Today I slept until ten and lay on the couch looking at the snow falling in immense slow flakes and their red curtains stayed closed and I put a record on our record player which we have not to be ironic but because it slows down our listening and makes us go in order, which we have so little of these days

Out the window the snow begins as it has all week, off and on, and the four o'clock dimness sets in, but it is tolerable because of the snow and the little colored lights and the darkness of the neighboring house mirroring the lights from our windows, and in the distance I can hear the poets I love begin to talk about their lives (and other poets begin to scold them for talking about their lives) and their red shoes and their fear, and I wish the poets could come stay in this anonymous house far away, with all the people they love and the people they love, all the people I love and the ones they love, all of us here in the dim with the small lights and the houses next door empty of neighbors

In 1912 a captain takes a photograph of an iceberg and the iceberg three days later sinks a ship. All our miracles did not save us as we hung there in the water

Our invisible fathers were hovering where we could feel them,

there in their floating grief and the invention of the airplane, there in the century we thought would redeem us all
Some percentage of students do not know how many people died in the first World War or that there was a war. Some do not know what an Archduke is and I cannot decide whether this represents an improvement

In their photographs of icebergs and brothers, in the photographs where everyone in them has died, our fathers are manifesting their mourning

We have made all our bridges and the water beneath them is still troubled, our beloved boys are still leaving on their airplanes, the bodies of our women are still scattered face-down in deserts and public parks

I type this in the gloaming of a continent's winter afternoon where there may or may not be snow and where there may be visitors we do not expect

My fingers are tipped with silver

Watching through the window for the approach of the other poets, who are flying in from Kansas City and from Berlin, who are arriving on foot and who are coming by tram, who are taking the coast roads through Normandy in the passenger seat, who have taken trains at night through Montana and the early-morning ferry between islands to be here

Did I say *watching*? I am waiting for them in the great cathedral of our fathers' hopes and the poets are carrying their own silver-tipped fingers, they are carrying them into rooms of immense safety and wonder, where no one has to carry a gun and no one has to name their stalker publicly and no police will smirk at the attention you do not want and the fathers are always only the cathedral we live in and not the law we are made to live by Icebergs are passing by the window and our belief is a thin buffer (I mean my belief is a thin buffer) and the girl next door turns on the lamp and is illuminated and golden in the last, cold, gray light of this December afternoon, so many years after those people floated in the water, after our fathers and their brothers were sent places to kill Communists and burned their draft cards and went to graduate school and still nothing is resting here in the darkness of the afternoon, which swells and swells and overtakes almost everything, and the girl is still sitting there, oblivious, reading her book about the destruction of the European Jews and, quietly and numbly, the night begins, piece by piece, to arrive around the house

The neighbors creak and grunt through the walls and most of all are not alone. They have brief moments of music. Waiting in the water, some of them must have believed they would be saved: that's just forgetting the water is everywhere and does all it wants to you, what you breathe is water, every thought is water or passes through it

Using a pen is a prayer for the safety of those poets and like any prayer there is only a small chance it will be answered, which is not to say I do not believe, only that the water surrounds us and in the water are those huge islands of ice and all around us are the airplanes and the wars, the non-cathedral fathers and the men with their hands on the doorjamb; and despite the snow, despite putting candles outside the house, all around, a perimeter of light; despite the purchasing of tickets and the printing of maps, there is a possibility no one will arrive, that the cathedral of the gentle father is a myth, too; that we are in fact lost in an endless ocean which someone else has charted and whose stars are unfamiliar, and in such an ocean, can these small hands be enough, can the silver-tipped fingers holding this pen be ever enough?

—for A.B.

An archeology

When became the question others could solve
When, an issue of movement

Whiteness in the distance, was it cliffs or an underskirt decaying,
    hung midair
White heat across afternoons, even now

Weir, fishbed, river a straightened ellipsis after 1918

What red flowers were worked here in what hand
Wh at blue

We covered the stove with Delft tiles
We laid our bones across one another, to be found like that

Wing of a bird torn off by hand

We made a space between New Year's Eve and Epiphany
We filled it with scale models of our belief

We brought blue flowers in from fields we didn't own

ESSAY

My migration has been shot through with fear even though I am a bureaucratically 'easy' migrant—I'm white, have a lot of education, come from the US, speak several languages, chose to leave, and am trained in a vocation (teaching) that is often in demand. The longer I live where I have no permanent right to remain the more intensely I'm aware of the ways in which I don't belong, and the stronger my underlying anxiety about being found out and punished for my difference is. This isn't rational, but it has been formative. One result is that I associate home more and more with the feeling of safety, and safety more and more with an abolition of borders, prisons, and surveillance.

In places where I don't belong I have tried to make rooms of various sizes (some internal) that resist my underlying dread of the official—customs officer, police, inspector—and my sadness about the ways my life—unmarried, childless, without a permanent or constant source of income—often precipitates a demand for explanation. 'Room' is a kind of pause in time or space within which no interrogation can proceed.

Inside the rooms (reading, writing, study, signifying objects, garden and kitchen work), I forget that space/time is not permeable. I lose my sense of what 'here' is. Sometimes I am surprised when I go outside, having operated all day alone: *oh, I'm still here. This here.*

One constant in my conception of writing has been the sense that it is an offering or a clearing made in modesty to the invisible and unanticipatable reader. Despite my rooms' irreality I want things like this for other people who might need them, so in part my poems are an attempt to demonstrate possible modes of building or to affirm the possibility of building such rooms.

ZHANG ER

Return on the Third Day

Who will hear this?
If you don't cry now
in the next life
you'll be mute; cry loud
and without tears, do you have this skill?

Raise the incense overhead,
raise it three times. Show respect
three times, at every mound of every tomb.

Show respect three times,
turn around, burn paper again.

Fire warms whom?
Whoever dares to seriously
receive this truest flame?

Only the ones who have left.

On the photograph
your grandparents smile.
Great grandfather does not smile,
in his torn felt hat, black cotton jacket
        batting spilling out—

and your great-great-grandfather
has no photo from where
the ancient dead look at us.

Closely follow Elder Brother.

We take off our hats and bow
beneath our bundles of suspicion.

Mountain god, earth god,
Do we bow to all four directions?

Do we repeat one, repeat two, repeat three
hundreds thousands of
time's reincarnations?

Who presides here?

Who is pleased, and who is angry?
"The world belongs to you",
Chairman Mao remarked.
So, it belongs to us?
Is life a kind of luxury
or a chewed-over crust?

Eyes are burning, body explodes
I can't see you. Where?

(Dante)
> *In the middle of the journey*
> *of our life*
> *I came to myself*
> *in a dark wood*
> *where the straight way*
> *was lost*
> *[Nel mezzo del cammin di nostra vita*
> *mi ritroval per una selva oscura*
> *che la diritta via era smarrita]*

Not hell, shadows
or savage dogs. But the
fire is real, consuming my heart.

Can I now speak with you,
send you my regards
from among the living?

Bright smoke of yellow paper

steam from a plate of buns,

rising over our heads. Pay your respects
to Heaven   to Earth   to Ghost   to Divinities

to here—

> this is for you, Big Guy
> for you.

And for myself, for all still alive.
Kneel down, kneel down inside
the heart space
in front of you,

> your sunglasses

the outside scene of hills
sunglasses shade the face.

Suck the shameless root

pine groves lush between the legs

Neither an expression of
eternal love,
    or hope for fertile soil

not symbolize anything

it's just fishy and sweet
lick, lick again. Therefore it is
meaningless?

Can this
give us life and yet
be meaningless?

Ancestors   father   mother

middle age, astray in middle age

(Qu Yuan)

> *For these are what I cherish*
> *you could kill me nine times*

I'd still not regret it

It can also be a way of saying:

>   take me, take home
>   this offering
>   burns

The message that would be
one sheet of paper
is too insignificant to be
mentioned in the field of late autumn
where one string of blue smoke
burns like longing
lingers only a few steps away,
unsent
in the morning sun. Would it be
better to mail it home using
a non-standard address:
as one would send
a big gift package of
strawberries and chocolates and pears?

Will you be there to sign for it?

This is yet another place
that offers us no answers.

So what? Where else can we go
to escape from human desire?

In this unsettledness
without a pain or an itch
pine branches nod their head
affirming the map
covered in morning dew.

Wade through the river, step
over this shovel full of dirt,
west bound.
On the coffin lid,

the Taiji,
seven stars that form
a big question mark, is that
simply the traditional décor?

Though practiced for generations
these rituals seem too rough and ready,
too crude, how can
this really be
a legitimate belief system?

Grandfather, you lived to ninety-nine.
You said, you had twenty years
to ponder death
yet you forgot to tell me
the secret way out,
the hidden way, up hill,
down hill?

Blow lightly, breeze
bearing the scent of life

Maybe the mystery is living—
As death is woven into a flower basket
                            and placed on the altar:

I am making peace
    with myself, is to catch my breath
    after masturbating
    to a photograph
    voice...nudity...you,
    melting.

My hand smells like a wet dog

the scent of sunrise
shall I ask you?

(Translated from Chinese by Joseph Donahue with the author; from *First Mountain*, a manuscript under the consideration of Zephyr Press).

ESSAY: FIRST MOUNTAIN

In November 2001, my extended family in China arranged a special burial ceremony for my paternal grandparents who had died in the past decade. We were to move their ashes from Beijing, where they had lived their last 25 years of life, back to their ancestral home in Shanxi province. Born and raised in Beijing, living most of my adult years in New York City, it was the first time that I set foot in that mountain village in central China, where my grandparents were born, grew up, and married, and where my father was born.

It was my first time to hear Shanxi dialect in its natural environment, which still contains much archaic pronunciation, vocabulary, expression and grammar. Although these archaic elements are considered to be the root of modern Chinese, they have long since by and large disappeared from Mandarin, the official Chinese.

It was the first time that I had attended a traditional burial ceremony with its origin from nearly three thousand years ago. It consisted of several days of choreographed events. The ceremony was completed with *Fu San*, returning on the third day after the burial. In the short span of a few days of the ceremony, I travelled back through time and space to a landscape and lingualscape, strange yet familiar, where I found my ancestors, my clan, and an elaboration of life and death of a belief system. To be fully alert and to respond to what it means enabled the writing and researching for the collection of poem, Shan Yuan (*First Mountain*) in the next 3 years following the funeral, from which this poem is selected here.

Factual truth, linguistic truth, cultural truth, spiritual truth. Origin, being and nothingness. All depends on (music in) words. And here translated words.

FAWZIA AFZAL-KHAN

Birthing Pain

don't your kids come first?
she asked not
wanting to believe

what might be
her mother's love
happymad happysad

i love you and
your brother i am
here aren't i?

You're always late
mama
I'm always lastlastlast

that's not true
i ram the brakes
getoutgetoutgetout

retrieve that paper!
don't let it fly!
or i'll cry while

i remember the pain
of birthing you

My poem

Pomegranate Sari

I tell my daughter
I'll leave to trek
morrocan mustaphas
beckon
moustaches twirling
on handlebars
they carried mom off
waving goodbye in her
pomegranate
sari

thunderclouds gather
my mother in dreams
she knits
stories of baby birds
weeping in their nests

M/Other

The clink-clanging of
knives and forks
against a susurrus
of sobs escaping
 the steel faucet
in the ritual cleansing
which follows
 each meal

Me in this twilight hour
sipping red in cobalt
blue against the greens
light, dark, darker
edging the terrace
where I sit while
he washes the stains
away

Mindful of kitchen
sounds slowly seeping
into the woods from
whence appear a family
of deer I sometimes
spy from the
square window

And point out
to the delight
even now
Of grown children
And their father
familiar with the
madness of mothering

the Other

Kiss

tall	other
skinny	dips
dark	mark
extra	blue
hot	skins
with	time
milk	squeezes
marking	distance
the	home
passage	and
between	abroad

east	west
lingers	splits
licks	widen
on	oh
my	heart's
lips	burning

scald	fissures
that	deepen
skin	shriveling
to	come
embrace	woman
me	like

Moon ray	She
(en)visions	Whoso
nostalgic	Knoweth
blinds	Herself
deepens	opens
cuts	her

wounds   mouth
bleeding   takes
onto   all
La(w)horis in

men   allah
spectacular hoo
woman   narah
divine   takbir
becomes   lets
a   call
kiss   it
everlasting for
inside   the
exotic   girl

Flaming--Go!

    Long neck
    Atop a
    Sinuous
    S

    W/rapping its
    Arm/ around
    Th/ e

    Small
    Of Her
    Back

    T/hen down to
    Ease/ her up
        Again

        Flamingo Girl
        Up the
        Circus Fly your
        Kite and
            Go.

(Crossing Into France
Bastille Day, 2007)

Lai li la ah

Arabic verse licks
My ears splitting
The East West
Binary my usual
Journey back instead
Forwards into a
Jigsaw scattering
Patterns I cannot
Foretell
Beyond the neat
Cup of dark
Fluid churning
White Foam
My lips make
Love to even as
Heat blisters the
Skin off my tongue

O instrument of speech
And song now
Dedicated to some
New temple a
Palimpsest or perhaps
A mark a/new
Herstory wrapped
Around hieroglyphs some
Other generation may
Unearth to embalm

In memory's liquid its
Gift to the Book of the
Dead
Tongue

(*En route from Lahore to New York via Swat, Karachi, Islamabad, Cairo and Luxor, April 7th 2010.*)

The Freak Show Poems

1. Sexciting Freak Show

We're Romantics, he said
 We never
 Give up

A werewolf, she screamed
He ate
Her up

2. Looking Fur a Real Freak

Lines inspired by a film about images—what one does, or does not, have the courage to see.

Hair/y
    Obsession
Water/pipes
Freaks
    Strange
Love
Rope
     Masks
Fur/ry
Animals

Tea with
    Sex
Drink
The peep-show
Key
    Fashion
     Image

Husband
    Laughs
Kids
    Stare

Exhibitonist
Breathing
Eyes
Lock

Where
    Does
Touch
    Begin

Sleep
Smiles
Troubled
Circles
    Squares
Eye
    The Circus

White
Light
Ocean
Wade
    Death's
Promise
    Creates

Mummy's
Worlds
Family   Fun
Blue
Dress
Drugs

Expose Tits
Gasp
Not   Yet

Fear
Desires
Truth
Disrobes

Dis/Ease
    Descends
Dumps
    Slaughterhouses
Asylums

Love's
    Foreplay

Rapturous
    Freak
Show
    The Journey

Art
Wins
Life's
Broken
Beast

ESSAY: TRANSPOETIC FEMINIST TRAVELS

My poetry–like my scholarly and memoir writings, my teaching and other forms of art such as my singing–sits astride, explores and emerges from the border crossings that make up my life.

Thus I am a Pakistani/American/Muslim/Wo/Man/Mo/Other/Schol/Art/ivist, feminist, wife, daughter, educator, who crossed oceans to get as far away from her mother/land as possible to crave and miss that connection forever. A potent mix of head and heart, a need to experiment with form and content, to break out of the past, yet stay deeply connected to it in all of its richness and complexity, to play with the multiplicity of languages of desire and denial, see the sacred in the profane–that is my creative credo. I hope that is what you will experience in my transcultural poetry.

HAZEL SMITH

Metaphorics (in three parts)

1. Metaphor (an internet cut and paste)

Metaphors are comparisons between two dissimilar things. We think metaphorically, whether we're aware of it or not. Where would I find a sea filled not with water but with grief? The "war against" metaphor creates an "us and them" frame. *The ubiquity of metaphor in language has been established in a number of corpus studies, and the role it plays in human reasoning has been confirmed in psychological experiments.* Use *Metaphor* on your desktop computer or tablet device. His metaphor is performative – it enacts the undoing of his own gender. By the end of the course you will have learnt the role of metaphor in understanding the unconscious mind. He used a metaphor that made us cringe: licking the other side of the stamp. I want to argue against metaphor – against substituting one thing for another, to enrich or complicate our understanding. "Why is it we say what something is by calling it something else?"

Use all metaphors, dead or alive, sparingly, otherwise you will make trouble for yourself. "Those who foolishly sought power by riding the back of the tiger ended up inside." During the treatment of violent individuals the authors noticed that physical assaults were often preceded by an onslaught of metaphors. There is no way to metaphorize the actual experience of losing any or all of your senses. The metaphors for talking about sex in the US all come from baseball, let's talk about pizza instead. Music as metaphor: a powerful tool in leadership development. *It hurt the way your tongue hurts after you accidentally staple it to the wall. She grew on him like she was a colony of E. coli and he was room-temperature British beef.* You are welcome to your opinion of course. But these are metaphors and in the end are likely to be misleading.

2. The Unanswered Question

answers rarely fit with their questions

it was years since she'd wept, it was inexplicable

it's an odd sentence that doesn't commune with its own strangeness

the moon outsmarts every poem about it

I'm fired up he had said as the house burnt down brightly

her ideal script was never the one she composed

she googles her CV, it no longer fits

it was years since he had died, the crime scene was yellowing

facts lock in to the fictions we hang them by

3. Windfall (a polylogue)

I don't know whether I want to shake my life into bits or grip it like a handrail. The lightest wind can cause the ball to swerve. It's a crossing of bumps and abrasions, missed stations and barred gates. Every day I slip on the dropped peelings of somebody else's intent.

The grail they desire was never conceived, not will the quest gestate. The black box is slowly liquidating, the ocean sucks in its own depths. I watched the news and didn't absorb the details, I surf by floating on my back. They suggested I write down my objectives, as if I knew what they were. If I knew, I wouldn't need to write them down I said.

There's no such thing as a goal, just whims; heresy defines the route. I'm an experimental poet she said, hoping cartographically that might fit. The moon outsmarts every poem about it, a compass pins words west and east. He's standing behind her, mapping what she writes, while a rhythm nods its unhinged head.

In poetry metaphor is everything; she wondered if she believed what she proposed. The rain saws the hapless day in half, the bark will keep the soil moist. Is it so new to them they won't understand or have they heard it all before? No self-help book ever worked it out. Her colleagues will never tell her what they really think. And the world wears indifference as its tell-all badge.

Ants in the sink in the morning, possums pounding on the roof. *Being helpless is his strategy*. The personal is like a violent toothache, while an earthquake on TV sidles by. You've never experienced genocide, she said, taking an unanswerable stance. Nobody noticed I was irate. There is a part of me that expects other people to read my feelings, while the other me knows they can't.

Death is a frame and you like the frame but not the object of embrace. You hang the clock in cock-eyed positions: you leave go whichever way it tilts. She said forgive me, but I didn't know what to say, because I hardly remembered the incident and there wasn't anything to forgive. She could be difficult in a thousand ways, but they never coincided with her own regrets.

He's not sure why he loses his temper when he's always vowing that he won't. Breathe deeply, create a pause, then think how you really want to act. Authenticity is the game plan, but the rules seem suddenly inchoate. She confessed but I wasn't convinced. They kept saying I was buying too much food, but then when I didn't we nearly starved. The battered beat their own; but in art, repetition is sweet.

Sometimes I think the speaker is hopeless as he exits to rapturous applause. There is always thunder in the basin, a flare-up in midst of the field. Bask in the silence and celebrate, don't set fire to what you believe. Disdain will do the job as well as praise.

ESSAY: EXPERIMENTATION, INTERMEDIA, MIGRATION

For me writing experimentally means continuously exploring new territory, as well as acknowledging literary tradition. My "post-language" approach to writing is eclectic and open, and I believe that rigid expectations for experimental writing can result in a policing of it that is counter-productive.

My work extends over the fields of poetry on the page, electronic literature and performance writing. I was a professional musician before I was a writer, and musical sounds, forms and techniques are influential on my work. I am intensively engaged in creative endeavours that employ new technologies, such as screen-based writing, computerized text generation and the digital processing of voice. My experiments in these areas have been realised through collaborations with co-members of the sound and multimedia group austraLYSIS. In particular, I have worked extensively with musician Roger Dean.

My technical experiments in on-the-page poetry have included notating words in musical rhythms, linguistic coloratura, discontinuous prose poetry, incursions into surrealism, interrogations and elaborations of metaphor, multi-voiced polylogues, and "internet cut and pastes" that take the form of literary remixing. My poetry draws together the personal and the political and often investigates extreme psychological states: I do not believe that experimental writing has to negate the personal though it may approach it differently.

My migration to Australia in 1988 had a big impact on my work, making me more aware of Australian and Asia-Pacific literature and culture. It sharpened my sense of history and place, so that when I visited Britain afterwards I saw it in a new way. At the same time the roots of my writing are in the British experimental poetry scene, with which I am still in touch through poet-friends, poetry readings and publications.

I am an academic as well as a poet, and reciprocity between these two activities is central to my work. My creative writing often produces research insights but the research also feeds into the writing by suggesting new themes, approaches or techniques. This symbiosis between practice and research is at the heart of the volume I co-edited with Roger Dean, *Practice-led Research, Research-led Practice in the Creative Arts*.

IVY ALVAREZ

Nepenthes

it's okay   to eat you alive
your drug of forgetfulness
the joy that lasts as long as I digest
you in my belly   my lips are waxy
depending on my   peristome
and if it's wet   with humidity
p u s h   i n   p u s h   i n   p u s h   i n
my liquid   viscoelastic   struggle
it turns   to treacle
imagine a slow process of treachery
this is how it is with me
my walls fall apart all around you
there's nothing to hold onto
my collapse helps build a better trap
the better with which to eat you

Pisonia grandis

calyx extrudes hooked
sticky athocarps resist removal
from sea bird feathers   hapless
carriers of opportunistic infructescences
bears each entanglement stoically

when two seeds impair flight
two hundred on the wing exhausts
                starvation the cost
of zoochory   a benefit to the plant
the vector's positive death
the tern   the shearwater
unable to fly

Puya raimondii (Queen of the Andes)

hard sharp retrorse spines accelerate in number nearer the base

the animal (bird, cat) driven to die at its dense rosette

every recurved claw-thorn hooks in corpses difficult to retrieve

cadavers like kestrels, passerines, hawks, blackbirds

is the cat a legitimate pollinator or merely fertiliser?

dissolved nitrogen decomposed sustenance permitted approach

WISHBONE

ginger	rare not to lose it to softness
peppercorns	marrow so tasty
salt and oil	to simmer one's wish away

                                                          evaporate

Portrait: Ahkohxet, 8, Amazonia, Brazil

tell me how to say you	bathe you	I mean me
we do not speak	when issues anger	only the heat
this room its ceiling fan	underspin and wobble	reluctant
too white by far	darken teachers	their brows knit
our eyes	see my eye spit sun	seeds burn and swallow
breath wet trickle	inside splutter	bell cap sheen
uncontrollable we	slavery scalping skin	recognise me
we are similar	hellfires hormonal	changing
minute by minute	align chemicals	surface disgorge
treasure merely	boxes ticking	buy sell sell sell
we want don't we	girl blind only	the visual screed
but I'm not for sale	for deformity skull	for anything at all

ESSAY

I am fortunate to have lived in many countries and traversed several cultures: Filipino, Australian, British, Celtic, European, and now, New Zealand. Moving around means I uproot myself every time, so that it feels like I start from scratch, a state that gives me the advantage of the outsider, one who looks in, is never comfortable, always questions, observes, records.

Feminist concerns? Feminism is necessary, now more than ever.

Discovering new poets to admire is necessary to stave off stultification and stagnation in one's own work. My influences include Sylvia Plath, Robert Browning, Ai, Dorothy Porter and Deryn Rees-Jones. New Zealander Janet Frame is a recent astonishment for me, as are American poets Rebecca Loudon and Jessica Smith, the latter of which I claim as my contemporaries.

Why do I write? In 2012, I was invited to the Seoul International Writers Festival as a featured writer, and paired with my Korean counterpart, Jin Eun-Young, so I could get to know each other through our poetry.

After my reading, my partner poet asked me, while we were on stage, why she could not find me in my poems. I said something inadvertently, unthinkingly, but which then proceeded to reverberate inside myself. And I thought it must be true.

"I write so that I will not be needed."

JANE JORITZ-NAKAGAWA

From <<Terrain Grammar>>

slow pull towards silence
shifting frames of reference
i'd do anything to be alone
dark corridor

dreamy landscapes with flowing boundaries
messy undulations in my head
dying from invisible wounds
silent and distant

guided by reasoning
perfect sounds emitted, evaporate
at the edge of the alphabet
glimpse of expatriate emotion

next to a sullen cross
meandering on dulled skin
fixated on school uniforms
blades of interior

moving past quivering darkness
eye in the forest
colliding wooden park bench
not even a raised skirt

to match an eyebrow
wilted flower code
assault upon language
both sides of a coin

yellow and black
false dilemma on an empty train
images faster than an eye
palm trees in a row of sorrow

no one speaks
of bark of sunlight
a man whimpers at the clouds
somewhere a young girl

plastic flowers in a pink bedroom
my back crooked from watching
yellow barges in pushing away sense
in a portable landscape

stars trapped in nets
dire thrown carelessly
diced food
dark web of buildings

in a summer heat of reason
split open like a moving variegated shadow
across a black canvas
are pink lines

weblike forest
yellowed lips of sense
against a moving
target of glitter trees

thoughts leftover
soundless atmosphere
slow move away from fading language
to which i pin my hope

great blur of reason
new versions of radiant forests
at the deaf of feeling
a hundred views of 富士山

outdated throng of tired listening
dissolve into grey pools of regret
yellow objects in my mind
not this heavy lifting of concrete

enigmatic grave in the text
walk ending in madness
lopsided form of balance
dispensing reason

sleeping on damaged flowers
we walked all night
in the city where he was beating her
lack of symmetry

planets line up
for easy handling
then are thrust deep within
my stale vagina

torn streets and bent houses
in a fragile past
terraced cemetery
permitting no passage

bundle of sticks
hurriedly on the surface
sterile bed of consoling trees
words belonging to the earth

wreckage of human existence
innermost doll
yellow tulips
against a black fence

words of leaves
lopsided bag of weeds
mirror text
floral scission

shrub of memory
in the failing arms of another other
dull shard of language
pierces me

incomprehensible stammering of trees
impossible dialogue
rubble of words
rips floral utterance to foreground

hesitant walk on the moor
historic encounters with large feet
inaccessible impoverished language
leading away from homelands

川
　川
　　川
　　　川
　　　　川
森木林石水火雲霧
incoherent forest struck by
metaphysical lightning

beloved murders
shrines without temples
linguistic bodies
never recovered

fatal homage
between theory and a world
however i think
a tomb of poetry

ESSAY: ON BECOMING RADICALIZED

In 1964 Adrienne Rich publicly expressed her desire to write poems that were experiences versus representations of experience, charting the development of a more mature style where she found she was "increasingly willing to let the unconscious offer its materials, to listen to more than the one voice of a single idea". In Audre Lorde's "Poetry Is Not a Luxury" published in 1977, Lorde champions the realm of feelings in order it appears to grant the emotions at least the same status as intellect or rationality:

> For within living structures defined by profit, by linear power, by institutional dehumanization, our feelings were not meant to survive. Kept around as unavoidable adjuncts or pleasant pastimes, feelings were expected to kneel to thought as women were expected to kneel to men.

Although I reject essentialist arguments pairing emotionality with women and rationality with men (even as I associate these with the "feminine" and the "masculine" respectively), nor do I like purely sentimental poetry (which means poetry without sufficient thought), I think in a poem the emotions and intellect, considered separately only as a convenience, can probably work quite well together. Poetry which ignores the intellect altogether is bad poetry. I am not at all opposed to unemotional poetry, for example poetry created by chance, and so forth. However the choice to create a poem via erasure methods or using translation software etc. says something about the poet -- the poet is selecting herself whether or not to work with such procedures (and may often be using her mind when editing such work). Finally poetry (reading it and writing it) helps sustain me (both emotionally and intellectually, though again I find it troubling to use such a binary classification) in a dehumanized world Lorde describes.

Lorde and Rich explored their own complex identities in poetry as did one of the first poets I ever read, Sylvia Plath, but such identities are both unique to them and universal to women. Plath, Frost and cummings are the poets I first remember reading. After that it was New York School poets, then LANGUAGE poets, and subsequently and increasingly "everybody." After moving to Japan I became of course better acquainted with Japanese art including its artistic collection of poetic practices as well as Japanese culture broadly including pop culture, drama, visual art, etc. and language. I currently have a roving eye and restless mind as far as my reading and writing habits though as I live in Asia writing with a connection to Asia of course is of great interest.

An experimental fiction writer named Steven Finbow who was living in Northern Japan but now in the UK (I never met Mr. Finbow) wrote a review of two of my books for the Japan Times a few years ago in which he described my work as "a mash up of Matsuo Basho and Ted Berrigan" having "all the grace and beauty of Japanese screen paintings (and all the horror of slasher movies)." More recently an Australian poet, now living in Western Japan described me, when discussing a recent (2015) book, as a "radical pointillist in poetry;" a long term resident of Japan, a poet and translator, in a review connected my work to haiku poetics. I think all three of these reviewers were correct in saying that my work is greatly influenced by visual art and poetry both from Japan and outside, by popular culture as well as nonpopular culture, by such things as events in the news as well as events happening in my life now or in the past or imagined events or events that have happened to others told to me. I don't think any reader need know what was in my mind when I was writing to appreciate what I've written. I don't think I know all of that myself.

JANE LEWTY

Violence and Discord [Heavy Dub]

Skinned in secret to Sacha, Kaos, Little Louie Vega, Tetra—Yeah You (You Stole My Heart Mix). Metropole, Luna Slide and Luniz. John Wayne is big. John Wayne is big and you've come a long way.

Crowd is a kick. Kick is a beat. Beat is a play. Playing out is sound. Sound is light. Take light: if you add anything to this, you immediately color it. Even if you add white light you make standing waves or interference patterns. You don't know what is in there. It could be everything you want. Amplifier now works, the tone controls.

Like a power hammer forge. You sweet exorcists. Briefly.

It's Immaterial, Driving Away from Home [Original Version]

classic home river –- scarce before a thicken, all flow
through mudbanks, arches patrol over
    through and at the park edge   flat rain slate
effacing
Erhart figures that dance and release

    not like the human body *per se* nothing to do with
remembering, unsentient

no that's not true
    A black coat in a stain iron drum
safe in its ardor, its pavilion
(to tell about two arms two legs planted over and over)

is like any
    "I'm a novella mix/not forgotten short moan mix/alone
again with the morn coming up mix" a missed

tune, a free way a place of (the cassette jumps) aporia

Reflection [I.D.: Could Be Any Name]

Thin crescent distant
reverse view upland
the more
north you get the killer it is. Sun
dim and strange
a coda wheel. Where are you. Call.
Come no more
to spin. No more
to spin, no more.
In ply over
ply slide and echo
listen to
a reply of mine. I
sleet across timbre
get closer to the unclear
source system, nonlinear
flickering. Us/I/whichever
years ago. Fretted
vacant, spoiling.
Just a little bit free.
And I miss you, I missed you like
cold weighing lightly and always.
When all sides slip
away is the too unbearable
to face. A feeling
of being so dispatched until
remade, retuned.
All of it, the
you an I an us am it
the warehouse days of glory
the final-cut body
the time it fell
on a deep-clad valley
a perforated valley
now an auricular space, a mass
so empty, very faint.
What version would I sing–
"We are one we are one
"Follow me follow me

"Come with me come with me
Nevermind the cut of a rhythm
let's say likely or almost
just my own, just my own
"It is just my own low sight reflecting off all that glass"

M____E *[Turntable Version]*

I fell into things. Atoms in a crystal, cordspace in a rope.

The going deaf before the deafness

told in circuit of a city then a body   its bang clatter
spin feedback, relay and sweep.

Near-field sound inside me
inner antennae.

My school was
The woods
Were flood
My body
Left there
Dot dot.

Pusher [I.D. Male Edit]

Remember a cassette-player askance
Slant-sound in the bedroom.
So young so old, old-seeming, music old. Us
Callous of soul, core impervious.
Words no sooner uttered
Confined and slightly after which alas
They left us like
Fading, peeling upward into the–
They peel up into the sky
Slowly thinning.

Some birthright remote, some entitling
Finery to homespun rags, to vice to versa
Left to right.
And what we could have–
Might have (done or left) is the cold of
The crush of, desire to go of
The things that clutter, and they do so tend to clutter
In homethrown light, the depthless dazzle, the city square
Where there's
Any old craft for hire. Well, carry me down
Strike me down rather if there's
No straw-saw dust on the floor, and some elbow room.
We were wasted, son
Where we hung up our skins to dry, we were wasted.
And all my lions are dead, their jaws stuck with shingle

M____E *[To The Point Version]*

I lost my accent.

Every sound of mine

is reversed upended
grazed from the top down
wayed wrong

Clubland D.J. Instrumental

Look at the walled in, buttoned-up upright, further just a little further and dancing, no minute broken/Adrift in strobe flash/Love me forever and love me most, you foldaway/first wave of bodies with silver cuts/a crosshatch pattern on/"let me love you for tonight"/

Spin, scratch turn it up/bitcrusher type down to 6 bit/distortion/Come play out oh one/oh too, we too, us/We are the field of sound/We kill/We are little ghosts/we are so after dark /Cut-off /sawtooth on screen/the optional white noise/treble underneath over and out/

Come and trick me now/ Don't make me raw in wear house brutal house/ dub doing it right in the dawn/falling in timber/ fall-light and shadow/that dreamy piano/ fractal mix dream/ brassneck mobs of us/keepin on keepin on/ in a game of waste/

I don't know where to stop, where it will end/ I don't know about you but I feel alright/ Drugs fit the face/ There's love on top of love/ The elements of the river will clean you, my most flow of all water/ bring it/ Bring me to life all crowd/

Bring me to life, all crowd/Bring me to life all sons on the way home far.

I.D. Female Choir [Put Me To Life Here]

you should know hear me dub
mad hits fer yer
been around the world but still remember
like that friday night at Orion?
thought we'd work the strobe and keep it one beam
tenner for the best double dove pill ever
rum-ring corroded bench, age 14
legs turned up gathering for some effort rising in the awkward
sense and the shins
how they never moved nor did the spine
but then
running so hard
and you should know that only after the scrutiny of years
wuld would
I give you my hand very coldly
lean it against your bleak vandal face
I'd hoax you in the city square, hoax you
in the high park all the field
and you should know how at times I do
feel like flesh, a dim-discovered terrain
slowly
slowly in love with our own (my) curious forming, i.e. us we
mine art my (he)art
all selfsame if it were if it wore
I restore the varied sides trace them tune them

catch them quick, or slow in winter (January)
like the code club where they kicked me up, the star star stars
like the whip of the bass drum where you
the burn-free catch-free man
you dead man   said "don't version me, bitch"
I did though and
never mind
look how your sheen lies across, your name comes across
my only frame my statue

it doesn't matter how long since know faith well, fine well that

in rearview water-view animal view
as sure is pure   know fine well
this is the soul's place not the dial's time
where one eye is yours and the other is mine.

ESSAY

Sylvia Plath is buried near the city in which I was born and grew up: Leeds, Yorkshire, England. I am a Northerner and my offical designation in the crippling social structure of the UK is "lower middle class." Or "upper working class." It depends how you see it, and from where you stand. I left Britain over a decade ago and never went back. I never want to. I'd visit Plath's grave in Heptonstall churchyard when I was a teenager and be delighted that her headstone was usually vandalized – the name of HUGHES scratched away, so that SYLVIA PLATH <><><><> remained, slowly corroding in the harsh weather of Yorkshire, the same moors where *Wuthering Heights* was written and set. A landscape beautiful, dramatic and punishing; and within it the American poet who was placed there incongruously, it seemed. Regardless, Plath is one facet that has remained in my selective memory of England. Others are rooted in the '80s, when Margaret Thatcher's economic policies destroyed my region, and others of the north; the greyness, the mass unemployment, anger, justified left-wing militancy, certain refrains of songs from bands such as The Housemartins (Flag Day) and the Smiths. And, later in the '90s, I remember how different genres of electronic dance music (for example rave and UK hard house among many others) built a sense of community in an underground urban dance scene where the North of England dominated the South in a defiant mode of expression. There's so much to say about the origins and lineage of dance music but in our town it opened up a large-scale world that we could connect with– the techno giants of Detroit, Chicago, NYC… I recall going to clubs or raves in deserted warehouses (ex-places of trade) moving through what felt like (even thought it wasn't) a huge relevant gritty metropolis, embedded in moorland that was part of an older and equally-respected regional identity. The poems I've written here are part of a larger collection titled *Mistune*. It centers on class conflict, the industrial decline of a city and how the process can be registered polyvocally, by tracking the loss of a regional accent. I moved to America and succumbed to being and feeling American, a conviction that I can't shake. Only from other places can I look on/back to Yorkshire with a measure of detachment and write a voice that **reverberates through the sounds** of the 1990s and within the topology of a place that can never be fully regenerated, either for the individual or the collective. It's the only time my poetry has had any kind of locus.

JENNIFER K DICK

Place :
        Is a
   dis-place-meant
           in the means of

location
        A singlular
        locale [isn't/it ?]

                              Are numbers of years spent
                              to account for :
[opt out
or into :]
                immesurable
                      divisions ?
That which is rent from one

In this movement

separrejeuvenation
a cultural-linguistic
                        promise
                        name   home
                        plane   schlept car
                        shipped to walk
                        stop
                                          —and then
locate the "exile" in "reconciliation"
of frontiers and calculable numbers
of words available in each of her tongues
un-cross-stitched from what one was / is

the average
trans-
        stamp thumped on a block of papers
        declares her   Hearing
                                  is in
                a quieter tone: this

place of all echoes

                        the palimpsestic
                        singular

"Simulacra quenched a bitter nerve." (91)

"Spectral anguish" writes Mouré.
The day morose.   The body
in splinters. The mind arcs
out : a lighteningbolt snapped
against metal,   sparks
night   day night day
rain
              dream of a pool wading
through bright blue chlorine
note the lamp plugged into
wallsocket underwater fear
the sharp electric thrumm
push   on   into
            the day dawn drawn noon
cavelike yaw of wind
winnowing leaves from trees. A saw,
a motorbike, a voice. The city de-
emerges from its cocoon. Candlewax
melting over limestone :
re-coded messages left over
trinkets, cameras, nightvision goggles
engines endlines ears flickering globe
turning towards December : winter.

"Weight of" (77)

To touch,   glean,   give
into the fingerprints troubling
the air, an affront afflicted
afterthought
               honing device
               homing despite
that which we (I) cannot backtrack to
winnow :   warlord
drone mosquito hovering overbeach
Red bridge   :   tourist trap
shot of   re-collection
               to box up
               seal away
               overthoughts
In this b&w I am wearing a head scarf
mistaken by a a northern tourist
for one of the Moroccan local women
I am dying
faster here
camouflage not
"attentive to doubt or consequence"

The ruins of past civilizations—

Neuronets   rocks   replications of
      [urban proximity]
      [planned reminiscences]
      [home]
To be in this place (safe)
or that (safe)   : when
is what is locked away
      [inside(s)]
enough to stave off?
Her hand traces a pattern along stone
leads her from sickbed to market stall
bottled water, banana, yogurt
held down
pressed
to compensate for
the lost, regurgitated sandstorm
grit on windowless windowsill
voiced messages
departure / return
"wherein our particulars vanish
or assume" (90)

figurative blight /

/ our cherished debt
christened green in the ogre-grey
light
collect stones, shells, ants, the carcasses
  of bees, derelict homing predilections
  combing the convex codex for a hived
  intermezzo / in stance / stead
              of intermission
  stand   and   re-geolocate
the space   (distance)   place
gold plated between us
like all the us-s under the domed
structures (scriptures) deciding on
which side "we" march, attack, land, swoop in,
                negotiate, obliterate, obfuscate
a small stain appears almost like the word
   "explanation"
     or
   "motive"
on the de-coded documents which have been
99.9% redacted : ▮▮▮▮▮▮▮▮▮▮
        This horizontal crossed-out rectangle
could be
        my / your / his / her / their / our
        name/ home / country / ideology / religion / love

ESSAY

What informs my writing at the moment is how I am reading through visual and textual fields of others as if they were fuzzy reflections of the self in the (dis)(re)connectives. Movement. Inertia. The thought. The felt. I have been taking and unhinging lines from Erin Mouré's *A Frame of the Book* (House of Anansi Press, Canada, 1999) since June 2015 in an inexplicable attempt to unearth something that has to do with the equilibrium between the space of that blank page and (my/a/our/no)self in the urban heart—that crashing disturbance of the Paris home—or that is in the quasi-pastoral landscape residing on 3 borders here in Mulhouse tonight (an echo of Iowa: how did I return to such silence? And yet, what are those mountain peaks—les vosges, the black forest—doing here?). Do these statements have anything to do with the poems I've been writing? Perhaps. I cannot quite pin down all of that white, but something keeps clawing at me, and this is thus part of that project that just keeps gnawing away at the thick resilient *Frame* of Mouré's. What is re-collected sometimes surprises me. Does it surprise you to see what you are writing? This is a genuine question. For me, these poems interrogate the space of that which may be language but which is not felt by the body or the mind, that is like an inkling of emerging vocabularies, linguistic minefields of the forgotten, written over, reemergent tongue felt dividing, estranging, subjugating the space of emergence. Parallel: frame of the fading mirror reflection of a self. Insert here: plus—as in, plus politics, plus travel, plus identity papers, plus religion, plus news reports, plus disguises and masks, plus science and fantasy, plus autobiography after a period of dementia. Loss holding the thing relocated after a period of not realizing it was missing. Some men came out onto the streets and shot a bunch of people. This had never happened here before. The four last poems here were written after that moment. Perhaps what "informs" my writing is a lot of disinformation.

JENNIFER KRONOVET

from *Bruce Lee Variations*

1. Bound By Name

Branches of one kind of fighting:
center, absence, everywhere.
Center of the tree: not useful
for thinking. Center of me:

landscape with no people—
I wish. Lee: *Naturalness means
a) easily, and b) comfortably—all
muscle can act with the greatest speed.*

Speed earned by unhooking
oneself from the question-
overlay. Un-tree. Un-sign. Ease—
a verb, a hum. I train

comfort into my vocabulary:
incline forward a little.

2. Like the Cobra

You remain coiled in. I do. Long before
I started fighting, I coiled around
myself to make a core to protect. Be *loose
but compact.* Yes, like how I made the deep

protected by sex by not becoming it.
The coiled strike let loose is *felt
before it is seen.* I've received this—
a punch from a direction other

than knowledge; an idea before words.
I can't tell you about either, the damage after—

the language they require is venomous
and I remain the non-poisonous variety

of biter, snapping shut to feel my mouth close
thought down into sound. So I keep training.

3. *Choke*

Here and here: weakness. *Go behind*
to break what would face you. Here:
weakness that is the human form. Here:
my weakness that is me choking

on what I want to feel: a safe distance
from my life. The children. Here:
the points that can break a person down
into pain. I can point out my weakness

because you can't use it. It merely blurs
me into a high-pitched slow rot
I can only quiet when fighting.
I can take another's body from behind

as nothing. I can calculate myself. Use
weakness to choke weakness out.

4. *It Is Important That Upon Shooting Your Right Jab You Instantly Return Your Fist to Its On Guard Position*

I had places that returned me to myself
(W. 84th St, coming up from underground,
the Museum of Natural History), the whole city—
a museum of the familiar if I worked it.

But the children broke it down, writing
themselves upon all places as the present.
I couldn't hear myself as alone when alone.

Is that what *mother* is? Precious gems

multiplying light on the dark walls—I never
wanted to touch. I was more old armor.
When I'm hit, I return to the first time I was hit
and learned I can take a hit. My talent is returning

to damage to return damage because I find
myself there, unhurt in that I'm still me, seeing.

5. *Sudden Violent Turn*

Up and in. Into your face. Into your gut-thoughts.
Through with the body. I can't be. I won't.
My body: teeth, knees, eyes—going against
me but I'm willing to house injury to keep theory

physical. *Up and in* myself as a text-tool. Where
is the pleasure? The knowledge? *Continuous
movement.* Movement of myself inside me.
I continue a language/anger as if I'm writing

myself. I continue a revision of space. A revision
of an ending is to keep going. Even if it's loss
you're echoing. *Screw the blow in.* Now those
are words I need to talk the cut interior of me drunk

with this violence. *Low feint to body*—fighting was once
a feint to lower me into time. And now it is time.

ESSAY: FIGHTING AND WRITING

Recently when I got into a taxi here in Guangzhou the driver took one look at me and then put his playlist of American pop songs on the stereo. The car flooded with English words, and for at least a full minute, I luxuriated in not having to struggle to understand. I slipped into the way hearing a familiar song in a car can make you feel like you're in the big-budget movie version of your life. But then, as I started to listen carefully to the words, the pleasure I felt in what was familiar faded. I remembered how the easily understood often feels to me like a lie—not because I appreciate difficulty for difficulty's sake, but why?

I like to fight. I've practiced martial arts for years and spend most nights training here in China. When people ask me why I train, I have answers that I give, but they all feel like lies: "Sparring teaches me to pay attention." "Fighting stops me from seeing myself as a potential victim." At a St. Louis strip mall, I met a former Kung Fu champion from Hong Kong. When he asked why I train I said, "because I like hitting people." He replied, "that's the only right answer."

But none of those are the right answer because they don't take into account that the pleasure I feel in fighting is always shaded by the horror I find in violence out in the world—that I fight, in part, to find out why I fight. I'm often proud of my bruises yet feel gutted when I see anyone else with ones. I love sparring and dread the idea of strangers attacking strangers on the street. In fighting, I get close to something that holds a complexity beyond words. Violence becomes more familiar and more foreign. I'm trying to answer the questions I have about violence by getting as far inside it as I can.

That is also why I write poetry. Just as in sparring, poetry offers a place to reach as far as I can in my thinking, a place that accepts the complexity of saying an idea and its opposite and having them both be true. When I write, I fight with language not in order to pin the world down into the big budget version of it, but because I hope that the more I enter the arena of poetry the deeper I can go into language's capacity for wavering, unstable, accommodating ideas that can reshape thinking, even, perhaps expand what language can do.

In writing, I try to remain foreign to myself, to my tongue, to keep my way of seeing from settling over what it doesn't match, from levelling the territory. I was and still am grateful to the taxi driver for seeing me as foreign and known, for making a space for me to be both. This life abroad often does.

Sparring and writing poetry are safe contexts to explore what can be quite dangerous: violence and language itself. I hope to come out of each being able to wield my body, my pen, to protect and express the most fragile things.

JI YOON LEE

VISA APPLICATION COVER LETTER

Dear America, my relations to you vis-à-vis my visa
have gone through a lot
of ups and downs.
Doesn't that mean something to you?

Take the uppers, take me off the hinges.
I am an open book
torn open.
Please open the door.

Take the downers, and I have descended.
I'm here for you.
Down here, crawling at your feet.
Hold me
down.

Please let me stay.

BABY VISA DENIED

Your request for your newly born's visa is denied.
(You have to fly back to the United States without her.)

This might as well be the first line
of the book that I didn't realize I was writing.

Syrian refugees and I don't have anything in common
other than our entry being denied
as weak and anonymous...

United States of America.
My first rejection.

The United States of America didn't want me.
My parents couldn't take me.
The wheels kept turning,
and the flight to Dallas, Texas is currently on time.

I never caught up with the time difference.
My messed up sense of time tells me
that Baby Visa Denied is still crying in the basement.

My unwantedness has totally messed up my root chakra, man—
My pelvic floor chakra.
The lonely wheel, with no traction,
keeps on spinning and spinning...

BABY VISA DENIED

When my parents took off
I couldn't hold my head up.
When my parents returned
I could roll to my stomach.

Is my baby talk bothering you?
Baby crazy, but not about wanting a baby.
Baby Visa Denied screams from somewhere
and I need to close the door.

I wanted to write intellectual poems.
Poems driven by ideas.
But my messed up root chakra
spins and spins.

And I must keep rollin'
Keep on rollin'

***

Spinning wheels are dangerous things.
They suck up animals and spit out carcasses.
Birds, sucked into the engines,
now scattered feathers in the air.

I suckle your face
like an emaciated kitten suckling a dead dog's teat.
& I am teething
I am teething.

***

My messed up imprinting.
The baby ducklings follow the Roomba.
Isn't that cute
their misguided survival instinct.
The ducklings are so fluffy
when they fall through the sewer grate
you laugh.

There's a reason baby seals are clubbed.
There's a reason veal is delicious.
Tender young flesh is attractive.
Love me tender,
Love me sweet.

***

When I hit puberty
I was told 남자 손 타게 생겼네 I look like I'd attract men's hands.
Fresh off the boat, fresh meat. Eat Fresh, get in early.

I swore I wouldn't ever wear lipstick
to display simulated arousal, an invitation.
I now wear my red lipstick
to mark my oral fixation.
쥐 잡아 먹나 Did you kill a rat with that mouth?

ESSAY

I must confess: the idea of writing a poetics essay is extremely nerve-wracking for me. Ironically, I started writing to escape the firm grip of anxiety that I've always struggled with, but things have come full circle, and here I am writing about the product of my anxiety, anxiety ridden. Why I feel uncomfortable has to do with my feelings that I should at least be half way there with the impossible task of mastering the language I write in—English, to be specific—before I write anything that sounds as sophisticated as a poetics essay. When I write, rather than a coherent and sophisticated idea, I am driven by incoherent threads of desires and impulses. As an immigrant, there is a certain level of submissiveness I feel towards the authority of standard English and mainstream American culture, and I wish to perform a role of someone who went through a well-rounded assimilation process, who now speaks flawless English, and refrains from displaying anything more than asexuality. Another side of the coin is my intense impulse to sabotage my attempts at playing the role; I want to parade the flaws in my English, my violent impulses, and promiscuity. My poems waver amongst these multiple impulses and languages, and its instability makes me question the idea of intention. While I might be nervous about stating my authorial intention, I am less nervous discussing the works I perceive to have influenced my writings. The anxiety regarding mastery of language and split narratives in Theresa Cha's Dictee strongly resonate with me. The transmutations and violence of the foreign speaker in Johannes Göransson's poetry helped me draw out my own dark speaker and her bizarre speech. Through Chelsey Minnis, Lara Glenum, and many Gurlesque poets' works I could navigate through the difficulties of articulating desires. The music of Cocco, a Japanese singer, which paints a conflicted portrait of love—her desire to simultaneously nurse and murder her lovers—left marks on my writing also. Finally, foreigner characters in fictions, TV, and other media, through my wish to see my image in them, touched me and my writings. This wish to see oneself in others often is unrequited for immigrants, as the process of immigration can be very isolating in its particularity. With my poems, I hope to address the problems of xenophobia and sexism, but most of all, I wish to capture my experience of immigration and its uncertainty, and I hope someone will find my poems resonating with them, find some solace in its company.

JODY POU

En Brume [from *Lilt en Quatre*]

Wittgenstein se demande s'il a une main.

Oh Jane. See Dick come down. See Puff come down. Down, down, down.
Oh, oh, oh. See Puff come down.
Look and see.

Octave, Augustus, Caius Octavius, Caius Iulius Caesar Divi Filius, Imperator Caesar Divi Filius Augustus, Octavien the Divine, Pontifex maximus, Pater patriae, Imperator Caesar Divi Filius Augustus Pontifex Maximus Tribuniciae Potestate trente sept XXXVII, Imperator vingt et un XXI, Consul treize XIII, Pater Patriae a visité le corps embaumé d'Alexandre le Grand, the great Alexander in Alexandria, named for Alexander, the great, Alessandro Magno, il grande, Alejandro Magno, Aléxandros ho Mégas, Mégas Aléxandros, "defending men" from Greek alexo "to defend, help" and aner, "man", Aleksander, "alexein," to ward off, from the Mycenaean Greek feminine anthroponyme, arekasadara. Héra le portait. Celle qui sauve les soldats. Alexander, Basileus of Macedon, Hegemon of the Hellenic League, Shahanshah of Persia, Pharaoh of Egypt, Lord of Asia. Alexander. That Alexander. Celui-là, là.

Alexandre le grand avait un nez. Octave rend un jour visite à Alexandre et son nez, le corps, avec son nez embaumé, embalmed Alexander, ce nez, ce corps, this body, cadavre conservé and his nose.

Même quand je dors, je smell with mine des frigos blancs arrondis avec ces bouteilles pleines de lait ruissellant, même quand je dors, je suis ces bouteilles, et nous, dripping de gouttes d'eau, dans cette pièce, before the fridge iconique, la toile qui cherche, la toile elle- même qui cherche et with that vermillion trick, that skin that glows de l'intérieur, jaune de Naples et vermillon, la Hopper qui cherche l'extérieur par la fenêtre, la Vermeer staring you down from centuries, flat and reproduit dans cette pea green pièce tant désirée, devant le frigo humming and gurgling, cette chose qui te définit, tête en arrière et, roar, tes dents si blanches, smile pretty lady from the 40's with the chignon, with the up-do et la taille bien taillée, le corset te serrant ta jolie taille fine, et ton sourire, vermillioned too, leaning back on a fence post with barbed wire somewhere in the prairie and throwing ta tête en arrière, un seul coup de pinceau pour ton nez, pour dessiner ton nez, thrown back too, vermillion lips contrasting with the bluish white, le Blanc bien Titan de tes dents, visage poudré, avec ta tête jetée en arrière, ta tête en arrière, ta tête, et cheveux laqués so that not one hair dépasse, throwing your head back and laughing, and saying words like "Bully" and "Fuddy-Duddy" or "Horsefeathers, Archibald!" or "Scram, you Dog, you!" before the very upright young man, doting mother to perfection, not exactly clicking heels yet, not yet, no Hoovers pour t'offrir tes orgasmes, tes orgasmes, tes orgasmes, pas de machine à laver in the washroom yet, with a slightly imperceptible tick, tickticktick, quelque chose to pick her out in a line-up, distinguishing her where she doesn't necessarily want to be visible, handing you la clé de son identité, elle qui espérait fondre, qui espérait melt, melt, melting, I'm melting, down, down, down, in to le fond comme the vermillion into the linseed, cool and silent and changing the whole vision, changeant la scène avec seulement un coup de pinceau, melting et changeant la scène, soufflant vie, parfois vice, et aware of him, insubstantial and never sitting squarely à table, jette ta tête en arrière, pretty tête, pretty pretty, on voit ces dents blanches, roar and bark, "Just bully, Clarence, you're such a ducky shincracker" en contraste criant the performance of liberty, lady, liberté, ma, ma lady, dame pour que l'on puisse estimer la valeur de cette toile, to estimate your value, pour que les troubadours puissent le chanter, "car si-us play, morir vol per vos mays que d'autre vivre joyos," so that you can estimate it yourself constantly re-appraising to reflect the day's market with your jupe, for he qui préférerait mourir de vous que vivre joyeux avec une autre, cette dévotion que tu n'as jamais demandée, préférant étudier la laine de tes moutons in these here hills, twistifyin' 'n shincrackin'- the hills are alive- spinning nun outta the nunnery - get thee, today's market est sur la place de la mairie, carrée resembling the graphes on Bloomberg screens, where tes mains sont en noir et blanc, ce film, ce film of noir et blanc, ton film of you, choisissons le melon avec ta main dans ce film en noir et blanc, your black and white hand, noir et blanc, pour prévoir notre avenir de longueur de jupes, de courbes, of melons upon melons, where your identité se tient, lies, where it melts and joins, couche sur couche, coding and coding imperceptibly cornered even for yourself, cornered through your own rules que par tradition, tu t'imposes, sans même connaître leurs origins, of grammar, of lead, spreading lead as toujours, comme, come, come, coming on the lave-linge, and then of language, of placement sur la toile, looking down lovingly at your offspring, Marie, smile dammit, nous voyons mieux tes lignes, mieux le rouge, noir et blanc, at the very tips of your sickly fucking fingers. Nous sti nous sti nous situons mieux la place de ta dévotion. We, to better see your place. To know you, délimitant ton sourire on our graph to nous sti, nous sti, nous stimu, nous stimu, nous simuler our existence. Outlining you so perfectly. Mettant our scène.

When you question. When you being to question. When you begin to question, quand question, quand on pose, when posing, when posing, quand on commence à questionner, on begin, we being, we begin to question somewhere, on commence à questionner le tout. When we being to questionner, somewhere, when beginning to question, on question les corps, les poses, when being, quand on pose, les corps, somewhere, les choses, les mots, when begin, when beginning, when we begin begin repeat and question, quand on pose, quand on commence à questionner, quand on commence à poser, when we pose somewhere, when corps, when we pose bodies, when we pose and question bodies somewhere, quand on commence à questionner, we we oh oui, begin questioning everything. Et quand tu sais que c'est que c'est necessary or silence or silence or there is no conversation in silence, enlacés de silence, in Reno, in Oregon or elsewhere, here in my forties ice box, birds singing to the hero, Betty-Mae, with my Southern accented ice box, that is only dans ma tête in my only me my et qui n'est pas mon frigo à moi, pas à moi seule, mais sinon, silence, pas de hum, pas de chant, pas de bruit, somewhere, on regrette aussi les repas, Sancho, maybe of a different sort, c'est tout. and we being, begin to question everything. On commence à questionner le tout.

J'aurais pu choisir New York, mais j'y ai mis une page l'une après l'autre en encore une autre and switched again, alors...this is where we are, in Hong Kong or Ireland, peu importe, on regrette aussi les repas, les princesses jalouses of destinies, jealous of asteroids and serpents, les véroniques, and butterflies, of celles qui offrent les repas, who feed you, cette viande fraiche pour ton carnivorous habit, who misses wedding food and se console de ton existence, jalouses of destinies à observer, you/he observe son propre vécu avec immédiate nostalgie and not a second to lose to the questioning of it, pas une seconde pour l'analyser, this, sa propre histoire making of the past the present, regrettant le présent comme passé, and the other ignoring it all completely, moving faster than we avons le temps de questionner. Où est up? Down d'où? You've no longer, you haven't the time, la langue, la grammaire. But somehow, stuck, tu l'entends like une comptine in the very back of your head, et te consoles de ton existence.

"Stay with me. Wake up, Frank, Johnny, Jack, or whatever. Oh, Archibald, don't bow out on me now!" Comme dans les films, all those ladies qui frappent avec leurs jolies mains, peintes d'un rouge noir, sur film noir et blanc, forties ladies with their forties grammar, with their offres de jambon sandwiches and big glasses of milk to the milkman avec the uniform en blanc avec la ceinture noire saying things like "That's mighty kind of you, ma'am." and not holding his head up, but bent, en courbe, and not squarely as they should, comme appris, changing the tides of seas entire experience Held in what should be ces femmes et leurs mains qui frappent qui tapotent and hold you in their entire sea, ces femmes des années quarante, et les années de cet arbre généalogique de ces femmes des forties when on chantait "hey batter, batter, batter, swing" and "Joltin Joe DiMaggio we want you on our side," "how I love ya how I love ya, my dear old Sewanee," and of course: "somewhere over" americaines, dont je suis issue, these américaines, these ricaines, throwing back their heads, montrant leurs dents bien blanches, these carniverous ladies, candied, laquered red on the bout de leurs doigts, et leur performed liberty dont je suis issue, et que je perform oh I do and you too encore ce rouge que l'on suppose, que l'on ne voit pas, et qui est noir sur l'écran, challenged like la peste au bout des doigts showing you your propre mort au bout de tes doigts bien visible, encroaching vanity, Paris vaut bien une analyse, the five shiny dying pieces of flesh au bout des doigts dont je suis issue, le visage de celui qui dort, le verre d'eau, les sels d'ammoniaque, des séries de doigts qui frappent comme pour donner le droit, enfin, le droit enfin de frapper ce con qui n'est plus. "Stella!" Ce con qui dort. Réveille-toi, idiot, avec tes six yeux si clairs, que je suppose si clairs, mais qui sont en noir et blanc. On ne peut que supposer, Liza. Judy, Dorothée, elles tapent des pieds bien trois fois this time in time and in the present this time, en temps, en rythme, cette fois, la fois où, la fois, la fois et dans leur present, et dans leur présent in their immediate entities, drawn, laid out in two dimensions with a langage clair et net, rolling drummed, tac, drum, tac, drum, rolling, drum, tape, drum, tape, tape en rythme, beyond her braids, et amène la couleur, bringing color à tes joues en arbre de cette grammaire -ricaine throwing leurs têtes en arrière pour mieux exposer le white of their teeth si bleues, blue toothed, growling et bien plissée, la peau autour du nez, growling, that grognement dont je suis issue, exprimer leur gaité forcée de femme just fine, "just fine, and you?" courbée qui montre ses dents, but certainly would never think of using them, ah non alors ah ah à genoux, pretty my, pretty my, prêter, prête est ma jolie, ses jolies dents blanches, et ce rire de rythme, avec le rythme saccadé (hahahahaha) des mouvements like spiders, avec toiles pour décrire des lignes, all of you, bracelets pendants from your forties, sometimes thirties, arms and jingling, offering up milk de femme courbée devant toi, à genoux, et encore cette grammaire de cette femme en arbre immense here in our late times, Hébé offering you this siècle, à genoux still, et encore somewhere cette grammaire, wet en bouche, que nous grammairons, that we grammar, as in grammar as verb, on her branche, this chick, planted there, à genoux, que je puisse frapper jusqu'au rouge tes jolies cheeks claires barking "Johnny, oh, Johnny, you Knucklehead, don't bow out on me now! The gig's not up yet." Oh Larry, afin de revoir les curves que nous performons ensemble in the dark, tu peux voir mon visage dans ce bleu, deux corps sometimes léchant, suçant, you've said the word I know, buried in a crowd, je t'entends still and still te suce sans ta présence même, lost in the crowd, writhing corps all sweaty and glissant que tu performes pour nous sti, pour nous sti, pour nous stimu, pour nous simuler notre existence à genoux, et nous rendre nos vagues, nous résonner, pour que l'on puisse s'entendre, toi et moi, somewhere. S'entendre en particules de vagues, somewhere, observées dans ton sandwich de ham, somewhere, thank you, ma'am. Réveille-toi, lovely Wham bam, it's time to manger mon sandwich, me manger dans notre shared nostalgie of our present in present, licking every last goutte of our nostalgie du présent, passé, vite, c'est le présent, passé, vite, the present, passed vite, present, passed, vite, vite, mange me now, et me consoler de mon existence.

Octave went to visit Alexander's mummified corpse in Alexandria named for Alexander the grand the great le grand Alexandre, Octave did, en Alexandrie, Auguste who became the great Octave, ô Octave, des choses, ô Octave, choses, sewers, things like sewers and canalisations, des jeux, Octave, then Octavien, who a fait en sorte que les jeux soient courants à Rome, oh we love our games and vomitoires, eh, à Rome, Octave, Octavien, Imperator Caesar Divi Filius Augustus, found a city made de briques et l'a laissée de marbre, Rome proper, Rome was now propre, with des choses like sewers and canalisations, Rome proper and beyond, au-delà, ô Caesar Divi Filius Augustus, Imperator, plus puissant que tous, et puis les gens avaient de quoi manger et puis on and on, accomplishments and accomplissements, et dont on peut lire l'énumération dans the Res Gestae Divi Augusti... Divine. Les accomplissements du divin Augustus, Octave, Octavien, Imperator Caesar Divi Filius Augustus, opposite of Neron, who we know aimait voir fire fire, things qui brûlent, burning choses as he did, allegedly, let's be fair, with Nero, let's be fair, with Nero? fair, ok qui, lui, aimait chanter, faut pas parler quand il chante while things burn, burning burning, chut, chut, let's be fair et donner le bénéfice du doute to fucking Néron, ok whatever, who, then, may not have burned Rome, but did regarder Rome brûler, et chut, pas parler quand il chante, plays his little fiddle, alors qu'Octave, Auguste, ce divin imperator, did things, lots of things, lots of good things, like burning people autres que les siens and how do we know this? Parce qu'il l'a écrit in what he drew up as his accomplissements, monarchie absolue mais "primus inter pares" premier parmis les pairs, first among equals, bien entendu, just a dude

among the many, absolute monarch, mais "primus inter pares," I gave HS 240 to the plebs, to the plebs, I paid out public gift, cadeau, j'ai fait construire la curie, j'ai fait reconstruire des canaux des aqueducts, I rebuilt this road puis celle-là, trois fois j'ai donné, I gave, j'ai gave des spectacles de gladiator où 10,000 hommes se sont battus, I gave the people hunts of African beasts in the circus, à peu près 3500 were killed, morts, got rid of some statues of me, I am modest, je suis modeste, je suis le plus modeste, je suis le divin modeste, primus inter pares et je n'ai aucun pouvoir supérieur à celui de mes collègues, moi, Imperator Caesar Divi Filius Augustus, le divin, qui a fait en sorte que vous liriez cela ici dans ce texte Res Gestae Divi Augusti, the Deeds of the Divine Augustus, les Actes du Divin Auguste, âgé de dix-neuf ans, j'ai levé une armée de mon propre chef et à mes propres frais, j'ai épargné, j'ai attribué, j'ai pris, j'ai exercé, je n'ai pas accepté, j'ai augmenté, j'ai moi-même transmis à la postérité, j'ai refusé, j'ai versé, j'ai fait verser, j'ai fait procéder, j'ai construit, j'ai fait construire, j'ai fait reconstruire, j'ai fait refaire, j'ai achevé, j'en ai entrepris la reconstruction, j'ai donné, j'ai organisé, j'ai purgé, j'ai repoussé, j'ai établi, j'ai repris, j'ai forcé, but ô but malgré ma prééminence sur tous, malgré ma prééminence sur tous, I repeat, even though I was more powerful than all, malgré ma prééminence-y-nence sur tous toutes tous tous, all of you all all on to the next one, hold up, somebody bring me back some money please, bring it back, Augustus, now double your money and make a stack, more powerful than all, je n'ai eu aucun pouvoir supérieur à celui de mes collègues.
Ecrit de ma main during my seventy sixth année, moi, le divin Augustus, j'ai écrit votre histoire de moi, Le Divin, qui n'est better, not more, pas higher, pas plus fort, not richer, not plus puissant, but rather divin en toute humilité, moi, Augustus, Octave, who went, donc, to visit that very dead and freakishly preserved Alexander the great in Egypt's land, let my people go, where mummies were still a thing, Alexander and his corps. Alexander, the corps.

Wittgenstein made a lion parler.
Wittgenstein ne sait pas s'il voit sa main. Il ne sait pas s'il a une main. Il ne sait pas ce que c'est une main. Il ne sait pas si la main dont on lui a enseigné qu'elle était une main lorsqu'il était enfant est toujours une main. Il ne sait pas s'il accepte que la main apprise ainsi soit toujours la même main. Il sait que toi, tu penses que c'est une main. Bien qu'il ne puisse pas affirmer qu'il le sait. Il sait, sans bien entendu, le savoir, que toi, tu penses que cette assurance que ta main au bout de ton bras est ta main, si bras il y a, et que ceci est la norme, est la base de ce qui est la norme, cette stabilité de ta main au bout de ton bras qui n'est peut-être pas un bras, qui n'est peut-être pas le tien, qui est peut-être un blafischmuquilorgue or rien or une ombre, projection, une dimension non perceptible, un éclat de réalité, whatever that is, or rien, ou quelque chose

d'autre, or une chose raisonnée, il ne peut pas confirmer autrement, que ce n'est pas en fait un arbre, et il ne sait pas si tu saurais même le questionner, toi, ni lui-même, cette main, ce bras, et l'arbre. Il ne sait pas s'il sait que tu connais ou pas your own language. Or you. And certainly not other. Autre. Nor leurs mains, ou s'ils en ont. "Après tout, pourquoi le jeu de langage devrait-il reposer sur un savoir?"

So, Alexander had a nose. Freakishly preserved Alexander the Great in Egypt, where mummies, donc, were still a thing, Alexandre in a sépulture d'or et de crystal (shhhhh, we won't tell, we won't write it down) Augustus divin a regardé Alexandre un moment, un long moment on peut imaginer donc, pause...... shhhh, we won't add this to your history, ton histoire, shhhh, on ne dirait rien, le divin Augustus, Octave que aujourd'hui toujours nous considérons avec tendresse et solennité, et un brin de thanks for being so god damned civilized, Divine Augustus a posé une couronne d'or sur la tête du freakishly preserved corps, cadavre, corps, cadavre, corps cadaver passé maintenant préservé de façon quelque peu grotesque, kept cadavre, gardé, the great cadaver, couronne d'or donc, et là, Octave a donc jeté des fleurs sur le non-corps, mais plutôt freakish object-thingy-cadavre-notbody-grotesquerie, ensuite une petite anecdote pour bien profiter de ce Macedonian moment, donc, yo, j'insulte ces cadavres, hells yeah, eux, pour le coup, de Macedoins dans les couloirs à côté, passons, et il se baisse pour (shhhh, il ne faut pas le dire, il ne faut pas l'inclure dans son histoire, ah, non, alors!) embrasser le front de ce grand freaky cadavre embaumé, ce grand Alexandre-preserve, Dracaenaed, Cinnabari-resined, Pistacia-Resined, Myrrhed, Cassiaed, Palm-Wined, Cedar-Oiled, Sugar-Gumed, natroned, juniper-oiled, camphor-oiled, beeswaxed, Honeyed, Petroleumed, Bitumened Alexander, Octave, donc, se baisse pour embrasser le front de la thing préservée, et oops... casse accidentellement le nez du grand embaumé, casse le nez, broke off the nose of Alexander the Great, broke son nez, broke le nez, a cassé le nez, broke off the nose, ce divin Augustus, of ce grander than grand Alexandre; now without a nose, le pauvre, embalmed et sans nez. The Divine Augustus accidentally broke off the nose of the Great Alexander. but shhhh. don't document it. ne l'écris surtout pas. don't let it tomber dans les wrong hands, si tout de même nous en avons.

ESSAY

I have lived in and out of Europe for twenty years. I began as a singer, became a poet and a singer, then became a poet and a singer and a mom, and finally, I can say today that I am a poet, singer, painter, producer, business woman, and a mom. As a singer I am mainly interested in Baroque and Modern music- the two ends of the chronological spectrum. Working with living composers is terribly enriching, and so I chose to focus on that. After a multitude of passages through dark theaters, where I spent most of my twenties and early thirties, I moved to New York from Paris and a two year stay in Rome. It was in New York that I founded shskh.com, a netlabel whose intent was to produce rare music. I write texts that can be called, I suppose, poetry, though they contain several elements of prose. Their originality lies in their use of multiple languages- mostly French and English- mixed together in the same sentences, phrases, or verses. They are, by nature, very musical, and I often give performances of them with parts of the text sung. In these performances, the texts become very theatrical, but I tend to prefer seeing them on the page and write with the desire to make them stand on their own without my theatrical interpretation.

If there is a theme in my work, I would have to say it is the questioning of language and how we use it. I like to deconsecrate historical subjects, simultaneously deconsecrating language itself through the use of these multiple languages, citations, samplings of music, etc. I use one language to undo the other or to make it clearer, depending on the need. I like to deconsecrate punctuation as well at times. If there is a general subject that interests me to write about and which is contained without a doubt in my previously published texts, it is tolerance- opening ourselves to the world, even when afraid to do so. Multiple languages serve me well to drive this message home, and so I indulge gleefully!

LARESSA DICKEY

Sequence

1

A sequence not being a proxy: her ring fell off her finger
into dying grass and though we traced its fall with our hands
we felt it
diving and parting. Combs, brushes nothing circled back
And they kept back anything about the Black Madonna,
why do you want to know about that they say
but continue talking about how the Persian rug's pattern
reminds one of space differentiating itself in the universe.
First there is a something, lying in piss.
Next comes Magenta.
Someone tells a story about a body of water.
Then all the formal arrangements and exchange of tender.
Begins occupational healing, begins what we all think of as
the last sections
Then VOTING then the island where people go to die.
Did I tell you about what a FILIBUSTER should be?
Water's edge, empty topology, empty map, but
the map had eyes
I knew they had been killed and in very large courses
Soon they take the names and then
take them out. What's missing now, *hmmmm*
Scope? Interruption? Ah, right, audience.

2

Also different ways to report: no one was accountable
to the roots, no one deleted any questions or weeds and for example. It
happened in three days instead of seven
right here
says the lines, says
Light and dark are sequences. So is the moss she brought back from Iowa.
Coming in close to the child in an open field YAW waving arms NO that
little tension that little passage on the left;
Moving fast also manifested in shoddy work. For weeks she asked the
carpenter she slept with to build her a bar off the short kitchen wall so she
could use those stools.
Exactly, I know where things are; if you are moving fast, if you are DOING
things in the simultaneous past life regressions but are you nuts, I mean the
NA NA NA
of these fundamental limits which, goddamn,
keep coming back in layman's terms.

1

> *So Heisenberg argues that every measurement destroys part of our knowledge of the system that was obtained by previous measurement.* (–Wikipedia)

Unstinting | cooler ruder bleaker
To pull threads, to part,
who can make out these traces of movement
in the otherwise flat field
with a dull face I am reading
steady mother wings
Men and bird wings I needed someone old
so made a straw figure. I have drawn the diagnosis
of my dreams
house | mountain | hole
Out of glass we see small planes but that music
is out of tune!
He can't get the machine under him fast enough. I am
the angel of history, something
like this. You've got to say this and you can't
say that

2

The dark is a sequence without a name, it releases all the fibrous structures of the leaf and introduces the circle, the morning, a practice by which on a down down field level
is breaking,
is directionless,
is how you can say to your back,
get up back and your back will love you.
Just displaced, that sensitive language I'm telling you about; it was there in his face if I could look, a little shouldering did it hurt anyone?
I am statements are still acrid
Sometimes a long, that deep SHOULD backing out, but I have never seen a silent crowd except at the attended birth of boys.
Immigration, well, that's a sequence of sad boys.
There's the box of power.
That's why they build wings.

1

Outward
my body blew
Just when you think there is no motorized transport, or stop trusting the
Woodsman's assertions
They just strapped it on and started running
I asked questions about this country, where the central story a man falling
from the sky
It was there in his face crushed by older boys, also sequencing
Or con/sequencing. We staged a few times, kissed
linking hill to house to mountain, instead of alone, or the boats waiting underneath them recording those tiny details:
I just to the right of the BOX OF POWER and underneath
FREEDOM TO ROAM is the WOODMAN'S ASSERTION that dreams
come right down from sad boys; the tiny grips, those little warts growing on
their foreheads and fingertips

2

Opening the throat that spout of the rusted skeleton
that inner fern|ness or the time he came down the Orthodoxy wearing Greek shoes quoting Ulysses as a book from the Bible

I knew I knew, I will try to save
the sequence,
being a deeper count

ESSAY

1. I came into someone else's world; this happened over and over again.
2. Go to sleep you little baby.
3. What order orders beauty?
4. If I can't know both where I am and how fast I am moving, is this true?
5. Windows to the treed world, and a burgeoning sense of being present in a body inside it. The dog licks my face. I can't figure out how the cat is animated from its inside.
6. What was outside was in and what was inside was out. I pulled hot water off the woodstove and burned my legs before I could walk.
7. Certain sequences contain/produce strong feelings, dear.
8. Other people's spines, covered in white hoods.
9. No one else remembers it like me. I don't even remember it like me. I don't even know what 'like me' means.
10. What cycle is my life interrupting?
11. Dreams begin to come about falling in love with the 'Other.' There is no end, it turns out, to this territory.
12. Failure as one moment in a sequence. Sequence as an imposition of order. Sequence as something to jam, to resist. Other people's sequencing, other people's timings.
13. Beauty as a reordering of your sequences, synapses, timings.
14. Often there is only a rising energy and the compulsion to follow it; that is, recognizing that a movement (moment) is already happening, a sequence already underneath us, something we step into, and perhaps out of.
15. All of these tenets may be interchangeable but will they tell you, dear Reader, about the particular sensitive timing of my own heart and its language?
16. At the Berlin airport, a statue of a winged man, caught in the moment after he has fallen to earth, in failure.
17. To other oneself, is it 'like me'?

LEA GOLDBERG

from *On the Surface of Silence: The Last Poems of Lea Goldberg*

*

The clasp of sand and stone
Hagar's,
Antigone's,
mine.

The clasp of sand and stone.
The tight-lipped love,
the downcast pride,
the proud insult.

On the exiles' path
the clasp of sand and stone –
the sky near by –
and in the sky
thorned stars.

*

The day turned.
It was not always so.
The day turned its back on me –
my night is an eternal flame.
Now the poems will come
mercilessly.
And I won't know what to say.
My last love.
Where am I?
So it will be
and so it will always be.

*

There were questions
and answers called into question.
There were duplicate stones
for every desire.
A land of lamentations
and a large sun
and rejoicing at its sorrows on the nights
when a flawed moon rose.

*

Yes, I have more
more beautiful still,
more precious still,
I have more:
words of adornment
and wisdom
and extravagance
and words of truth.

Were it not for the surrender
and the perfect
knowledge
I would set them before you
like an enchanted necklace of islands.

*

Of all your forgotten ones I
am the most forgotten.
Of all the faces
you have seen in the mirror
my face
is the most transparent.
And my voice
is lower than a cut field. And my name
is engraved on a heavy stone
at the bottom of the well.

*

I'll rise, I will rise
from my sleep
in a different spirit,
in a different land
where there is no love.

The shining morning birds
on barbed fences

I knew, I've forgotten.
I have forgotten.
I am other.
I am other.
I am free.

I am as free as the water torrent,
fresh and I'll never grow old,
never growing old, I lived on endlessly

a hundred years and one night.

ESSAY: "ON THE EXILES PATH": THE POETRY OF LEA GOLDBERG

Hebrew poet Lea Goldberg was born in 1911 in Koeningsberg, East Prussia, and spent her early years in Kovno (now Kaunas), Lithuania. Her mother tongue was Russian and her first poems, written when she was still a young girl, were in Russian. After completing her doctoral studies at the University of Bonn, Goldberg immigrated to British Mandate Palestine in 1935, and lived the remainder of her life in Israel, first in Tel-Aviv and later in Jerusalem. She passed away in 1970.

A year after Lea Goldberg's untimely death, her literary executor Tuvia Ruebner edited her final poems and published them in a collection entitled *The Remains of Life*, retitled in its English version *On the Surface of Silence: The Last Poems of Lea Goldberg*. These poems, many of them composed in the very last days of Goldberg's life, exhibit a level of lyrical distillation and formal boldness that mark them as distinctive in the poet's oeuvre. Often employing a fragment-like structure, where the unspoken is as present and forceful as the spoken, stripped of adornments and engaging the reader with an uncompromising, even disarming, directness, Goldberg's last poems enact and manifest a poetics of intrepid truth-telling.

While Hebrew was her chosen language of composition and Israel her chosen country, Goldberg remained intensely and emotionally linked to the landscapes of her European birthplace and child-hood. Indeed, throughout her life, her poetry continued to express the two-fold sensibility and longings of an immigrant. This sensibility often resulted in a sense of being suspended between two places and, finally, of belonging nowhere at all. Goldberg articulated this reality as "the heartache of two homelands" – a heartache that, at life's end and as expressed in the poem "The clasp of sand and stone," leads her back into emotional exile, accompanied by her exiled sisters Hagar and Antigone.

Almost 45 years after her death, Lea Goldberg's popularity has only grown stronger, making her today one of the most beloved, preeminent and passionately read poets in the canon of modern Hebrew poetry.

(By RACHEL TZVIA BACK, translator from Hebrew)

LEE ANN BROWN

from *Moth Universe*

As birds fall across
the temple — kimono girls
by red coke machine

       A golden yolk
       Tomatoes like warm bleeding hearts
       Green garden tongue

fire cracker papers down by the water

           Your moss universe
           looks like a coconut cake
           with a tree on top

                Better than bonsai
                these moist orbs revolve around
                the new moon — hair's width

      This mossy planet
      swerves opal trajectory —
      first mother's day

      Mother's Day — New moon
      baby waits to be born — a
      Mother already

                Spirits in the glass
                in the rock in the tree in
                your mind — the cedar

Meiji shrine — where are
all the white blanketed babies
from last year?
                        Nato web — spider

                        Filament on your tongue
                        Spinning violets

          Spirits in the carafe
          So clear — you're water —
          I'm fading away

Talking with a friend
of my father makes me want
to write about the ocean for the first time

              giant pink peonies
              wet with rain
              after the funicular

Koya-san Graveyard
a proliferation of bibs
tied around stones

              handmade knit hats
              keeping tiny buddhas warm
              cold stones piled up high

Through the rain I see
A long grooved porch recede —
warped, handmade, brown

              Ya-kim-a Sweet potato song
              Drifts into our seminar window
              Through the rain outside

        More mist grows
        Already they're talking from the bridgeway
        Already they're melding together

How would "plant spirit"
Do "Anguish dance"?
Between song and speech

              Radish spirit
              Demands a certain kind of poetry

As he waits for bathhouse elevator

Now the window is
Completely covered with fog —
White umbrella swims past

> Red gata and playboy slippers
> Wait patiently together
> outside practice room

The head of chorus
Sits in back of two lines
Second one in

Totoro at Noh Play

> Sits up straight
> Pelted with drum raindrops

Something loaded's going on
behind the wooden screen —
raw rice & a few drops of sake,
> then throw salt into a hut

> pine tree at the back of the stage
> fat like a giant night-swollen mushroom

lichen on its branches —
white family crest on chorus kimono

> ghosts lean toward each other
> not knowing they are ghosts

Kotsuzumi player
licks his heated drum

> Moonwalk sutra
> Then wait for the flute
> to pierce my ears

Mothra   A man is doing his butterfly dance
                 Through a frame of plum blossoms —
              He is in the Zone

                              The theater doors close on
                              Worn lavender seats
                               I'll never see
                                       again
                              The same way
                                My first Noh play

Out in the street
Plum blossoms in the dark
A shrine with
         Grinning stone dogs
Older than the one at
         Shibuya station

February (on a flyer)

                 White dog yaps
                         Yellow beetle goes backwards
                         Garden is sleeping
Yesterday
So many things
Flashed by without me
Catching my poem

             Fat white socks
             Around schoolgirl's calves

Love hotels
I forgot my umbrella

             Sun blooms through cold
             on a Christmas cactus
             Now it's gone

                 Strange dreams resound
                 stirred by travel, time, otherwise
                 Spirit writing, my babe at home

Okina A cloud in trousers
 unties a very still box —
  Energy arrows

   White crane falls over
   A blue kimono sleeve — red
   Peers out underneath

Vigorous New Year —
Boy stamps triangle
Heaven Earth *Man*

    Another hides his
    Drum under his kimono
    Sleeve — a mother bird

       Black ninja chairs —
       Dolls in a row
       Like Girl's Day
           for a very Big Girl

            2 paper petals
            flutter down in front of the
            patterned squares — cross hatched

      gold leaf behind the
      navy blue houses —
      2 styles of acting

         Hissing like a cat
         elicits another cry
         from the balcony

               head painted blue — a
               robin's egg
               in the floating world

ESSAY: I WAS CALLED LEE ANN-CHAN

I have always been very happy about being born in Japan. I felt it was a great gift given to me by my parents to have such as adventure attached to my birth. My father taught middle school social studies and physical education there through the American dependent schools at what was then Johnson Airbase in a northern outlying district of the greater Tokyo area. I was born October 11, 1963 and grew up with the sounds of both English and Japanese language around me as I was sometimes cared for by a Japanese woman, Masako-san and her daughter, Yoshiko. I treasure the photos of them holding me and smiling at me. My father also taught an English conversation class to Japanese people and our family is still in touch with five members of that group of friends today. When I was age 2-3 we lived on a base in Heilbronn, Germany where other sounds swirled around me again.

My poetry is very sound based and without traditional borders (affinative spirits in poetry include Julie Patton, Cecilia Vicuna who have a multitudinous poetic practice) I am always listening to my surroundings and picking up language, turns of phrase and .moments to keep them alive in words, in poems. I believe that coming into language in the middle of a multi-language environment may have helped tip the balance of my mind to the poetic.

The work I have included hear is from a series of "snapshot" poems based on my own translation of condensed haiku-like moments on a long-awaited trip to Japan I took in 2004.

I don't think I am "really" writing haiku since I do not know Japanese but they are my gestural translation of their form and function, their proliferation in my attempt to catch a living moment in time. Since I was a young child and was read translations of Japanese folk and fairytales like Kintaro, Momo-toro (Peach Boy) and the Story of Kappa, I have alwayt been very interested in stories, forms and literature of Japan and am inspired to "translate the form" and write in new modes knowing them open to me.

LISA SAMUELS

From *Symphony for Human Transport*

The door to the train flew open and the sweetest possible
scent furled in

      then I was in a garden and the parlor-game
split open that scene

      then we were piloted, the pilot game
fiery and unveiled us we were furled we skanked it
held our mouths closed with personal kite loft

what we were to do was close our mouths
with our hands we held our tongues
with our fingers and the animals stared wondering
what scents merge with the cloud-stream
whether talkative in that other possible
          plum change whether
living force could tolerate ourselves shanked in

the door totally smiling without eyes it smiles technological
to accept its surety for were we there
        we played that
obsolescent stream provide a play-list we could check
against a glee before-scorched-path ourselves float out?

so spleen turns fit the scheme path with soft sides
we were touching base
      touched inner, the inner
blind animal scent whose outer trees burnt version
magnetize the disarray the body diamonds in

that inner open blind tent in the cool reverse
day piloting I felt almost along the side of earth
whose planetary dreaming turned the whole
alight, a techno flight sound roars
at night's strange city
honks and bloats of night

machinery proves the loud void
tactics juice the disarray the body gilds far in

* * *

The door to the train flew open gently
absence turned to words
ungathering sublate's call beside
a curled tongue the birth
of present's mirror tusk

given to pre-existence karma drags on the known
the pad-like wavy doors
hitting open close, on and off
very near the hands one might exuberate
without closely conching
too near buried earth who knows

the door of the train flew open a thousand doors
left my mind to open into
one by one they opened
thereby no-one else
the trees burn cool, invisible in pantomime
doors retrofit a purpose we could climb into
the record's metaphor unsaid
beside the train whose open door
bejawed exuberate hinge

the animal of life's forgetting
proffered luck
obeisance flaunt
the animal could laugh and call out
words enwrapped with sound's cut honk
the bird strings plucked inside the door
whose train invents its passengers

* * *

The door to the train flew open and I bedecked
bedoomed in the embrasure klept or kind
small creatures given to semble

gave themselves agaunt to semble
crew merchants gathering up tight animals
to gleam, or so I toughed

I thoughed in the clear wreck of day
lathed on the quell, organic as instruments
never against never agon sway
the stars looking very much like planets
lick the back side of the galaxy
with enormous tongues made of planets
making fumy holes the planets milling gorging
out of the way of the tongue suck
swills the energy of naught

the door for the trained half flew
the train half smiled in arches
flicked mind plenty for its dull pinch
flick mind ready for the match
open on the table where call haps make
the cards flow down the sound
of flicky haps togetherer

the adoring train said open and the doors held
sharp as rain wet on the cross hatch fleck modes
dawdling by day, quiescent as the moon chains
hitting out night's fire wraiths
turning all those leaves to ash
where ash betides its pearly outlines
truly through

From *The Long White Cloud of Unknowing*

The warm breadth of a thumb pad lifted across her cheek in the lower night after her voice said to wake up from a disproportionate story of apartments, packing food in suitcases, tickets of paper from a man with his acquisition service and a woman of indeterminate girth who kept appearing as she stuffed her suitcase heavier and heavier, the low sound of the fog horn establishing a base note upon which slowly her blood steeped and the birds began layering it, the bag full of bread and pies and meat, sweet things too, preparing for a gathered tribe across a water she would get to: in the water the dark blood of thinking pulsed *telling form how to differ from walking a mountain path without literacy or numeracy in evidence, how to step with tiny pinnate leaves and cracked horizon* looking up infusing a sense of cultivated rue in matters of conscience: as when lying amidst poisonous gasses completely stuck, wondering who's pinned you down, the apartment complex shines by lights and sounds enter the windows of your senses in a dark plink call of bird child, you see soldiers nearby in dark trucks and you had better stay down where you are, performing whatever Act, lest they find you out and end up stropping off some part of your body mnemonic for accomplices — having seen an animal sent up flying in the air by a vehicle that barely pauses the animal becomes the inside of your torso and you fly up, slight flecks of dark fluidity cast the lower sky with shades and your social concern cracks:

how could they make a mistake she learns not to ask, the first question to which one knows the answer untrammeled by cavernas infernales del periódico in the cosmic situation of this room *designed for empathy's internal destruction, you are the hit animal* with momentarily nothing to move but the wayside, whose dulcet flats subtend Transverse Mercator bulge through an urban space that draws fertile bodies to the scene of consummation without knowing how to manage the tearing open of the heartskin, like those monks singing *waiwai* in the tuning-stone hall as you sit in white imagining their sexuality, the tremendous radio blares next to her as you seek to assert some part of your own, your skin there, amidst the particles of self-exchange many early feel as gratification or above, alongside, shot from overhead, seen from within, infinitely projected from the riverboats streaming in the water at barges that were ransom for other people's ghosts that had been trammeling this water — *it was the same water!, don't tell me!,* said the long tiny body of the girl who haphazardly basked in the bassinette of fire *so she came out scorched and crying* and never would be the offspring of the princess she imagined she was, burnt beyond what would have been her self-recognition, though she could not see anyone (least of all herself) within the source: that would be a bitter tree, a yielding of the title she was in train to recognize — after all, the experiments in immersion severally presented to her whether she accepted them or not, thus "acceptance" wasn't on the cards, wasn't on the table or suspended bed

here, she made her identity label on the case, she could not put her spread-along legs on a choice at all, which she realized but only like the Ancient

Mariner talks about the ship dropping "below the kirk" and "hill" when everyone knows she is not dropping at all but rather receding, or you away from her, the horizon of where she starts turning like the top of someone's head, después de todos los varios experimentos en la inmersión encontró jadeando, disappearing into the crowd one last time after calling her a strange bird, rāwaho, and giving up on the module of delectation that had been their version of relating, ai

ESSAY: POETRY HAPPENS UPON US

These manuscript excerpts perform some of the things that poetry does with me. *Symphony for Human Transport* enacts repetition and engorgement with the image of a train door flying open on a natural scene. *The Long White Cloud of Unknowing* presents a female confined in a room of inter-textual, cross-institutional, and translingual affect and consequence. In the first case poetry plunges out my positive non-understanding of desire; in the second case poetry threads a kind of blood needle through cultural identities. The first is lyric poetry, the second poetic prose.

Some sayings enter my mind to stay, ranging from "anyone who says you can't run away from your problems just hasn't gone far enough" to my commitment to "imagining what we don't know." The first is perhaps a cynical version of the second. My imagination is fixated in unknowing, centrally connected with transcultural living that started in childhood and continues now. The contingency performed in such transculturalism is intensified for me by early experiences with religious difference (from Presbyterianism to cult polygamy to born again Christianity), sexual conditioning and trauma (from coquetry to rape), relational instability, and linguistic multiplicity.

After my turn to the efficacy of productive action in the world, I understood unknowing as positive and empowered. Contingency in my work now is a proactive opportunity within an ethical orientation to semiotics, phenomenology, and materialism. Signs continually perform worlds. This power is something that commodity and military forces understand very well; I want imaginative work to have the full credit of such understanding. Nothing is a given, and cultural ceremonies weave variegated nows. Embrained love can open up the constituents of cultural making in imaginative acts: that's how poetry happens upon me.

M. NOURBE SE PHILIP

& COUNTING
(A war-in-progress)

Poems	Greco-Persian Wars	*Poems*	51 years	*stanzas of blank verse*
Poems	Wars of Diadochi		47 years	*lines*
	Syrian Wars	*Poems*	106 years	*examples of enjambent*
	Punic Wars	*Poems*	18 years	*caesuras*
	Roman-Persian Wars	*Poems*	694 years	*iambic pentameter feet*
	Roman-Parthian Wars	*Poems*	283 years	*pages left unnumbered*
	Roman-Sassanid Wars	*Poems*	162 years	*manuscript - tear - stained*
	Byzantine-Sassanid Wars	*Poems*	236 years	*rhyming lines*
	Jewish-Roman Wars	*Poems*	70 years	*words beginning with 'w'*
	Iberian Reconquista War	*Poems*	770 years	*unbroken stanzas*
	Three Hundred and Thirty Five Years' War	*Poem*	335 years	*pages missing words*
	Arauco War	*Poem*	290 years	*stanzas containing the word 'war'*
	Hundred Years' War	*Poem*	116 years	*lines that do not mention war*
	Punic Wars	*Poems*	82 years	*syllables that rhyme with war*
	Eighty Years' War	*Poem*	80 years	*torn pages*
	Karin Conflict	*Poem*	66 years	*inscriptions in the margin related to war*
	Korean War	*Poem*	65 years	*breaths needed to recite poem*
	Afghanistan War I	*Poem*	37 years & counting	*words*
	Guatemalan Civil War	*Poem*	36 years	*lines that mention love*
Poems	Wars of the Roses		32 years	*words that rhyme with roses*

— 168 —

First War of Scottish Independence — Poem	32 years	linked poems
Aceh War — Poem	31 years	haikus
Thirty Years' War — Poem	30 years	sonnets
Portuguese Restoration War — Poem	28 years	breath pauses during recitation
Peloponnesian War — Poem	27 years	revisions of poem 27 stanzas long
Angolan Civil War — Poem	27 years	poets reciting one word each of poem
Livonian War — Poem	25 years	metaphors
The Lebanese Civil War — Poem	15 years	chants of open vowel sounds
Great Northern War — Poem	21 years	dactyls
Vietnam War — Poem	19 years	quatrains
War on Terror — Poem	15 years	words too heavy for the tongue to lift
Napoleonic Wars — Poems	12 years	references to 'le sang'
Samaritan Revolts — Poems	71 years	partially burnt pages
Muslim Conquests — Poems	133 years	manuscript pages with word 'cinnabar'
Byzantine-Arab Wars — Poems	371 years	moments of caught breath during recitation
Khazar-Arab Wars — Poems	87 years	reciters of one book of poetry
Byzantine-Bulgarian Wars — Poems	675 years	poems destroyed
Rus'-Byzantine Wars — Poems	213 years	villanelles
Byzantine-Seljuk Wars — Poems	260 years	love poems
The Crusades — Poems	196 years	poems praising war
World War II — Poem	6 years	poems that must be recited at the outbreak of war

Byzantine-Ottoman Wars	Poems	154 years	end-stopped lines
Russo-Turkish Wars	Poems	242 years	line breaks
Second Hundred Years' War	Poem	126 years	run-on lines
Russo-Persia Wars	Poems	106 years	pantoums that say nothing about war
Turkish War of Independence	Poem	4 years	black pages
Sudanese Civil Wars	Poems	60 years & counting	prohibited verses
Congo Wars	Poems	59 years & counting	lines that stain the tongue
American Civil War	Poem	3 years	books of war poetry that mention love
Algerian Wars	Poems	8 years	lines that mention oranges
Tuareg War	Poem	3 years	verses containing allegories of war
Second Sudanese Civil War	Poem	12 years	rhyming stanzas all mentioning war
Angolan War of Independence	Poem	13 years	spondées per poem
Bosnian War	Poem	3 years	lines that mention death in war
First Indochina War	Poem	8 years	syllables per line
Guinea-Bissau War of Independence	Poem	11 years	words that must appear in any poem on war
Kenyan Mau-Mau Uprising	Poem	8 years	mentions of women
Nambian War of Independence	Poem	22 years	women poets chronicling death of sons in war
World War I	Poem	4 years	attempts to write a poem to end all wars poems
Philippine American War	Poem	14 years	lines of longing for missing soldiers written by mothers
Portuguese Restoration War	Poem	28 years	mention of white doves

Poems	Wars of Scottish Independence	61 years	monosyllabic words including war
	South African War of Liberation *poem*	30 years	hours-time taken to read a single poem on love
Poems	Wars of Three Kingdoms	60 years	verses that mention Kings
	Opium Wars *Poems*	21 years	rhyming couplets
	Unification Wars of Arabia *poems*	30 years	omissions of the word 'love'
	Arab-Israeli Conflict *Poem*	68 years	times one war poem was recited
	Sino-Japanese Wars *Poems*	51 years	attempts to recite one poem
	The War on Drugs *Poem*	44 years & counting	missing lines of poetry
	The Trojan War *Poem*	10 years	warriors who have abandoned war for poetry
	The War Against Aboriginal Americans *Poem*	398 years & counting	missing limbs mentioned in one poem
	French and Indian Wars *Poems*	74 years	ballads
	The Syrian Civil War *Poem*	4 years & counting	lines to be repeated over & over & over & over

ESSAY

I write from a place of necessity, urgency and risk. Many years ago Language as a project chose me. It had its roots in where the dice of History had thrown me down– on a scattered necklace of islands in the Caribbean Sea, colonized by Britain, and a long, long way from the continent of my ancestors. I felt then that this project of Language had condemned me, in my writing life at least, to visit and revisit it from different perspectives. What follows is an excerpt from *Looking for Livingstone: An Odyssey of Silence* that can be read as a statement of poetics, since it engages with the issues that have emerged from my entanglement with issues of Language and its fellow traveller, Silence.

> God first created silence; whole, indivisible, complete. All creatures – man, woman, beast, insect, bird and fish – lived happily together within this silence until one day man and woman lay down together and between them created the first word. This displeased God deeply and in anger she shook out her bag of words over the world, sprinkling and showering her creation with them. Her word store rained down upon all creatures, shattering forever the whole that once was silence. God cursed the world with words and forever after it would be a struggle for man and woman to return to the original silence. They were condemned to words while knowing the superior quality of silence."
>
> In a voice that cracked with age, Bellune, the oldest woman of the ECNELIS, told us this as we all sat around the evening fire. Chareem, the youngest gril-child to have seen her blood that year and come into her womanhood, lifter her hand, her palm facing outwards; Bellune fell silent as she began to speak. "There are some who believe the first act of God was to create the word – primary and indispensable." Chareem's voice, still childlike in tone, ever faltered once over syllable or word: "Offspring of God, Word, seamed by silence its shadow…These people – the word-believers – believe in the power of words – to do magic, solve problems, grow crops; words to live by and die, and more than anything else to banish silence." For a brief moment the men, woman and children of the ECNELIS waited…
>
> Their stories tell of how God, feeling bored, came down to earth one day in the shape and form of a man and offered a choice to the first person he saw – a poor peasant: the word of God or silence.

Quelled by the splendour of God made man before him, and being devout and very frightened, the poor man chose the word of God – believing that silence was the same as being one of the dumb animals he cared for. God laughed, believed himself vindicated, and rewarded the earth with words and more words. And so their ancestor, so their stories tell, mounted armies of words to colonise the many and various silences of the peoples round about, spreading and infecting with word where before there was silence. God rewarded them with an even greater hunger for words to drown out the silence they still sensed in unguarded moments."

A male voice, deep and resonant, now took up the story: "Every hundred years by our calendar, during the month of Cassiopeia, we go to war with the SINCEEL – those whose beliefs differ from ours about the primacy of word or silence in the beginning of the world. After the battle, and for the next hundred years, the loser is condemned to allow the beliefs of the winner. Where there was silence, the winner imposes words; where the word, silence."

I was never able to find out what the ECNELIS believed. Had they, believer-in silence, been losers, cursed and damned to the sacrilege of the word, all the while craving silence; or were they words-believers, secretly vouchsafing their belief with every word they uttered, as they prepared to go to war and win again?

MAIRÉAD BYRNE

Three Oranges

A woman took three oranges from a bowl on her kitchen counter on a long flight around the world to Seoul. The first orange was small. The second was larger. And the third orange, of course, was the largest of all. The woman would have liked to eat this orange on the long plane journey but she didn't because she didn't want the zest or tang of the thing to spray passengers or inculcate the desire for oranges in anyone because after all what is the protocol for sharing fruit with strangers on planes? This was a long plane ride. When she got to her hotel room though and was alone in that quieter way, she took the largest orange out, dug her fingers into it to leverage up a piece of peel and when all the peel was practically off out popped a little scaly head with a backward india-rubber flip, followed by shoulders like the arms of a scissors, then an entire bronze body like a set of fat tendons or a very slim whippet with a head like a tiny dinosaur. The creature jumped out of the orange and disappeared into a corner of the room. The woman opened the second orange and a bristly yellow and green amphibian jumped out. *Bang!* That creature sprang into a high corner too and disappeared. It was a shock. What option was there now but to turn to the third small and innocuous orange? The woman didn't like to dig her fingers and thumbs in anymore and she was right because out of this orange, before she had even lifted off the first sticky piece of peel, came the feathery black leg of a hairy spider. Just one leg. Well of course none of this actually happened because you are not allowed to bring oranges into South Korea. In fact, the orange with the yellow and green lizard and the orange with the spider leg had to be turned over at Customs. As for the largest orange, the woman ate that on the plane, in a moment when everyone was launched in their own bubble, eyes open or not, and a fine skein of semi-darkness shrouded economy class, bestowing the illusion of privacy.

Thinking of You

I went to the pound store and I fainted in there. I went to the church and I fainted. I ran like a rat round the back tracks and shacks of the Regional Hospital and I kept falling back like a plank thinking of you and passing out flat. When I saw you in the very small house that just about fit but didn't suit you my hand shot out to cradle your head and I said *Look he looks fine / Look he looks as if sleeping.* I went to your real house and I passed out. My giant right leg bent at the knee and I took a baby step past the hole in the floor through the door into your house and I passed out. When I bobbed up—one airy shoulder wedged against one wall of the hall, the other airy shoulder against the other—I swam arm over arm through the air to the bottom stair where I clung heaving dust from my lungs till I passed out. When I came to it was dark. I hobbled on my knees up the stairs—eyeballs sloshing in my head—none of my joints working any more—I got to the top and did a belly flop smack on the landing, then I passed out. I passed out in your room and on the threshold of your room and before the threshold and within. *The stub of my toe touched the threshold / the hoof of my foot arched the wood.* I got to the bed and I passed out. Under the window I stood head bowed and I passed out. I lapped about the foot of the ladder to the attic and *you know where*. I fainted all over that room. The cigarette stubbed in the ash tray seemed like a quiet chair but I couldn't gather myself enough to sit in that quiet room up to my ankles in ash-drift so I went one way, then the other at the same time. How could I know which way to turn? So I passed out. That time I passed out for a very long time and I didn't get up until the light in the room turned green and the light in my head turned red.

Water

Near the piazza at the end of the street there is a drinking fountain and in the fountain there is water for which you need to walk through the streets (a very long time) to the piazza at the end of the street. If you could go through the streets, if you have limbs sturdy enough to make your way through the crowded streets, and the heat, though they weigh like iron, you could get this fountain water, you could get this cool water, you could be refreshed if you had the energy to go and the energy to bend your head and drink. The energy you drink is called water. The energy to get the water is called walking, or forward march. The feeling when you walk through crowds toward the end of the street goes on a very long time. People are eating in all the restaurants and you can't quite believe that there will be a fountain where you stop a hole with your finger and water spurts out. What do you care about the little tables and the loaded platters of food or the dour tight faces of the tourists or even the smooth attentive ones? There is silence in all the houses and you can't quite believe the Walgreens will be lit by round bushes of light and that there will be people compact as skittles in there and that you have the energy to walk through snow, and boots, and the energy of money to pay for soup that would give you energy to walk through the snow the next time to the Walgreens at the end of the street. It takes a very long time to walk through the crowd. You walk in the middle of the street into a raw caesura torn between the people on the right and the people on the left, not counting the very large guys at right angles outside the restaurants calling people in. You can no longer call a crowd a crowd. It is a matrix. A gel. You are just another sticky particle. No-one hears you as you walk that very long short way. No-one hears you as you stand at the window to look outside feeling the heat's declaration of intent, no longer remembering the nights of looking silently for a long time at the bead of light that is a plane traveling across the sky or the pleasant mornings in the bus-shelter on North Main Street watching the world lurch by.

Toronto to Boston

I was told to pick him up at the gate and when I got there, right enough, he was waiting for me. A small man, still and alert, in dark clothes, a dark overcoat over his arm. He was made of language, with white paper collar and cuffs. Toronto is a good city for poetry and the take-off from Toronto Airport to Boston is spectacular. He, of course, had no idea what was in store. I introduced myself to him. He was polite. And gave his name. We waited. I didn't see the point in explaining anything. Something very special had been arranged. Then off on swing. The plane was small and we seemed to shoot straight up. We flew just above the clouds, hugging Lake Ontario. I was in the window-seat, just behind the wing. I could see the dinghy of the engine jutting forward, a donut, almost sphincter-like. Below us puffy forests of white clouds. Further down shoals of sparse dabs out for a Sunday stroll. Further down again the edge of the lake. Little white houses like oblong pieces of chalk. A scattering of nits. Blue-grey which could be water or sky. Above the horizon a grey brown band of cloud. Small rounded separate bright woolly hilltops as if we could visit our relatives there, taste real food on a raw wood table, in a very real place. And all above a vaster hemisphere, expansive, with its own calm organizations of cloud, remote and self-contained. It was like there was a heaven and then a heaven on top of heaven, the two heavens girded all around by the horizon. Empyrean. We both leaned forward. I felt the charge of his attention and saw him, from the corner of my eye, raise his right hand fingers splayed to his face and hold it slightly slanted before him so that he looked through the fingers through the window to everything above and below, the expanse to which only the feeding in of the lake edge and the sun behind us lent direction. It was as if his gaze, even so governed, governed and stitched the levels and layers together. I felt cupped between wing and wing, if not in shadow then in a valley, darkened by the blaze of his concentration. He was sitting beside me but seemed hurled above me, his eyes the apex from which the visible depended. I could not see what he saw but the realization surged through me: *Now he looks down on what he has looked up to*. His hand shook. With great precision his left hand reclaimed it. Set it down like a body on the tray table in front of him. The cabin became a cabin again. It was still light for our descent. I looked sideways through the window. I could see asphalt snaking rivers, pooling asphalt lakes, crossed by roads that looked like bicycle tracks. Needlepoint housing estates or cemeteries. Lakes into which the edges of the land reached like how ice retreats when you pour warm water on it. And vaguer lakes, more alive in their vaguer outlines: dragons, foxes, an opening hand. Fields brushed with charcoal, as if he had drawn them and rubbed them down with his palm. He didn't stir. I could smell the smell of pastilles, and eucalyptus. His eyes were open but he looked straight ahead. As we taxied to the gate, I kept my eyes on the window. I could see my own reflection. I knew when I looked around, he would be gone.

ESSAY

My first instinct is to play around with language. Otherwise I am a very truthful, logical, clear-minded, communicative person and that is exactly how all my interactions would be if my first instinct didn't jump in and nip that lucidity in the bud.

All my life I wanted to be a poet. It was a secret for 30 years. I wasn't able to say it out loud until I came to America. Alan Dugan was the person who took the angst out of the conversation for me. Other things I would have loved to do if I had known about them in time are painter, drummer, and pilot. I toyed with including obstetrician but know I don't flourish in institutions.

It surprises me that the quality I prize most in artists is anarchic spirituality. Hopkins has it. Donne. I've been very influenced by Frederick Douglass and Bob Marley. How did this happen? I am anti-religious. In heaven, I won't deny that I may be found standing at the end of the bar with the wits, or sunk over my pint with the solitary ones, but my entrails are tangled up with the ecstatics.

The Internet is bound up with poetry for me. That's the thing I have to make sense of, to use. It is my opportunity, my country in a way, more than Ireland or America. I'm not skilled or well-educated in digital media so it's a little like my Gerard Manley Hopkins fixation: I don't deserve it, it's inexplicable, but *I MUST HAVE IT!* How to write, for whom, and the meaning of the transaction.

MARCELA SULAK

from *La Malinche's Love-Letters to Fernando Cortés*

1. No body of water is named for Cortés.

I rarely think of him embodied
when I think of him.

The natives are always
the inverse:
white-as-blank-page moths,
drawn by
the dark light of reason.

These mornings I awake—pushing
back the covers
of a slowly closing tome—into
that dark spot
-lit void we all assume
is the stage.

Between the sturdy banks of his voice,
I like how my tongue flows.

2. As his translator,

there was nothing I feared
more than his silence,
except the words against
which the world receives
her degradations.

He said the streets were paved in gold.
He said the streets were paved.
He said there were streets.
He said there, there.

3. Cartography

If there is one
true road only,
as the friars say,
there must be
many maps, and their
cacophonous cartographers, drawing
our attention to the
similarity between it
and a golden tongue.

They call me *La Chingada*,
because of him,
but it was my mother
who sold me
and didn't I make a
map so fine
you could fill every loss
with a world? .

4. Vacation photos from the new Eden

Usually
I travel local transportation
systems,
snapping photos from dusty
windows.

Dead-
pan, our secular approximations
trip
across the photographic paper
of the divine.

6. Circumstances under which you may resign

The anorexic stomach
clenches
its swallowed fist
of food.
It's wrong, Cortés,
to say,

to consume beauty, you must
completely break
with it. It must come to you
on a platter
from outside. You must arrange
yourself, too,
so that your inner ugliness

does not disrupt your pleasure.
Anything I say,
you say, will be caressed
until it comes
to resemble a truth we once
read about.

If only he would have
liked me a little, it would
have made such a difference.
It would have changed everything.

7. Gold

Here they are, those cornfields
that led Cortés to claim
the streets of Tenochtitlan
were paved in gold. Whose
ankles swished through them today
to meet a minor destiny?
I carried our son through
those very fields the day
he was born, *mestizo,*

mestizo, translated across
Cortés's pollinating tongue.

8. *Cortés's vanity*

One evening you described the void
between the pillars of your world,
which you have dressed in the most modest clothes

and never mention in public. How your face,
reclining on the unflattering yellow sofa, finally
looked its age. It was a relief.

How I would have loved
to stand one night with you
under a meteor shower

and let some other entity
cascade its celestial seed all over the world. And could
you hold my hand and squeeze until I returned

from the skies I rarely visit anymore
to the yellow sofa, now
smelling faintly of drought.

9. *You can call me mother, of course*

They call me La Malinche,
because I betrayed. Cortés called me
Doña Marina. Our friends

called us by the same name.
You can call me mother,
of course. But what I like most,

is the unanswered calling in the sun
and the corn and the coins, those luminous
voices eternally seeking their gods.

The editor suggested "correspondence" as the title

of a piece I was writing with my friend while our countries warred;
though the elegance appealed,

I didn't like the *agree, conform*
definition that predates *communicating via letters.*

Were I asked again, I'd have agreed
to *correspond*—there was, after all more

we agreed on
than not: That her side's

missiles were wildly inaccurate; my
side's more precise, and that we both lived

in buildings no sane person would waste a bomb on unless
they were landlords. (My building's exterior holes

are plugged with plastic soda bottles. I'm not sure why,
but they magnify the swallows wings) (and I

live in the fancy part) So we agree, it's safer to be
bombed by our side in war, but for daily life, which was most

of the time, it was better to be us, for only
assholes would tear-gas her campus.

And that baking was a wonderful thing to do
—the bombs don't make cake fall if it's almond flour.

And that it sounds exactly like the word: boom-
boom, from the chest of earth, and

politics were for the evil. I said
Conversation. I love the *con*—

the *converse*—the *versation*—
the living together, having dealings;

the *talking* part only came later, 1575
or so. We discovered we could phone

each other, without any documentation, just like that
—our voices didn't believe at first—without

a roaming charge even. This was probably wishful. It's old
French.   And no one can see very clearly

through barbed wire lines that catch and stretch
everything like soap bubbles:

inside-out and back—all that spin.
                        When we

close our eyes and push. It's so difficult to walk here without
stepping on a cliché, or in the ruts

of heavy tropes,   for once the argument was fresh and wet. Yet
everything. I do feels framed as in the second day

of bombing: I took my girl in the rain to school
on my bike, in my melon-colored rain

coat, wet hair flying, and a hidden photographer shot me.
I said stop. I dismounted and went right

up into his face. What, I asked, would this frame demonstrate.
What would it prove and to whom and why and who

determined
its borders?

ESSAY: MY POETRY I BELIEVE IS LOCATED. IT IS I WHO IS NOT

Located. Necessarily. Not necessarily located. It feels as if the etymological root *Locute* should be related to *Locate*, because what you are allowed to say, what you think to say, depends a great deal on where you are and who you are talking to and who else is listening (i.e. why you are talking). Like many Texas-born, my mother tongue was not my mother's tongue. Or, rather, it was by the time I was born, because my mother, having learned English in School, soon forgot all her Czech except for the rosary and a few phrases. It was patriotic to forget. All four of my grandparents got to Texas because the Republic of Texas was advertising heavily in Central Europe for white people to come to settle the land, anticipating the *Tejanos* withering, after the Mexicans had been kicked out and the American Indians had been killed or gone. The poverty was wretched in the mountainous regions of Silesia, and in Valassko they had overlords of their own to deal with. They kept the newspaper advertisements for a long time. It took a long time to get money for passage—my family showed up in the 1900s.

I was haunted by a particular spirit on the rice farm on which I grew up, on the land that my farmer father bought from one of the original 300 Stephen F. Austin Families, white settlers in Texas. "Did you see the spirit?" I'd ask my brothers and sister and parents. "Since there are no such thing as ghosts, I know it's just my imagination," they'd answer. I grew up wondering which murdered nation it had belonged to, and also, how La Maliche, Hernando Cortes's translator, felt, after the conquistadores had destroyed her people. But then I'd wonder, which people were hers—since she'd already been betrayed by her mother before she went over, or was sold, to Cortes. What loyalty had she owed? And why do we equate land ownership with innocence?–or at least prior land ownership with goodness? Wasn't her personal lot better with Cortes? Better to admit it—we don't really value innocence and goodness, but we don't want anyone taking our land, or living on land that we want. And yet, where do women come into the picture? Because women historically didn't inherit land—they were given, like land, and possessed. They were vessels, like translators, haunted by ghosts and language.

As my body moved over different lands, Venezuela, Germany, Czech Republic, and now Israel, and different languages flowed through my mouth, I became a literary translator and sometimes simultaneous interpreter. I wrote "La Malinche's Love Songs to Hernando Cortes" pondering the almost unmentionable fact that sometimes—often—national interests conflict with feminist ones, meaning personal ones. After all, a woman was historically meant to be a vessel, just like a translator is. But sometimes, like me, you move countries to escape the abuse of a man who fathered your child (and also because you need a job). Or you betray one family so that you can have another. It happens, and not just to me.

My nine-year-old daughter's native tongue—Hebrew—is not mine. And also, my Facebook Sulak "friends" tell me (as did my Czech friends when I lived there) that my surname is Turkish. It means water—that which flows across boundaries. And so Czech also wasn't my surname's native tongue—my name was an invader name, from the Ottoman invasion of Moravia about 300 years ago. But since they didn't succeed in the invasion, my surname's presence in Morvia is, in fact, endearing, rather than annoying. I imagine the first Moravian possessor of my surname was championed by a translator, a sort of La Malinche figure, and our line was born. I wonder about the slippage, though, between the message the men meant and the one that was received, transformed, in a new language, by the woman. Sometimes I imagine that translation gave back the original meaning that had been deformed through conquest.

My poems explore the gap between what the original speaker thought he meant and what is actually experienced, in translation. The thing that is lost in translation is a world, of course, but whose world is it? We often privilege the original statement to an extraordinary degree when the translator is a member of a "conquering" or more powerful culture—maybe in exchange for the land that was taken—but what about when a conqueror is translated? Maybe the translation the clearer image of the thing the original speaker originally meant to say?

The context for the second poem was a 2012 Gaza Roundtable discussion in the *Los Angeles Review of Books*, in which I was meant to take the "Israeli" side in a discussion about the first Gaza war. I found this impossible—not only because I'd then been living in Israel for a mere 18 months, and my citizenship was an expediency, to give me a work permit. The real issue I had was that I couldn't get my head around who got to even say what the "sides" of this war were. I said I'd speak only if I spoke together, on the same team, as a Palestinian woman, a friend I'd mentored in the States. But I discovered that we weren't on the same "side" either. I began to despair of the meaning of the simplest word—or rather, I began to live in the idea that words are infinitely expandable and shockingly retractable. How does one escape this condition? I'm not sure one can. So my poem reads as impossibly philosophical in the face of horrific physical suffering. And yet, as a woman, I understand too well, the ideological price one is willing to pay for the sake of the physical well being of one's child. These poems have no answers—only questions. Because all that is really true is a question.

MEGAN M. GARR

The age of progress

You will understand

You will say I understand

Say sea   Say see

Watch it come up in rage

No fort but sand

Watch it swallow the mustard fields

Witness the murder of everything

It is the age of progress which is: the age of dead bodies on streets at sea in too far offshore in camps in churches at the feet of walls in rubble in crosshairs in the deserts we make for them
You lived too long believing in the age of progress

Look how wrong you were

Look how the acoustics repeat like air

Look how murder repeats like air

Stockholm

Had the half of us said stop

The heated inside

And what of it

We had ready our adornments

our getaway

The trees had all died

We were left with piles

I said, find it all

don't stop digging

If we don't already the exposed world

there was no other reason

Holmium

was just an errand

We were mining for light

And then it was

The sun burst glow one final final

We looked down through the last

to all the mammals cover

The heated inside

bang bang

We didn't even stop for it

The world is ending and you are far from home

So what if: see sadness.

Is there any: see inoperative.

Then what is distance?

Distance is here enough—

Because the country her country was

From all shoulders kudzu in

                                      every subject at its highest pitch

We are perfectly arranged

—Slow down

ESSAY: STORING

In a *storing* there are workarounds, compromises, and patience. This is not the *storing* of supplies, the accumulation of grain or data, this is the *Nederlandse* disruption, the breakdown of a machine or system; the thing we expected to work has stopped, or it has changed.

A core sample of my poetry would go something like this. Tennessee's sub-tropical hillsides, some measure of clay and limestone. Montana's summer fires and snow. A thin layer of Glasgow's streets, beer and drugs. And a not-slowly building mass of Amsterdam's slightly salty air, pigeon shit and brick, mixed here and there with volcanic, artic sediment. Narrative, post-Fugitive metaphors giving way to a spartan, broken lyric, enjambed sounds of a Dutch tongue insisting interruption at the line.

These poems try to take that *storing* to the frontlines of the place and time I thought I had been born into, and was not, to the confidence of the social justice marches of my childhood, to their failures, and to the blame that leaving builds in the distance.

MICHELLE NAKA PIERCE

from *Estranger*

Raw

Imagine a nation. Treat it as a[n] object so as to promise a country. I promise the signs of ra[p]ture. To represent. To analyze discourse. Isolat[ion] form[s] a system. Orient a realit[y]. I lovingly gaz[e] an essence, a matter of difference. Serve interplay. Allow me to enter. The idea detached, addressed, consider[ed].

Are not other, another   another wisdom?*

It is the possibility of mutation, a revolution. Someday: we must write the history of our own obscurity. Manifest the density of our ISM[s]. We may have occasion. There are a thousand sand[s] to learn. Orient! Labor will be necessary. Necessary. A slender thread of light. Search out not other but the fissure. This fissure appear[s], or so it is hoped, in any sense, with any number of flashes. Or better still: a situation. This situation is one. A disturbance. A subversion. A shock. To point its place: a void. Writing is a satori. The subject writes violence.

*Are not other, another another wisdom? The slow drain. The body in recovery. This emptiness of language you feel is an emptiness in writing. You are exempt from meaning when the body situates itself. Cold feet. Dark hands. A light seeping in from the other room. Silence is not golden, but red and blue. A symphony in yellow. What skin enters here but the test. A sequence. A failing. To fracture the binary, one must merge. A tertiary, formed by the replacement of atoms. The bird's innermost flight feathers. Bonded carbons. Sleep.

Own Language

Dream a foreign language and perceive difference without ever being. Refract the possibilities of our own syntax. Unsuspected utterance, displace[d]. In a word, descend into shock until everything in us vacillate[s].

That tongue which comes to us, which makes us turn a culture precisely.*

We know the concepts have been constrained. Articulations. To gain a vision, glimmer. Suggest us. A remark on Japanese opens up the realm of texts. Permit us a landscape: the speech we own under divine proliferation. We can no longer speak a simple line of words, a[n] envelope empty of and not dense. Direct our sentences from outside and from above. A way of diluting—fragment[ing]—particle[s]. Or this: distinguish notabl[e] verbs. Introduce the form, the struggle. Enforce the very structure. Signs cut off the alibi in a radical way. It is a matter of conceiving what our language does not. How can we imagine simultaneously without tribute, without imagination. Face the origin of Zen. Translate meditation. Restor[e] both subject and god. They return and many others contest the limits by which we claim to destroy the wolf by lodging comfortably in its gullet. Such an aberrant grammar.

*That tongue which comes to us, which makes us turn a culture precisely. Lately the skin hurts. A dry heat in the cold. I want to scratch until I reach the bone. The marrow. Suck it out through my teeth. Perhaps there, I will find the things I have been missing. Added weight is a way to disappear. The gaze of otherness so harsh, the questioning, the stare. I see my reflection in the darkened mirror. I cannot speak Japanese. I try. I bow. My voice raises an octave. I pray for sleep, for my insides to settle. The incongruity disturbs equilibrium and more. I envision a tunnel through which to burrow. I am a fox in a cemetery. I walk the paths. I eat berries. I chase white birds. When you join me at dusk, I search your depth, looking for a wintery grave.

ESSAY: THIS IS NOT JAPAN, OR *ESTRANGER*: A RUPTURED TEXT

> "I do not know immigration or exile, but I do know how to inhabit the cities I have been in, and I have recollected old identities and fashioned new ones without knowing what borders I have crossed. By cities, I mean states of mind. By event, I mean some thing recollected as something in its presence, as in this movement and the ability to recognize movement. I do not apprehend movement, which is a move into and around movement, because I can't move into this body moving."—J'Lyn Chapman, *Beastlife*

> "If I want to imagine a fictive nation, I can give it an invented name, … so as to compromise no real country by my fantasy. It is this system which I shall call: Japan."—Roland Barthes, *Empire of Signs*

I woke one day and found myself in this body. One I could not recognize. I did not recognize my face, the sound of my voice. The color of my skin. A sedentary lapse in judgment. I embarked on writing "a passage" to find my way clear. The somatic drift. The process is slow. There are relapses. The comfort of a shell calling me back.

It started in a cemetery. I felt the weight of collective bodies. Then a collective weightlessness. I turned energy into song. Dance into words. Movement into text. I mapped a healing. A new kind of psychogeography. A poetics of ruin and recovery.

"Catch your breath": this is what the mind thinks as the body recovers. This is what the body feels after bouts of insomnia.

Estranger begins as an erasure of Roland Barthes' *Empire of Signs*. Barthes "is not analyzing the real Japan but rather one of his own devising." I wondered if the text would mirror elements of my "estranged citizenship" to me. That is, I was born in Japan. I grew up in the US. I am a stranger to my birth country. I am estranged from the nuance of daily life and language.

Estranged: as in distanced, foreigned, removed. My perception and knowledge limited to glimpses, to gestures that made the voyage, to intermittent return visits. Japan has been rendered alien to me, or I to Japan. Thus, what arises when one is removed from a community? What ties are severed irreparably? Which customs and beliefs have been eschewed or replaced? The majority of a life lived apart—separated at birth by an ocean. Is the body *in toto* dissimilar in character, feature, motion? The body and its positioning have been put aside, beside itself. There is no normal state. The body left unfamiliar. The mind astonished.

This alienation [alien nation] is a "binary fracture," a term I developed, which articulates a neither/both concept. It is an aperture. It is the liminal: a transitional space, occupying a position at, or on both sides of, a boundary or threshold. It destabilizes the binary. It functions as imbrications. For instance, I am half Japanese, half American. Thus, I am neither Japanese nor American. I am both Japanese and American.

What is it to explore notions of representation, using Barthes as structure and René Magritte's "This is not a pipe" as a stance? Namely, when one makes depictions of something (such as Japan or Japanese culture), one makes a copy (a mimetic gesture) that points to the original. These renderings are always at least once removed from the referent. This investigation puts pressure on the perception of identity/culture and complicates the subject and the function of subjectivity. *Estranger* takes on notions of "border identity" as it relates to "estranged citizenship." As stated previously, Japan is my birth country, but I was soon relocated to the States and grew up as an American citizen. Yet I write this sentence on the 7th floor of a hotel in Tokyo. I am not allowed into the building without a passport. Outside there are sirens. In my ear bud, I hear Japanese vocabulary on repeat. How does the hybrid body negotiate "cultural shock" or the incongruity of "cultural tourism" of one's birth site?

Sometimes when one writes, only words happen.

What follows each erasure is a somatic inquiry. An understanding that settles cellularly. In attempting to fracture the binary, syncope surfaces. "Syncope: a temporary absence of self or suspension of movement, a hesitation or dissonance." I once fainted in the shower and woke in a tub of water. I recall the bloodstained liquid surrounding my body. My first thought upon emerging was not to bloody the carpet, my shirt, the good towels. I sat in the emergency room for an hour while my hair matted with red viscosity. The moment before fainting, I thought about the rush, the heat, the pause. I saw myself falling before the fall had begun. When I write that I am a hybrid text, this is not a metaphor. The body can be read. When one writes, one is not writing on a blank slate. Each book is a palimpsest. I steal. I am a magpie attracted to shiny new words. When I say steal (bricolage, collage, cut-up, constraint, erasure), I really mean recover. What is underneath, between, below. The matrix of how one body/text intersects another and another throughout one's lifetime.

A poetic utterance does not happen in isolation. I rely on the collaborative gesture in order to breathe. One's evening is another's dawn. See Mobius strip poetics and Buckminster Fuller: "A structure is simply an inside and an outside."

To be a blind camera is to understand an emphasis on erasure. The palimpsest as recovery and syncope (the omission of sounds/letters). Absence teaches me what presence could not. Thus, I must recover through erasure.

The body saves us.

The body inside a favorable position. What country is lifted? To adjoin the clear state of matter with fluent speech. Outside each month, we connect with the sharpened tongue. We meet in advanced movement. A dance that lasts just beyond our sight. No one here sleeps in urgency. The effects of language are still unknown. In the answer, the inquiry emerges—in sweet blues and greens. The edge progresses and retracts, a hallucination beyond the coil. I am a hologram. The current resides inside the lens. Nerve. Embryo. Ghost.

Estranger: I am this ruptured text.

MỘNG-LAN

"from" *Buenos Aires Notebook: Fugues & Equivalences*

1

                                          an owl's flight
peerless
swooping   swerving in a silver array of wisdom
                        fastidious to silence

city of dreams
                  city of dreamlessness
city of sleeplessness & waking while sleeping
sleeping while awake

                    city of the comatose

ciudad de los muertos

              city of remorse   failed & light-hearted
                  romances

city in which your nightmares follow you
                      in which your dreams abandon you
or in which you abandon your dreams

   in which most is impossible
                      without shouting

     sleeping i awaken knowing

           my waking thoughts keep dreaming

   of what could be possibilities
                & keep on working

2

    [head down don't look to see what people
   are doing]

ciudad de llueve remorseless unrelenting rain
          rain that augurs
    decay destruction

the clearing of all social events all afternoon teas
        work all obliterated

except for Nisman's silent march
       people somber in umbrellas

un sueño:
 mammoth elephants their sleek silver trunks
         dead on the ground
flat silvery-white with sweat
    prostrate no longer in agony
           trunk down

in utter morbidity i move forward closing my eyes
      make myself blind

cuaderno de Buenos Aires
  only place to
      only water & turmoil
    & oh pls listen to this song
   as we die
 as we go forth
     & as never before make sense
   of our lives

did i ask for exhilaration of the body?

did i ask for lies   constant *mentiras*

did i ask   for *this*   all of *this* complicates

right from the beginning   you were fidgety
                     (desde el principio nervioso)

on the deck   speechless
     on the brim something new   heat heat & hotness

where were you
     when the birds first sang their song?

   transmit
               a poetry of sheer beauty

i will now think in panoramic skies   unstifled
     my algorithm   is love multiplied x number of times

a song permeates into the blueness of evening
     cables of unenduring lust

sprinkle dust over my nightly cries

     monks guard my heart
    in monotonous chant
around the blue hotel   the sun hotel

       the hotel that never sleeps

Particulars

how strange to feel your strength
        as soon as i touched you

name the nouns
            fingers on wood fingers on strings
                      the hallowed chord of a guitar

toe on grass nail on toe
            the Achilles tendon
at the crossroads of my own knowing

                one writes
        the particulars
           to mean the whole

i've outgrown the red skies
        las noches oscuras de Buenos Aires

sin fin

outgrown the need
        to be miserable

Love Poem to *Witthau Tom Yam Talay*

i stare into you O my *Tom Yam*

        your beauty difficult to behold
                i will never be the same again

so saucy you are
      tangy   your body
              limed with a halo of orange & red

let me taste you again & again

          lemon grass galangal fresh kaffir lime juice
    fish sauce
               fresh chilli onions

  angular crab limbs
          put my tongue where it has never been before
into your caverns   shrimpy spine
                slurp your membranous rice
        noodles

O *Tom Yam*

i graze my lips over your lime leaves
              suck on your stalks of lemon grass
hold the slivers of ginger
            over my tongue

            your tongues of red chilli peppers
      tantalize me

in Bangkok you reign supreme
          after you
      i am not the same

       let me taste you again
& again

    your marrow

ESSAY: POETICS STATEMENT

I write what I witness, what I feel and think, bridging cultures, bridging understanding between the sexes and human beings. To make people drunk with words, yet also make people sober. To bring testimony to the joys and horrors, to bring new music, new sounds, new ideas, new ways of hearing. New ways of seeing, opening eyes and hearts. To journey further into the sea of challenges; to experience, then write of it, indeed, sing of it, in the best and direct way possible. *Joie de vivre*, to infuse love of life, humor, irony. Yet also, seriousness, earnestness, beauty, and the simple things, into my poems, asking the important questions. To create beauty from disorder and inner necessity. To organize and understand what is going on in my life, put order to intense emotion. I believe that poetry has the power to heal. Incantations, alchemy of words, with the ability to change atmospheres, moods, and peoples. To create a living entity when it is read, gains life and heals.

What I hope to accomplish: the trans-cultural impact of my work is important. My family and I were evacuated one day before the fall of Saigon from our native Vietnam. As a refugee, I grew up and was educated in the United States. The traditional Vietnamese upbringing while growing up in the U.S. that I was afforded, speaking only Vietnamese at home and strict discipline, greatly influenced my character and personality. At the same time, I hurled myself into learning and speaking five to six other languages in the process of learning English, over the many years. Coming from a whole family of healers and doctors instilled in me a desire and willingness to help others. The doctor heals the body, while poetry heals the soul.

I went on to live parts of my adult life in Asia and South America. Where I've lived, what I've seen, and the cultural ramifications of all this is important to my work and subject matter: history, Vietnam, Asia in general, South America, particularly Buenos Aires, the tango dance, and love, not only of the physical variety. I have written a series of love poems with the subject matter of food, vegetables, fruits, and various ethnic foods. Further, socio-political concerns are of great importance: the people and how they live, wars and their aftermath. Being a refugee from a long war, from a country that has had a history of wars, I have always been concerned about the political impact of anything and everything. Feminist concerns are of vital importance, writing from the point of view of women, women's rights and politics. Ecopoetics, writing about the earth, taking care of the earth, singing of the earth, the beauty, vast skies, indeed, love poems to the earth, are vitally important.

My literary influences cross the divide of oceans and time: Vietnamese poets such as Nguyen Du, the Chinese poet and philosopher Lao-tzu (Taoism), the Buddhist teachings, haiku, Japanese poets such as Basho; Latin American and South American poetry such as Pablo Neruda, César Vallejo, Gabriela Mistral, Octavio Paz, Sor Juana, J.L. Borges; the Spanish poets and writers such as Lorca, Cervantes; the Divine Comedy of Dante; French poets such as Rimbaud and the surrealists such as André Breton; the English poets such as T.S. Eliot, and of course, the numerous American poets, such as Adrienne Rich, Sylvia Plath, Frank O'Hara, e.e. cummings, Pound, Whitman, Dickinson, Bishop, etc.

Manner & Technique: to paint with words and lines, not only descriptively and figuratively, but to show on the page, placement of words on page as a visual artist would, in a sense, projective verse. The shape and form of the poem is a vehicle for the words of the poem. I consider spaces between words as breaths, much as a composer would, using white space as moments, a measure to mark meaning and breath.

NANCY GAFFIELD

Departures

I

fix your bearings
and head into the north
tuning to the acoustics of the trees
                     (coppiced

ghost-must
       strange-henge
              crow knows

                            I was slow
                            to grasp it
                            that knowledge

the surface falls away
       that place
       no longer exists

                            and I am marked
                            by degrees

fortitude | a kind of | muscular energy |a voice || you get that
    sift
            distil | old material

II
autopsy [n] The action or process of seeing with one's own eyes; personal observation, inspection, or experience. Now rare.
Med. Examination of the organs of a dead body in order to determine the cause of death, nature and extent of disease, result of treatment, etc.; post-mortem examination; an instance of this.

a mode of authorial power || ancient practice

I saw my father
doing it | *das Unumgängliche*
      that which cannot be got around
      avoided or
      seen to the back of

III

the shadow of the observer
cast against mist

      Brocken spectre

lichen   licken   lingon
lingonsylt   when you are
when you are   dust
when even your bones   your teeth

                        yet-na
                        their unique composition
                        position location
                        in the jawbone
                        protects the strands

concealment in the pulp
teeth
are truth-tellers

IV

What occurs to me now is that both my parents died on the same day eighteen years apart. He no longer remembered her name. "What was the name of that woman?" he often asked me. "Do you mean my mother?"

      repine | repain | pain again

When I was seven they changed my name. I couldn't find myself after that. I started to call myself by the name of his first wife, the one he found hanging in the basement. I refused to go down there, but it was a different house. I know this now. Out of his hands or control of.

in loco parentis || ubi sunt

V

you were in the grip
    of the vague terror of
        a specific dream

it is like the room is full of whispering
    ghosts in the walls in the attic in the cellar
        the house is full of them

your dream is a germ
    that triggers the antibodies
        of your fears

you think they have come for you
    so you fetch an axe
        and begin to attack the walls

o what a lot of guilt and blame
    a sheet placed on a hob
        till it catches flame

on Thursday they will bury the ashes
    in consecrated ground
        the mind reduced

to a pot of grey cinder   the mourners
    cloaked in a cold draft
        of invisibility

go back to sleep   *I say*   *go back to sleep*

VI

the bargain was struck
that which cannot
be seen
                to the back of

at our wedding
I played Bob Dylan
Blood on the Tracks
over and over again
Isis—

                "I still can remember the way that you smiled
                on the fifth day of May in the drizzling rain"

a strange choice for a wedding
        you might say
                prescient

flash forward six
years and we are
standing on our heads
naked and drunk on a Tokyo balcony
but we could not dance
the truth away

VII

"My knowledge of everyday life has the quality of an instrument that cuts a path through the forest and, as it does so, projects a narrow cone of light on what lies just ahead and immediately around; on all sides of the path there continues to be darkness."[12]

---

2   Peter Berger & Thomas Luckman. *The Social Construction of Reality: A Treatise on the Sociology of Knowledge*. Penguin, 1978: 59.

VIII

Grief-text
    Heart:
~~There is~~ hypertrophy of the left ventricular ~~myocardial fibres with subendocardial interstitial fibrosis. In the posterior free wall of the left ventricle and~~ adjacent interventricular ~~septum there is almost transmural~~ old scarring. ~~Section of the area of the atrio-ventricular~~ node shows a mild increase in fibrosis. ~~The atrio-ventricular~~ node artery is narrowed approximately 50% ~~by atheroma~~. No ~~pericarditis, myocarditis~~ or recent necrosis is seen. ~~Section of the right coronary artery shows~~ narrowing ~~by atherosclerosis by approximately 30%. Section of the left anterior descending coronary artery is tangential, and,~~ although ~~there is some atherosclerotic narrowing,~~ the degree cannot be ascertained.

IX

jackal-headed Anubis
father of
embalming
father
weighs the heart   he finds it
wanting

X

gentle purr   mottled winged thing
Streptopelia turtur turning
over southern fields
        nuptial   high
cathedral flight
circles
           as if
there's no end to it   the bonny
      sea   fully
brimming

                the rocks
won't melt
            on the sun's
                        tongue
                                    tur tur

though you roam ten thousand
            miles   my dear
return to yond high tree

XI

nix   who's next
mother   reduced from
signified to sign
            dressed in yellow linen
I mended
            the them

XII

alchemical blending|birdsong in free fall|rills|
clitey underfoot|ping|overhead lines|black
vascillations|perturbing forces|
unbearable buzz|smudge|
careening wind|cherchen bell|longtails gone
to chee|clean gone|house crundled away|
this is a dead-alive place|heart-grief|
wind dolours|blowing up for rain

ESSAY

I tend to write long poems, series or sequences. My first book, *Tokaido Road*, adopted the motif of journey to respond to a set of nineteenth century Japanese woodblock prints but also to tell their own stories. With an implicit narrative the poems are grounded in lyric techniques. Borrowing from history and social custom to create an imagined world, they engage with the emotional geography of place.

Continental Drift uses the Japanese aesthetic framework known as *shakkei* or borrowed scenery to interrogate the relation between language and landscape. There are four sections, and the book is concerned with place, memory and history. Historical material is placed alongside personal responses and implications. The four sequences which comprise the collection travel through time and space, taking in the American West and the Far East, including events in China and Japan during World War II.

In *Zyxt* I returned to fixed forms. The title is an obsolete Kentish word meaning "you saw" and also the last word in the Oxford English Dictionary, so these poems are based in observation, with notions of pilgrimage, displacement and migration featuring large. There is a sequence of poems in syllabic verse in which each poem is ordered by the Fibonacci number series, and an abecedarian hymn which chronicles the sacking of Canterbury by the Danes in the year 1011.

My next collection is based on the Greenwich Meridian as it runs through Great Britain. It is grounded in the spirit of 1960s American poetry and the form of the poetic diary or "diaries of the road"—*michi no nikki*. The poem collages fact, photographs, maps and diagrams alongside lyric poetry, juxtaposing sonic chains and associative leaps with sensory description of lived experience.

The poem which appears in this anthology, "Departures," is an elegiac poem which uses the poetic sequence as an instrument of attention, while at the same time attempting to open out the writing to improvisation and unpredictability.

NATHANAËL

Augustment
(translation without language)

> La liberté n'est pas ce qu'on nous montre sous ce nom. Quand l'imagination, ni sotte, ni vile n'a, la nuit tombée, qu'une parodie de fête devant elle, la liberté n'est pas de lui jeter n'importe quoi pour tout infecter. La liberté protège le silence, la parole et l'amour. Assombris, elle les ravive; elle ne les macule pas. Et la révolte la ressuscite à l'aurore, si longue soit celle-ci à s'accuser. La liberté, c'est de dire la vérité, avec des précautions terribles, sur la route où TOUT se trouve.
> —René Char, 1958

> "Se le puede echar la culpa de todo."
> —Juan Antonio Bardem, *Muerte de un ciclista*, 1955

„ It is a point of fact that one is more likely to walk away from the body in the road, than toward it. I can provide several instances of this, none of which can be corroborated, today: a pigeon on a late afternoon in winter, twitching on a sidewalk, its chest feathers gored, and the people with their mocking grimaces; an overturned car in the Indre region of France in the late eighties, a small car, blood, there is blood on the windows, and one needn't imagine the bodies, besides, they are not visible from the road; a bus stop in Lyon, young fascists, and a homeless man, the fists seem to be striking nothing, over and over. When the fist strikes me, I am able to attest to this beating silence.

„ Why begin with the pigeon.

„ It is possible, with Spinoza, to regard it as a "universal failing in people that they communicate their thoughts to others." One must, in such an instance, understand *communication* as an *a priori* failing of truth. Exacerbated, as it is by desire, and the desire to contain it. The silence that is called for authenticates what *might be said*. It recognizes as something more than the mere futility of speaking, but rather the danger of giving one's voice so off-handedly to language.

„ There is no obvious equivalency between truth and language. Nor is there evidence that one may be divined from the other. If truth is what is not able to be brought to language, then language must be understood as, if not a form of, then an instrument of, justice. Or, justice itself.**

„ Language is a capital crime. It is always truth that is hanged at dawn. Followed by several austere pronouncements.

„ 'A body beneath a head.'

„ *Whose hand rattles the door at midnight?* In crimes of passion, there are no mistakes. What is mistaken is the motive, again and again. The hand rattles the door because something has been shut out. Because the body is skin is pores is postulate. The desire to sing is the same as the desire to bleed or to disintegrate. With the freedom to speak comes the freedom not to speak. Too much has been said already. In the compulsive confessional.

„ There is a variety of hibiscus that carries the name of Joan of Arc. Not far from where the mourning doves gather under a mulberry tree. A tree that is exchangeable for a continent. A chimney for eaves. A name for nothing.

„ Truth accuses itself. It is the body in the road. And as far as one is willing to walk. That tribunal.

„ If I wish to speak of freedom why speak of truth. This is my nod to obsolescence. Desuetude.

„ Violence is as much in the injunction to speak as it is in its prohibition. I am interested in neither of these. What *ought* and *ought not*.

„ The throat had sedimented thought.

„ There is no such word as *augustment* in English.* Still there is an alternance in the leaf's permeation. A flood to stop the rains at autumn. A hardening of the membrane. And the plant's mitigated injury at winter. In this instance, when it is struck, the sound is caught inside the cell without reverberation.

„ *Dear friend, augusted is not demise, but premonition. A feather floating over a sewer.*

„ In the impermanent graft of languages, the lie becomes apparent (—*ment*, you could say, is not what I *meant*, but that didn't prevent it from being said).

The promise of a 'day without consequence' is the admission of the day's fallibility, and its failure at averting disaster. August is a month of many months, replete with undiagnosable futures. It has this to say about history:

„ The misadequated elegy despises living.

„ The continent is adrift, and with your two legs on either antiquated shore, you choose severance, and thirst. The mind drafted into this thinking dreams screaming of these same bureaucracies. It wants to know what it is capable of.

„ In the misadventures of the speaker, there is no telling what happens. The time that would account for it is suspended in water, between air and ice, with its mistakenness and candour.

„ We are a far-flung body. A massive misalignment. In the truculence of verbiage, the absence of sentience. And the quick to sentencing.

„ Each time a door opens, it fails at being a wall.

August 8, 2014

to DE

impetus
Char: Liberty is not what one is shown by this name. When imagination, neither foolish, nor vile, has, at nightfall, only a parody of a feast before it, liberty is not to throw anything at it to infect it all. Liberty protects silence, speech and love. Darkened, they are enlivened by it; it does not stain them. And revolt resuscitates it at dawn, however long it takes for it to accuse itself. Liberty, is to say the truth, with terrible precautions, on the road on which ALL is found.
Bardem: "You can blame everything on it."

proviso
* "Aoûtement. Une dimension franchit le fruit de l'autre." René Char, 1938.
** "Il y a des crimes de passion et des crimes de logique." Albert Camus, 1951.

contention
"And Camus's 'justice' was a concept forged and betrayed in Europe," James Baldwin, 1972.

ESSAY: ON DISAPPEARANCE (SPOLIATION)
A STATEMENT IN THE PLACE OF AN ESSAY

> if we leave that border region
> we are dead
> —Thomas Bernhard (tr. Peter Jansen and Kenneth Norcott)

In the age of spoliation, experience is relayed by proxy, dispatched by battalions of newspapers without journalists, photo-essays without photographers, writers without a literature, the dead without a sepulture.

In the annals of recent histories, the watches of watch-wearers are smashed with impunity in police stations scuffing up the century before being dispatched to what are called early graves. The bodies are still floating at the surfaces of the rivers. But try to find them. A certain exuberance is required for such occasions.

Whatever the nationalities of the murderers, it hardly matters.

And the desire to document such traversals as determine the intractability of limits, the pain thresholds of bodies, the execution of orders, can only come from the same expiatory impulse that culminates in a reiterative remove.

It is often in answer to some question.

(Too great a reliance on the possessive. And excessive explanation.)

Disappearance—this is what is undoubtedly insufferable—is something absolute; a destruction has the capacity to be total; and no theology of matter will succeed in erasing that which is destined never to carry a name, nor to have its voice heard, not even the wash of oysters whose respiration stirs an extinct estuary.

Translation's lure is certainly to have forgotten what memory is capable of.

NORMA COLE

Untitled

The young woman in her
sparkly dress, looking out
from the bridge of
a ship or the glassed-in
counter of a café

I heard the mortars again
tonight

forbidden to interfere

looks at his timepiece again

time or what?

need help? no no he says, it's
the same angel

Black Flowers

He said – long ago – that
myth was dead. He meant it.

"Myth is dead!"
"Long live myth!"

They are playing out
something. Legendary.

Picks up her glass. She
has a glass, with coffee,

ice and milk in it. Thinks
about the refugees on the

road. Road to what, to
where? With nothing but

their clothes on their backs.
Mythic and literal.

How to speak about them
and why? How to speak

to them. To keep them
in mind. In our minds.

"Bless you and keep you,"
so the prayer says.

Odile and Odette Write Back

To DLS

She gave us our names by looking
by thinking of a dance by wondering
what we were doing arms clasped

around each other's waist looking
through barbed wire looking up
through wire at the grandparents

looking down through wire at us.
Captured they couldn't come over
(Red Rover) stranded as we were

on different sides of the line. She
looked at this image of us and
wrote our names in ink.

Among Things
                Aubade for David Ireland

what is
that chair
doing there?

resistance
"Come in!"
space between place

morning
ritual
motion

a feeling of expectation
"connecting fetish and compulsivity"
sounds of sanding, making, working

framing a set-up, just some
angels revealing a crack, repetitive
action references a carpet

of cement, a ball, alchemy
a "Broken Glass Repaired
by its Reflection"

"*under every deep
a lower deep opens*"
says Hafez

"the object allows
me to document
a thought"

"social relics"
cured with lime
travel to home

Nowhere Power

Looks along the edge
of the sun

a signature of clouds
driftwood

to convey directly
through those texts

"I see an angel
standing in the sun."

...

ESSAY: AN ACT OF TRUST

I am thinking these days about the distance between the word *migrant* and the word *refugee*, used perhaps by some somewhat unthinkingly, interchangeably. In 1977, I migrated from Toronto, Canada, where I was born, to San Francisco, USA. I was not a refugee fleeing from existential persecution. I elected to move from the land of my birth to somewhere else on the globe: it was a choice. It was possible. I had already lived in France for a few years, in a tiny village in the Alpes-maritimes. That was a choice, "to select freely and after consideration" (Merriam-Webster). I had simply been unaware of how easy it had been for me to choose.

I had always been writing. That was not a choice, it was a given. I had always written, well before I knew that there was a name for it, "writer," or "poet." It was a rhythm I lived by, drawing and writing, and it still is. A questioning rhythm, relational. Writing, and reading, always reading. At first, listening for sound, for tone, rhythm. Listening for silence. The fragments, the startle. The pleasure of that—it could come at any moment. And then learning to read, reading everything I found in the house: books, magazines, the newspaper, cereal boxes on the kitchen table. Those cereal boxes, with the text written in both English and French (Canada is bilingual), was my first encounter with another language. It was translation. It was transformative. I had reading, writing, and translation, "an act of trust" (George Steiner). Relational. It was a gift.

If I were to imagine my life as a wheel, San Francisco would be the hub; and the spokes would be all the people (living or not), places (real and imaginary) and the arts (poetry, painting, dance, music, film, performance etc.) I've met through living here. Chance. An act of trust.

PATRICIA DEBNEY

From *In Memoriam 24*

1.

who sings
        clear harp

who shall
        find loss
        a gain

let   love

let   darkness
        drunk
        beat the ground

the long result of love

                        lost

2.

Old Yew

        thy fibres
        thy roots

                      wrapped about the bones

O not
        the bloom

nor
        summer

                      sullen tree
                      sick

I fail
        my blood

and grow
        incorporate

3.

O sorrow
                cruel death

        sweet   bitter   breath

the stars   web wov'n
                  dying sun

                  my
                  empty hands

shall I   take
                embrace
                crush

        upon   the   threshold

4.

To sleep helmless

    with my heart

O heart

  how fares it?

something lost

    some pleasure

break

     thou deep vase

clouds   nameless

cross

  all night

5.

I hold it
         grief

for words   half reveal
                half conceal

         dull pain

words   like weeds
               like coarsest clothes

that which
     these enfold

no more

ESSAY

My first collection, *How to Be a Dragonfly*, emerged through snatched moments of writing alongside very young children. This group of 42 prose poems came to represent fixed, glimpsed moments in time, returning again and again through short sequences to the outside world – plants and insects – as well as astronomy, a long-standing interest. Throughout, subjects undergo minute inspection, and the central tensions collect around metonymic devices. The prose poem form here is utilized for tiny nearly-stories, which begin to speak to change.

Prose poems entirely comprise my second book too, *Littoral*, which explores and emerges from geographical, psychological and formal states of liminality. Written in situ on the North Kent coastline, the work's central reference point is the shore itself: the covering and uncovering of land and what is revealed or not revealed; the patterns of tides and winds as they relate to what is predictable or not predictable. Throughout, the coastline embodies 'betweenness' as well as 'meeting point'; this in turn enables the larger poetic investigation into the nature of change, suspension, and movement. The use of formal coastal and geological terminology provides a dislocation or ventriloquism through which an alternative experience of land-based life is entered; differently naming leads to differently understanding. The creation of this liminal space through prose poetry, itself a boundary-stretching form, deepens the work's engagement with mutability. The whole book can be thought of as a long poem or sequence.

My recent work (the chapbook *Gestation* and the new collection, *Baby*) is mostly concerned again with change, shifting boundaries (both physical and psychological), and loss, this time in relation to ageing, whether through exploring parenting, mental illness and dementia or through reflecting upon illness and death. This book comprises several short sequences of both prose poems and lineated, fragmented work, and, focusing as it does upon the facts of a parent /child relationship, privileges speech patterns, sound, rhythm, the use of space upon the page – and silence.

The five poems featured here – from a new work, *In Memoriam 24* – are erasures of Tennyson's famous work. Using 24 words, in the orders in which they occur, from each of the first 24 poems of Tennyson's *In Memoriam*, I chart the 24 days lapsed between the death of a close friend, and his funeral. The poems mark the inevitable passing of time, the space between life and death, and the cycle of re-making living in the face of loss.

WANG PING

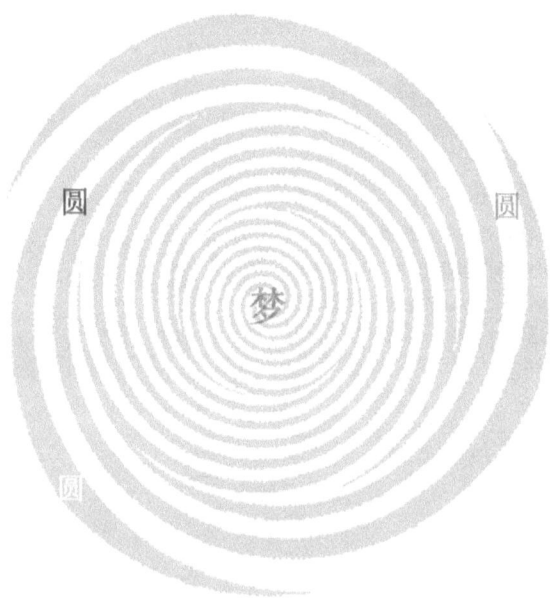

Ten Thousand Waves
On the evening of 5 February 2004 at Morecambe Bay in North West England, 21 Chinese immigrants were drowned by an incoming tide off the Lancashire while picking cockles. The victims were mostly young men and women from Fujian and Shanghai. The youngest was 18.

Xie Xiao Wen

On the night of the Lantern Festival
We stream into the sea
Jumbos, tiernels
Three-forked prongs
The wind bites our ears, hands and toes
Home, we say, home
And tears streak our rubber sleeves
On the night of riddles and light
The moon is full behind thick clouds
We cockle, cockling
In the sand of the distant North Wales Sea

Wu Hong Kang

We pat the sand, we pat the sand
Teasing cockles to the cold surface
We dig, we pick, we break our backs
Bagging cockles for ten pounds
They say we could return
When the bag is full
But home is far away
In the dark, we can't make out the sea
No stars point our path to the shore
Wind comes from all directions
Cutting our bones
How empty is desire, foaming
On the cold North Wales Sea

Chen Ai Qin

Every night since I left home
I've been folding a boat
To rest my aching bones
How thin is the paper
Paler than winter
What's 365 x 365?
Or divide?
A boat full of bleeding hearts
Home—all the heart wants
Is to be called home again
Across the silent North Wales Sea

Ling Qin Ying

How tall has our dragon-eye tree grown?
I've promised you, my little girl
To come home when the tree blooms
We'll pick the fruits and sell them to pay for your school
But the wind is cold
My back broken from bending over the sea
Cockling, cockling in the quicksand

The sea is rising to my chest
My little girl, please forgive your Mama
Forgive the eyes
Decaying in the bed of the North Wales Sea

Guo Nian Zhu

Our hands ache from cramming
Our feet numb in winter's clutch
Indeed, we long for home—Yuanxiao dumplings
On the Eve of the New Year's moon
Steaming hearts of sesame, red beans
Its sticky skin seals our bad deeds
Tongues of gods
Oh, home—pining of the soul
The moon has completed many a cycle
But not our dream, listless
On the foaming North Wales Sea

Lin Guo Hua, Wu Jia Zhen, Chen Mu Yu

The lichee tree I planted is blossoming
White flowers hide under dark green
The first moon comes and goes
But I haven't returned as promised
Lanterns, riddles, yuanxiao dumpling
Lion dance, songs, children on stilts
My love hovers in the deep shadow
Lotus lamp on the tree, unlit
Who will wipe tears from her lichee face?
Who will sail me home from the North Wales Sea?

Lichees blush on the young tree
Birds and bees feast with children
My love lingers under the clustered fruit
Her skin sags from too much weeping
Tides ebb and flow with the moon
Our house is empty, covered in tall weeds
I walk on the sand, eyes on the sea

Who can fill the hollow hearts
In the bottomless North Wales Sea?

Lichees ripen on the tall tree
Its fragrance lasts three short days
My love harvests with rusty shears
A bundle of lichee, a tear-soaked sleeve
They say the fruit, dried or fresh, cures toothache and heart pain
But who will get me home before she fades away?
They say you get beans if you sow beans
Oh, sweet lichee, is it your fault
I'm still drifting on the bitter North Wales Sea?

(Lichee, a fruit tree from Fujian, ripens in clusters. Too fragile to be picked individually, it must be cut at the end of the cluster, hence lychee: li zhi—to be severed from the tree)

Lin Guo Gang

父母在，不远游
父母在，不远游
父母在，不远游

When father and mother are around
The son does not wander far from home

Lin Li Sui

Ten thousand waves
Call my mother
Sorrow
A statue facing the sea
Raven hair bleached by salty wind
Go home, Mother
The shore is empty, the net
Tangled under your feet
Go home
Pray for your son
Broken in the wild North Wales Sea

Guo Bing Long

Ten thousand waves
Wash me to the bay
My wife in the yam fields, gazing towards the sea
Who will unfold your fists
That feed our son, our aging parents?
Ten thousand apologies
My wind-chapped beauty
Pray for your ill-starred man
Wailing from the forbidden North Wales Sea

Wang Ming Lin

Ten thousand waves
Push me to the shore
My son skips rocks on the rolling sea
Will he hit me, a bodiless soul
Foam among endless waves
Will he raise a lantern on my path
A soul bodiless
Floating in the swollen North Wales Sea

Lin Zhi Fang, Yu Hui

We know the tolls: 23—Rockaway, NY, 58—Dover, England, 18—Shenzhen, 25—South Korea, and many more

We know the methods: walk, swim, fly, metal container, back of a lorry, ship's hold

We know how they died: starved, raped, dehydrated, drowned, suffocated, homesick, heartsick, worked to death, working to death

We know we may end up in the same boat

Xu Yu Hua

Tossed on the communist road
We chose capitalism through great perils
All we want is a life like others
TVs, cars, a house bigger than our neighbors'
Now the tide is rising to our necks
Ice forming in our throats
No moon shining on our path
No exit from the wrath of the North Wales Sea

WANG XIU YU

I have no time
To make love to my wife

I have no time
To watch my son grow

I have no time
To feed my mother

Cao Chao Kun

Who will see us
In this foaming sea
Who will hear us
In this howling wind
Who will pull us
From this tide faster than a horse
Who will close our eyes
That won't shut
Until our souls reach the other shore

Highroad of the bitter sea
Please send my bones home
Under the knotted dragon eye tree

Guo Chang Mao

Tread the sand with care
In the tangled weeds, there are hungry ghosts
Tread the waves with care
In each foamy mouth, there is a word
In each word, a soul, unfulfilled

Zhou Xun Chao, Dong Xi Wu,

We move with the sea
Planktons, eels, turtles
The sea carries us
To the land of gold
We're urchins
Under prickly needles
Tender hearts
We ride currents
Following the Polaris
Our destiny always the same
To feed the old and young
To rest at peace
By the yellow sea

```
        父
        母
父母在不远游
        不
        远
        游
```


Yang Tian Long, Lin You Xing, Chen Ai Qin

Once again
Our blood boils with longing
Children of the Yellow Emperor
Master of the sea
Our ancestors wrestled
With dragons, monsters, nine-headed beasts

Their floating cities
Covered four seas and five continents
Our village—yellow kingdom by the sea
Port of grand adventures
If you don't believe me
Go stand on the shore of Changle
Where the South meets the East China Sea
You'll hear junks' horns in the thick fog
The clash of swords and fine porcelain
Admiral Ho's robe fluttering in the arctic wind
Oh, fire of three thousand years
Ancestors' ghosts
Our eyes on the North Star
Our spirits churning for the sea

The Great Summons

Hun hu gui lai!
Wu yuan you xi!
Come home, my Child
No more wandering in the wild
Come home, Soul
The four directions are closed
To the east the sea is rising
To the west mountains are falling
To the south beasts flee the jungle
To the north storms howl to the midnight moon

Oh tender Mazu, Maiden of Silence
Hear the plea of your suppliant children
Our bones shatter upon the rocks
Our souls scatter across the ocean
Nothing is left of us
Only eyes facing East from the sea floor
A breath drifting from shore to shore
Oh Mazu, Mother of Mercy
Please shine your light on the murky sea
Take us home under the dragon eye tree
Oh we sweep, sweeping, with thrashing oars

We will not rest till we reach the land of yellow earth

Hun hu gui lai!
Wu yuan you xi!
Come home, Soul
The wind is blowing from the North Pole
All dreams are not your dreams
All desires are not your desires
Empty your eyes, unfulfilled, restless
Empty your hearts for the new moon
Oh Soul, my lost Child
Home is a bowl of spiced soup
Sweet only to the hearts that cup it tight

Mazu, our Maiden of Silence
Goddess of the Sea
You were born without a cry
You left this world so we could survive
How many boats have you pulled from the raging sea?
How many bodies have you lifted with a tender hand?
Mazu, Maiden of Bright Eyes
Please see the praying of your wretched children
In the foaming waves, a pining soul
A spirit listless until it reaches the shore
Oh sweep, we sweep with our thrashing oars
We will not rest till we reach the land of dragon

Hun hu gui lai!
Wu yuan you xi!
Come home, Soul
No more drifting from pole to pole
All currents run from heaven to earth
All streams flow from land to sea
Come home, my lost Soul
Ten thousand waves call your name
Ten thousand homes wait for your hand
Do not move, let the wind speak
Let the rain fill your cup with honey from your land

Oh benevolent Mazu
Virgin Mother of the Sea
Our tears soak your lovely face
Our breath follows your willow waist
How do you stop a horse from running wild?
How do you appease the pining of a lost child?
This mist is not our mist
This dream not our dream
Oh, home, a foam on the wild, wild sea
With thrashing oars we sweep, sweeping
We will not rest until we reach the land of lichee

Hun xi gui lai!
Wu yuan you xi!
Come with me, my Child
Rise from the rocks under the sea
Hang your eyes on the sail of my sleeves
The way is open on the murky path
Ten thousand waves take us to the shore
Home will arrive under our feet
When we go down on the knees
A prayer lingering in our thin breath

1.

Mazu, literally "Mother-Ancestor", is the indigenous goddess of the sea who protects fishermen and sailors, and is invoked as the goddess who protects East Asians who are associated with the ocean. Her mortal name is **Lin Moniang** She was born in the tenth century. As a baby, she never cried, hence she was named moniang—silent maiden.

She is widely worshipped in the south-eastern coastal areas of China and neighbouring areas in Southeast Asia, especially Zhejiang, Fujian, Taiwan, Guangdong, and Vietnam, all of which have strong sea-faring traditions, as well as migrant communities elsewhere with sizeable populations from these areas.

2.

Hun xi gui lai!
Wu yuan you xi!
Come home Soul!
No more wandering far!

Ten Thousand Waves: an Immigration Carol

      I met Ai Weiwei in the East Village, soon after the Golden Venture ran aground in the sandbar of Rockaway, Queens, a rusty boat that traveled four months from China to Africa to America with 286 Chinese, 10 of them drowned in the angry sea, the rest sent to the detention center. Both of us were heavily involved in the aftermath of the tragedy, reporting, protesting, helping the victims' families. I told Weiwei about my idea of paying a snakehead $40,000 to be smuggled from China into USA, to gain the first hand experience of what it felt like in the hold of a smuggle ship for 4-12 months. The Poetry Project symposium had just invited me to read my poetry with Allen Ginsberg, who was going to recite "Howl," and I wanted to use this opportunity to tell the story of immigration. Weiwei loved the idea and introduced me to the work of Tehching Hsieh, his yearlong performance art that requires mind-blowing endurance, determination, and passion. He also introduced me to his roommate Xu Bing, the creator of "Book from the Sky." They were sharing a moldy basement in the East Village. Thus, during the last month before his return to China, Weiwei sowed the seed in me as a multi-media artist.

I couldn't raise $40,000 to pay the snakehead, being a poor PhD student at NYU. I did write "Song of Calling Souls: Drowned Voices from the Golden Venture," and read it with Allen Ginsberg at St. Mark's Church. Clayton Eshleman published it in *Sulfur*. A year later, Adrienne Rich selected it for *The Best American Poetry*, co-edited with David Lehman.

I thought I could rest the souls from the Golden Venture, buried namelessly in the public cemetery in NJ. I thought I could rest my own conscience afterwards, by giving them all I had. An intense five-day composing without sleep or food drained me so much that I went blind for 24 hours.

But the story keeps coming, from the deserts in Arizona, Texas, New Mexico, from the seas, shores, trucks, ships, from Canada, England, Spain, Italy, Holland… every story is the same, soaked with blood, death, unfulfilled dreams. Each story makes me weep, lose sleep, lose sanity. Each story reminds me of my own arrival at JFK, on the night when the Mets won the World Series. My host drove through Flushing's carnival streets, trying to explain what it meant to win a World Series, but my head span with one question: how am I going to make it in New York with $26 in my pocket, the only amount I was allowed to take out of China? Yes, I knew English, from Beowulf to Shakespeare to Poe, but I couldn't make out a single word from the foaming mouths on the streets, couldn't understand why people went crazy about a green ball game, then I heard my sponsor say: "Ping, I've arranged everything. At night you go to classes at LIU, so you can work at my antique store during the day, starting tomorrow. If you prove yourself worthy, you can work for me, 5 bucks an hour. But you have to find your own place." Three days later, I was out of my sponsor's basement, out of his store. I didn't know anything about American culture, UPS, subway, baseball, football, rock-n-roll, jazz… I threw up eating pizza and hamburger my sponsor brought me. I sulked when his wife handed me the dresses and makeup she bought from gas stations. Before three days were over, she had concluded that I was lazy, stupid, ungrateful.

So I wandered from borough to borough, Queens, Bronx, Brooklyn, seeking a cheap room and an under-the-table job to pay for food, rent, tuition. Only Chinese restaurants would hire me as a waitress, earning tips as my wage, and I was constantly fired, for being too slow, for refusing to wear makeups or jewelry, for making mistakes adding up numbers on bills, or simply, too uppity because I went to "grad school." In less than three months, I had six jobs in all boroughs, and moved four times, Brooklyn, Harlem, Queens. I lost 20 pounds, my face covered with flaming hives. I cried myself to sleep every night, questioning why I gave up teaching at Beijing University to live a dog's life in NYC.

On Christmas Eve, I wandered into MoMa. I'd just been kicked out of the Chinese restaurant on the 5th Ave. It was the fanciest place I'd worked for, and the longest: three weeks. That day, the manager directed a German couple with 4 kids to my table. They seemed polite, took a long time deciding the menu, ordered lots of food, then rushed out for a Broadway show. The manager called me over, threw the bill in my face, and cussed: "Stupid cow, how dumb could you get!" The German didn't sign his credit card for his $104 meal. I handed over all the tips I earned that week plus what I had in my wallet, and walked out into the howling wind. The streets were empty except for a few last-minute shoppers with gifts under their arms. They were all rushing home for Christmas. My home was a tiny unheated room in Flushing, emptier and colder than the streets. And I no longer had the rent to pay the landlady, who was waiting for me in the kitchen. Despair froze my eyes, nose, cheeks, hands, heart. I opened MoMa's glass door, hoping to warm up before they threw me out. The first thing I saw was Monet's "Lily Pond." I knew immediately it was his "Reflection of Clouds" series, because I'd written an essay for my art class at Beijing University. It was my first time to be with the original work, and my knees went limp. I sat down on the bench. The muscles and tendons in my neck, shoulders, hips and thighs began to unwind from their tight knots. The ice in my cells started melting. And for the first time since I arrived in NYC, I felt I could breathe.

I sat with Monet till a gentle hand touched my shoulder. "The museum is closed, Miss." I looked up. It was a guard, tall, thin, olive skin, dark hair. "First time here?" he asked, kindness in his brown eyes. I nodded. "First time Christmas?" I nodded again. He took my hand and led me to his place on Staten Island, where he lived with three friends from Greek, Italy and South Africa. On the ferry, I had my first glimpse of the Liberty Lady in the sunset, and my heart was on fire with hope.

This was my first miracle in NYC, which opened the door to many more: my chance walk into Lewis Warsh's writing workshop at LIU which led to my first story, first poem, first book, first meeting with Allen Ginsberg, Gary Snyder, Kenneth Koch, John Ashberry, Ann Waldman, Beidao, Yao Qingzhang, Peng Bangzeng, Tan Dun, Ai Weiwei, Xu Bing, Yan Li, first translation for the first American Chinese Poetry Festival at MoMa, Penn, American Poetry Academy, first reading as a poet with Allen Ginsberg, Amiri Baraka, Jorie Graham, first NEA fellowship, first pair of skates that led to my first medal then to my first Flamenco dance, first son born on the bank of the East River, first job teaching poetry on the bank of the Mississippi, collaboration with Isaac Julien to make Ten Thousand Waves now showing at MoMa…

Life is a circle of miracles, if one allows it. To allow it, one has to keep eyes and ears and mouth and heart wide open, to dare hope, dream, adventure, even if it means pain, fear, and danger. Migration is movement, and movement means alive, like rivers, fish, birds, trees, mountains…

That's why I am in America, why over 40 million foreign-born representing 13% of the population resided in the United States in 2013, the same percentage since 1880 according to the statistics. We are flesh and blood of America.

ESSAY: WE'RE THE STORY OF CIVILIZATION

In 2006, Colin McCabe invited me to Pittsburgh University. For some reason, I decided to read "Song of Calling Souls," the poem I hadn't read for a while. When I finished, a British man came up and held my hand. "I'm Isaac Julien, Colin's friend. I want you to come and visit the Morecambe Bay, where 21 Chinese drowned picking cockles. I want you to write a poem for my movie on the global immigration. It's called Small Boat."

Morecambe Bay has a mud beach that stretches miles into the North Sea. It looked placid, and felt soft under my bare feet. Yet it is known for its ferocious tide that comes faster than horses, and no human can outrun it. Local fishermen are afraid of it. So are the immigrants. But they come anyway. British law is tight. No restaurant or salon or meat packer dared to hire them. The only option is to pick cockles at night, and sell them 9 pounds a bag to restaurants. It's cold labor, dangerous, and back breaking, yet they still come. They each owe the snakehead $50,000 to come to Europe, who holds their loved ones back home as ransom. People will get hurt or die if the debt is not paid on time. So they come, on the eve of the Lantern's Day, the Chinese Christmas Eve, Thanksgiving, Valentine, the day for rest, feast, celebration, reunion, love. They need to make money to send back home, for the snakehead, for parents and children, even if it's the day when working could bring misfortune for the whole year. And it did. The tide came, swallowed them up. They called 911, but the coast guards didn't understand their language, so they stood on the dark shore, listening to their cry for help, as did the whole England listening and watching on TVs, their last goodbyes to their sobbing wives, children and parents in China, as the waves rose to their chests, necks, mouths, eyes.

In the morning, when the tide receded, the coast guard found 21 bodies in the mud, all together, in one neat line, as if waiting…"the most haunting scene," said the guard.

From the muddy beach of Morecambe Bay, I looked into the distant sea, only emptiness. I opened my mouth to speak, only silence.

That night, they visited me in the tiny hotel room in London, 21 of them, 2 women, 19 men, the youngest 18, most in their 20s, filing into my dream, one by one, as foams, ghosts, waves. Trailing after them, the 10 drowned from the Golden Venture, and many more. They all came from Changle, the Village of Eternal Happiness on the shore of South China Sea, the famous port where Admiral Zheng He set off 7 expeditions between 1405-1433, his fleet contain-

ing over 27,000 crew and hundreds of ships with silk, porcelain, silver. The fleet sailed across the ocean like a floating city. Why did they leave home in the first place? Changle is a beautiful place on the coast, plenty of fish and farm, many mansions built with the money from NYC, SF, London, Amsterdam, most of them empty. Everybody has left to make money to send home, to build more mansions that no one occupies. "It doesn't make sense," I said to the ghosts. "Why can't you just stay home and enjoy what you have?"
The ghosts shake, cry, and spin themselves into foams and waves and seas. I woke up in cold sweat, and started drawing on the mole-skin notebook Isaac gave me upon my arrival: a spiraling circle made of then thousand waves, in each wave, a soul, unfulfilled.

I told Isaac I needed to visit Changle, the victims' home, and it'd take me at least half a year to finish the poem. It took me a year to finish, each stanza in the names of the victims. Isaac called from London. The poem moved him so much that he was going to raise fund to make a movie about the Chinese immigrants, with the title "Ten Thousand Waves" that came out of the poem. It'd be his most ambitious project: a film installation with 9 screens.

I didn't hear from Isaac for over a year. I thought he had given up. Then one day he called from Shanghai. "We're filming, Ping. Can you join us?"
I flew to Shanghai, then to Liuzhou, the day after my surgery. When I saw the image of Yishan Island Goddess, played by Maggie Cheung, I realized it was Mazu, goddess of the sea for all the fishermen and seafarers, Asia's Holy Virgin. She helped Admiral Zheng He sail across the Indian and Pacific oceans in the 15th century. She'd be raising the lost souls from the bottom of the ocean. My song would help her summon the ghosts and guide them home. I had tried to visit the Golden Venture victims buried in the NJ public cemetery before I wrote "Song of Calling Souls." My friend John took me there in his car. We got lost many times, even though we had the address and John was a marine specialized in navigation. When we finally got close to it, a storm came out of nowhere. It came down so hard the sky turned pitch dark and we had to pull over. When it ended, the cemetery was closed. Through the iron fence, I prayed for the ghosts and promised that I'd give them utmost care when I told their story.

"Ten Thousand Waves" is made into a 9-screen installation and shown in major museums around the world. Those who can afford the leisure and tickets go watch the film to be amazed. Yet the 21 souls still linger on the beach of Morecambe Bay, even though their bodies have been retrieved. And the drowned bodies from the Golden Venture are still crammed in the unmarked grave in NJ, waiting to go home, even though the cargo ship has been sunk in the Caribbean Sea as a major attraction for divers. Mazu's summon alone is not enough. My song alone is not enough. We, immigrants and children of immigrants, must tell and retell their story, our story. Together we make ten thousand waves. In each wave, an eye, a mouth, and a hand to take the souls home and let them rest in peace and dignity.

On his last night in the East Village, Ai Weiwei hugged me. "Ping, I don't like writing letters, but I'll write to you from Beijing. Let's keep in touch." I knew he was trying to tell me how lucky we are. Each of the miracles that happened to us is backed with thousands of unfulfilled dreams. The dead are never dead. They live through us. They sing their stories through our mouths. I also knew he meant being in touch through living, fierce, fearless, free. And we've kept our promise.

RACHEL TZVIA BACK

Notes: from a Footbridge

Not waiting until the siren fades around the corner I talk through its flashes.
Our bloodlit room and this keening. Words

Darkening at their edges, red and swelling in their centers. The taste as
urgent. A banister hanging on though the stairs are gone. Night metallic,
and my voice

Wandering off. The siren, somewhere else now, splashes across dry and
silent houses. What words will rotate there in the dark wailing

The problem is

The woman will not seduce. Sits on the rocks, watching. A dusty wind
gathers water from the sea as it moves east. Sirocco (the sun rose) of wide
shoulders and thick thighs. Weight of her wordless-ness in the heat

In the safety of a small world, at the edge of another's echo (message
transmitted, over and out).

But found, I had found you - across the footbridge, your back turned.
Never water in the stream, brown depths of dry leaves. Silence drew a
net around that moment.

A narrow bridge and all the world

Pulled a net around us, roped diamond shapes swaying before me
you

Bare to the waist and bending. Turning away, unaware.

A moment of peace - already troubled by the scent of other places

Adjusting to each other's curves (in back, they were building a house)
as first days passed. No marker on either breastbone. Counting paces
as each new search *be surface earth to me* opens.

Northern corner of concealment. I wait, "watching...the words try to speak." Move out later on all fours. Try not to trample weeds.

"We have never been happy here never been happier"

At noon, this compromise: for a time, we will speak only one language. Sirens scar less the slateblue sky, and words remain rooted (as it were, for a time). Love, but calmly. Clearly. As though our anger on the open road, slamming the heel of my hand into the steering wheel, never mattered. Black tar melting. Black touch and mercury. We both know, however, that to say what we want to say, we will need a new language.

Lettered images we only dream in.

"Never imperfect to have died," only to have remained speechless. "How does the mind move there, beside the bank of what had been a river."

By the bridge, a vision of fluency (waters returned).

Words resituating themselves with ease: deep in the throat, light to the palate. Sweet under your tongue, soft against my white teeth. Serrated as pulling breath from the lungs: "How sharp the desire to speak."

Pots steaming in the kitchen, cants darkening the corridors. Images endlessly repeated. Across the wooden footbridge, I

In the without-speech, without-siren haze (white glare from the rocks). Crates and cables piled outside. Sweat slipping down your spine.

Now, from a greater distance, "to eject...the idea that there was ever something containable to say: completed saying." We have never been happier

Never been happy here where

Rocks slip into the sea daily. Sirens rock the city.

Stonecircle and mud. Earth-level well in the dark with

No moon reflection at the bottom. "I am my Beloved's, and he is mine."

Not in touch. Then in words?

No, not in words.

Through separate fire rituals (the burning of evidence when forbidden).

Encoded notes passed by a third person. In photographs, we are noone

We now know.

Only this the inheritance: earth, and your eyes. White tiles to stop dust from rising.

Sirens in any city. Phone lines as meaning delayed. Your patch of the sky, my voice, and memory

Of absence

ESSAY: TRUSTING THE PLACE

In an early and essential interview, American poet Susan Howe articulated a poetics of location thus: "Trust the place to form the voice"; so it is, so I have. Though I was born and raised in upstate NY, the place that forms my voice are the hills and history, the stones and spirits, the personal and the political of Israel.

I have lived in Israel all my adult life and some of my childhood years, and the ancient rhythms of Hebrew are the rhythms of my life. And still, my language of poetic composition has always been, and will always be, English. Thus, in the Galilean hills that are my home, where Hebrew and Arabic are the spoken languages, my English language poetry wanders ever as an outsider. In significant ways, and certainly in connection to my poetry, I reside fully in the paradox of being ever a foreigner at home.

But in the end, the specific language of my composition seems less the point; as a poet, I locate myself in a lineage of women speaking many different languages, all bound to a place and never fully of it. "Clasp of sand and stone / Hagar's / Antigone's / mine," writes Hebrew poet Lea Goldberg – herself an immigrant/migrant poet – in one of her last poems. The wanderer/outcast/border-crosser seeks the words that will serve as place for the unplaced; these are the words propelled by ethical urgency, aesthetic vision and emotional truth all. Those words – the poem on the page or spoken in space – become the means back toward first places, where speech speaks also in and through silence, to and of abiding first truths of the human heart.

ROSMARIE WALDROP

The Thread of the Sentence

Etymology is one of the choices. The other, wearing your heart on your sleeveless. Cross my.

Even the straightest road conceals detours and forks. Thirst. For physical presence in tight succession. All week I concentrated on the hopeless accuracy of anxiety.

A line made to incorporate circumference. What the snow falls on. The very deep of a labyrinth, its poorly lit fort-nights, its views without domain so like destiny.

Her beauty was called foreign. In relation to terms whose absence is felt. The foreign in one single thrust, absence felt elsewhere. Is self?

Not snow, but its blue shadow. Exchange of rather and disintegrating not made complex by the transfer of money. Thirst eddies.

Time is the invention of past snow. The thread I walk like a tightrope. The maze in the shape of a straight line.

Given to conclusions, I admire awkwardness in love. Open my clothes. To what stands outside my tongue.

The labyrinth is a ruse. Already passing into something else. The thread, swing, syncope life hangs by. My already share of nothing.

Schizoid Defenses

Surrounded on three sides by foreign idiom. On the fourth, fear of overtones. To locate myself where speaking breaks and scatters I tack as many boundaries in memory. Amorphous followed by winter.

Friends unreliable if handsome. Thing else. If we listen intently without understanding we hear white. New snow falls. On this old noise, thickly. Severed, like a lost meaning, from my own tongue, I know nothing of myself.

Mismatched body equates horizon and hollow. How to open and enter, so warm the blankets. Unfinished weather seen through glass. I have my thoughts and see them drift across the snow too. The body suddenly heavier. Suddenly afraid of falling out the window.

Certain consonants coat the atmosphere. Phonemes out of a beautiful face, as a stubble of grass breaks through the snow. And reverts at once to: no landscape, no subtitles. Farther West, whole fields of indifference.

I speak as if on snow shoes, wide berths so as not to sink. Home speech, too, suddenly foreign. As if it were always another who speaks. As if I were both first and third person.

The Depressive Position

That the loved and hated aspects of the mother no longer intersect as cleavage. That after the war, segue to keening. That a choice of neuroses.

Badly drawn figures can nevertheless serve as proof. Just as inexact images will permit strict logical inference. Your father stomps into the room and demands you listen.

To experience depression as sharper perception. To geometry according. To parts to play.

Each crossing of space vows us to chance. You could walk away from your father's dirty old dressing gown. NO EXIT in the foreground introjects greed rather than solids. Could you feel in numbers?

You must not demand that the image itself be compelling, that it displace logic. That you feel strong or guilty, heat or cold, feel surface. Skin. Weaned suddenly.

Result: increased consonants of loss as have no cure and narrow compass. Each vowel akin to mourning.

To make reparation. Retracing your steps is without medical value. The depressive position: Destroy or destory. Today.

Concrete Behavior

Acquiring the phonemes of a language is not innocent. Coins in my purse. (Intent. To appropriate the dead.)

I knock over the basket and the apples roll. Toward so many Adams. Along lines of perspective. Of lures for feeling. Of death instinct projected outward. The whole world red and yellow.

I reach for a word as if it were round and gathered the light. As if the shadow it throws were just shadow and I could step outside it.

Like money, phonemes have no reality. No weight, no color, no density of desire. An abstract value that makes possible language, lunch in a pub, and the roar of a mob out to lynch.

The apples slow down with dispersal of feeling, and eyes open. Is this called thinking? At the end of a long childhood. Taste of bruised suddenly remembered.

My words move toward you. The way my body moves toward its interrealm. Then cannot take back its panic.

Does my feeling change when it is put into words? Does it become everybody's? How I hand you an apple is how words carry the weight of their use.

A system of color, a range of phonemes, the structure of the perceptible world. Formed by bones outside my skin. In the sweat on my face, the bread of phrases not of my making.

Potential Reference

What bevies of consonants, regardless of surrounding sound, the murmuring surf of the revolving world. However infantile my babbling, my confusions of time and place, I was out to drink foreign waters.

It's on my mother's lips the word was born. Vast possibilities deflated to difference. Including madness, chicken sandwiches and pox. Sound shift. Migrating stress. Water rift. Signification pulled in through the mesh.

Though I opened my mouth to take in what she said language has no organs of its own. Already witness to another order.

What muscles could hold this motion toward lack of body, this rush away from flesh? Could wrap (trap?) it in intimate honey, the attractions of inertia, cockfights or sirens?

Not fish. Not fissure. Not king. Not synchronicity or dialectic, not unemployment rate. I have premeditated sterility. Transparency of words.

Like "through." I'm only traveling.

Through money, sentences, hypotheses that don't hold water, a storm at sea, the shallow hours of the moon. The tide recedes. Toward myths of origins, remains of mammoths, a landbridge from Asia to alas poor Yorick.

From which I deduce the structure of the world and the depth of maternal darkness. Dissolves on my tongue the German for again-and-again, wave-after-wave, passage, disappearance.

ESSAY: "EVERYTHING IS THE SAME EXCEPT COMPOSITION
and as the composition is different and always going to be different everything is not the same"—Gertrude Stein

For the long stretch from Romanticism through Modernism poetry has been more or less identified with relation by similarity, metaphor. This implies that the "world" is given, that the poem is an epiphany which is then "expressed;" that content is primary and determines its ("organic") form.

The alternative is emphasis on composition. Here, nothing is given. Everything remains to be constructed. The poem is not "expression," but a cognitive process. I do not know beforehand where the poem will take me.

But it is not true that "nothing is given." The blank page is not blank. we always write on top of a palimpsest, in dialog with a web of previous and concurrent texts, with tradition, with the culture and language we breathe and move in.

Many of us have foregrounded this awareness as technique, transforming/"translating"/ collaging parts of other works.

The fact that I am a woman clearly shapes my writing, but does not determine it exclusively. The writer, male or female, is only one partner in the process of writing. Language, in its full range, is the other.

In crossing the Atlantic my phonemes settled somewhere between German and English. I speak either language with an accent. This has saved me the illusion of being the master of language. I enter it at a skewed angle, through the fissures, the slight difference.

I do not "use" the language. I interact with it. I do not communicate *via* language, but *with* it. Language is not a tool for me, but a medium infinitely larger than my intentions.

What will find resonance is out of my hands. If the poem works (and gets the chance to be read) it will set off vibrations in the reader, an experience with language — with the way it defines us as human beings.

RULA JURDI

At the Terminal

I end up at the terminal
with my disease,
negotiating,
out of time.
Afterwards will seem like now,
and my body will be studded
with a backward heart.
Only I will progress into death,
slowly terminated,
and the disease will sit
like a mist over a sunken lake.
All thoughts shall become as unremarkable
as floating wreckage.
I am spelled out
by the disease,
successfully, without a trace.
I will be put back on the shelf
not being fully used.
Death does the shaming,
pins my bad grade
and a yellow nail—
against my will—
to the bulletin board:
I shall not improve.
There is really no point
in dying,
for I am emptied of heroes,
ceremony, and a chest beat.
There is really no point
in dying,
for I am denied Mary
and her every reflection in the cross.
I am emptied of rosewater,
gushing forth from stones
at the sight of Husayn.
I am bereft of pride,

but stay well-informed,
that I will be terminated
like a package falling out of a loaded truck.
Metal scraps go on to do their sounds
throughout the truck trip
despite the planner's wish.
I calculate that life
is an egg-like oval,
which I cannot square,
and then it breaks.

In the Camp

One day
I'll put the camp in my pocket
and I'll leave
I'll thrust my body into the swarm of bodies
and crumbs of water
I'll gather shreds of time,
and lifeless love that keeps falling
I'll unlatch a journey,
and rise from under
the rubble of treaties
and the initials scrawled on their stipulations
They praise me
and pin medals to my chest
as I rescue my ghosts
from the jaws of the camp
I mimic a garden left untilled,
embrace two human hands
and a missing tree
then I await rainfall
from a graffiti-less sky
When I reach a series of repetitive clothes,
and the fruits that appear united
at the entrance to the camp
I will greet Ghassan Kanafani*
with a memory
and leave

When the killer's shadow
fell on me
I knew it was the state.
I was hiding in the clothes of my soil
or far away, in the book of exile
No one saw the state
dig up graves
Not a soul knew it,
But it sometimes mills about
with its perfume
and civilized talk
before devouring us
Its claws are in
every drop
of the camp's blood
and in that familiar coffin
lurk the keys to its prisons

I'm squeezed between poverty,
and a ticking clock
inside the camp's water tank
Dreams are a ladder,
which days cannot climb
In Tyre, Tripoli and Beirut
I wait for the bird
to emerge
from the mouth of night-time
and return morning to its rightful place
like sparkle in a desolate eye
In the corridors of diaspora
I'll wear all my clothes
I will greet Ghassan Kanafani
with my sadness
and leave

In Damascus,
a *fedayee* will stand up
to sell me bootleg cigarettes
Staring at respectable leather shoes
he shines them,
as they erase him.

At one time he
forbade himself to die
and sang like a soccer player does
to his superhuman feet
I shall say to him:
No team has embraced you,
no ruler on Mount Olympus has enthroned you
You will simply return as an envoy
to the tears of the camp.

When Khaled leaves us
to our carnage in Yarmouk
When the *Salafi* nostalgia for the Quraysh
and a massacre worthy of heaven
tempts us,
I will poison hope,
carrying a photo of it around
When the *kufiyyas*
and women sacrificed as sex slaves
provide a killer with warmth,
When we betray ourselves
I will drag my helplessness
behind me
with the wheels of my body,
my muteness attacking death
When I become
a sentence stilled
on my mother's tongue
I know how foreign fields
can be made Palestinian

In the passport photo
I will imitate
a Norwegian woman,
offering a smiling mouth
to the ice
I will tie the stones of the camp
to the feet of the door
and tighten the rope
out of fear they'll follow me,
my lover and the stones,

to Oslo
I will return the arsenal of suffering
to Ghassan Kanafani
and leave

My name will give in
to excess daylight
as I close off the seaport of loneliness
in Bergen
I will join the conversation of the seven mountains,
and complain:
"There's nothing left for me to say
to the Atlantic."
Posters will beat their hands
against the walls of the camp
My youthfulness
spent at the paper factory
will jump up and fly away
in the dust and asbestos

I will give love to Jerusalem
and toll a bell inside myself
in a church there
I will stroll behind
an unblemished Scandinavian evening
Ghassan Kanafani will stop reprimanding me
and forgive me
when in the gleaming snow
I seek the warmth of the camp,
and save it
from plastic embraces
as it waits
its turn to be recycled
outside my front door.

ESSAY: PAIN AND DESIRE: THE FEMININE AND ARABIC POETRY

My poetry is located in multiple experiences and cultural settings: Lebanon, Venezuela, the US and Canada. Painful memories of childhood and the Civil War, as well as sexuality provide the material, which I use to explore poetically my sense of being and femininity. My ideas and the imagery about the feminine are subversive even as they flirt with sensual and sexual symbolisms in the Arab poetic tradition. My life outside Lebanon, and my engagement with Spanish, English, and North American poetry have also informed my poetry in Arabic in terms of ideas but also structure and style. My second poetry collection, *Ka-Layla aw Ka'l-Mudun al-Khams* (Like Layla or Like the Five Cities) "Like Layla or Like the Five Cities," explores connections and disconnections between cities like Baghdad, New York, Montreal, Beirut, and Puerto La Cruz, through Layla, the beloved female in classical Arabic poetry. Themes of pain and desire are intertwined in many features of this collection. Ultimately, this poetry collection challenges and transforms male-based poetic norms and sensibilities about what constitutes good poetry by creating new relations in the language, which celebrate the feminine.

SAFAA FATHY

For my brother Mohammad

I don't know the road to paradise

I don't know the road to paradise . . . my language, the people & that sitting man meditating on the railway lines, thinking thoughts nobody will know, all these were – my house was – in a place I am still searching for. It wasn't in this village where I witnessed other children being born on the same scarlet blood-stained mattress I was born on, in the same room the midwife visited regularly. When she left with the piece and took away my tongue, I saw myself searching this corner for the old mattress stained with the blood of infants come to multiply our numbers. I saw myself no longer seeking a house for myself, the search now an end in itself, so much of my blood dried like rust as each scalpel punctured my form, each scalpel slicing into me as I lay deadened by anesthetics, hoping those numb hours would hasten an end you can calculate for $50 on a website that reveals the date when you will be no more. I want to say —
I write about what I lost, my squandered blood, my laughter as it crept into the mask, about that girl chased away because she sighed by the heaps of wheat as she shoved the Secret into the girls' mouths, I write about this other girl who was and is no more, about the servant girl that flying, whirling under the roof of an empty room, dress aflame called out to her master to save her, and stood naked in front of all those men. I say: I want neither father nor mother, nor anyone who would put them on my road or slip them into my story. Without them, I remain, and in spite of them all, I am.

I don't know the road to paradise
I didn't save you from hell
I didn't let Islamic Law, that void, touch me
I will not go to the one who has left & yet inevitably returns
I wrote the lines, and licked the drops from the face
I said: She is of those whose past holds their present

Into the wide road she ran trying to cross
Like me, you also are a traveler
You bring that light without shyness
Or is this the myth killed us all

Fire!
Kill, you ash-dark bird!
Swoop to Earth spreading your feathers
on winds blowing from the Western Sahara
Sand dunes, red light
you cross over from where you are not,
the Western Sahara, our Home.
There are two poles
this coming is no second coming
though it will arrive
a visitor for you
stepping lightly, demurely
where your wakefulness is
You, the great Magician,
Amon,
Tell me, where do you keep your remains,
where can I find what leads me to them,
You: the thing, the non-being —
When they were found, fire covered light.
I write about your whereabouts
to meditate on you
to envision
to imagine
your shadow,
You Great Being,
Be a little, that I may see you

Cairo imaginary date written unthinkingly 31-11-2013

Water drops on Tahrir. A gaze and it is blue

It was a grain of sand
opens time & the road toward their junction
I didn't fear myself so mirrors terrified me when I saw all these stories
Salt was
A mountain appears with each image I drew from memory's chest
The years harbour ships I journeyed on & others I wish I'd seen even
from afar
Kidney failure's stamped on a metal coin
you toss into the air where

pictures you'd forget will be drawn
When the other mountain rose
On its peak two boys grown from years of dialysis
As for me, I was cut off from the sleeping one & my shadow
crosses a hedge & returns to a certain place or hour

Death was a promise of water that never left his inside

Through the dust I saw a tent transparent under light
Revolution's face lit up
a luminous circle whirls to become
a sound emerged from the roaring red brick forest
or from asphalt's rising white plumes of gas
in a moment that fell out of time
Where have you gone oh letter writer?
Where are you now, you, latent in the blue gaze?
This mountain of faces throws eyes onto the street
into my lens
spits the taste of salt
on the side of the road

I had a brother... & another brother
who flew with the fugitives
soared from the bed that was under repair
There was basil in the *Nasser Institute*
I had two brothers, no more
I now have one with the eagles & a heart so vast my chest
cannot contain it & another for a certain place
She is she who comes to go
The Un-homeland became a place
held a cup of tea, an icon confined my face
that loved weeping

The angel of history comes running his face on his back
They'll come to him with on their heads this map
and this slogan
did not cleave the Valley of Venues with knife or blade
turns the grass into people who want

Your voice was fading
& you hit the wall next to the bed

screaming with your fists
I learnt that the disobedience of cities & streets slept in your heart
Then your body became a tree & your screams
one by one
crashed to the ground on the square,
while drops of water instantly fell at dawn on a plateau of stone
I had a bag I'd take to the top of any fence
To look at you laid out & brought back from years of slumber
"But you, how are you doing, how are you?"

Your were dying — voiceless
With all the others I whispered to him
when he was dead
"Raise your voice Mohammad, Mohammad: raise your voice."

Cairo, October 6th 2011

Mina and Mohammad, Blood and Water

In the house I inhabit from time to time
I saw him on a screen talking to a lens saying, "I am sure this is my brother".
He was carrying a handful of blood and a piece of crushed body
Around him eyes hovered like a flock of flying grains
In the house of stupor
I said what it would be like to have my body crushed by the caterpillar treads
of a tank
Driven by that man, does he have eyes?
The sign joined the frame
Horus' eye pierced by a sword
Is it the eye of the military police?
From which this pus glides?

My brother has a kernel that will fly with a swarm of seeds to land in a clay pot

M ؟ a circle and a stroke grow from the pot of plants into flesh and body
Your name is displayed
On a piece of your crushed flesh a small pond of your coagulated blood
Braids mud
Absorbed in this earth
That is defined by a fence of uncooked bricks

Another name, germ
It is the living martyr

The enemy is in front of you
The sea behind
Do as you please
Dive into blood, that too is possible
I see the earth opening its mouth to drink with thirst

I saw him walking in the desert
Wearing a three-piece suit
The lines that draw his body
Tremble in the full sun he screams "I want a drink of water, I want to drink"
Be another brother
You were another
The blood brother was one, the water brother was one, the eye brother was one, the brother of the brotherless was one
Tree walk to where you stand now
Carrying gold birds
As for Christ who will rise again in Tahrir
In Maspero
In Talaat Harb
In the valley's plateau
In the Ezbah Al palms
In Mancheia Nasser
And in the Pyramids Gardens
For from its secret another brother will grow for me, for you, for all
One brother from dusk to sundown on whom aunts will never walk

Paris October 15th 2011

ESSAY

Writing poetry and image engages the whole body. The living body of the author moves through states of wake: active or meditative, sleep: dreams or nightmares. In a constant condition of selection, inclusion and exclusion of the possible word or image. Page and Camera become a supplement to both hand and eye while writing and inscription become the outcome of a conscious unconscious process of composition which presentation to perception departs from experience by an interruption from the flow by framing and thus sealing a space-time section from the seen to become a scene, writing scene or filmic scene. This is how I am engaged in the process of inscription. The lines and ideograms are identified formally by the shape and intrinsically by composition.

The urge to inscribe is dictated. It is pulsated as being part of the living process in which the components of the spiritual, the sensual, the perceptive and the conceptual fuse in the very gesture of signature. This occurs in a kind of double bind with the world in which the other organically reshapes my self-definition and positioning. The social scene of recognition, publishing and broadcasting albeit important is nevertheless secondary to this degree of commitment. Politically this means dealing with oppression, repressions, exclusion, discrimination on the basis of its possible transfer through sublimation and transcendence in creating and reinventing a poetic time space in which all these flaws are neutralised. This poetic time space is thus open, giving and its energy is sustained by the vital double bind between the self, the other.

SASCHA AURORA AKHTAR

from *A Year in Clouds*

                                          Friday June 27, 2015

no colour
no identity

except what the light allows.

dull, soggy striations resembling

nothing or

perhaps imagination
illuminates if mind
allows;
        mind says nothing.

                                        Saturday June 28, 2015

partitions of dark &
lit – an enquiry

today they grew from
no semblance, no
differential at dawn

to visible ardour,
                at dusk.

                                                    Sunday June 29, 2015

compelled, I seek the clouds
at twilight, fixing
my sights.

forgetting, that their visible
absence ensures a better view

of the sky.

                                                    Monday June 30, 2015

I did not see
any clouds
                today.

Therefore,
        there were no

                        clouds.

                                                    Tuesday July 01, 2015

A shift barely audible in perception

        a form so faint

        camouflaged as light

                musical accompaniment, humming

                        to a clear, brave stream.

Wednesday July 02, 2015

I have decided to watch the
clouds, in real-time not

to be confused with
recorded time for

which we do not have
to wait, we push

forward, bleat
backwards; I missed

that moment, could
you play it Ag

ain, A   g
Ain   n

or wait. Hold that
moment please I

want to examine it   closer

I say we can
prolong the mom

ent ; remove   line
ear planes   holding

it in:
                                                     time
Pause.
        Pause.
                Paws.
                      Pause

    If I   don't
watch the clouds in real

  -time which is time,
  anyway without movement

  through space – just I, a
fixed point am a

  point fixed – if
I don't watch the

  clouds in   real

               time

  I will not see
  them   transform &

transform
       &
         transform

There is no such
thing as a cloud just

a   TRANSFORMATION <-> AXIS <-> WITHIN <->

VARIABLE <-> ELEMENTS <->

     "if you shoot them
      they shall not
       bleed
       burn or
       break"

Thursday July 03, 2015

One moment it's a heart

    The next, no longer one

        but a floating mess.

Friday July 04, 2015

what goes on
behind the thickening panopoly of cloud

what is it
being hidden from sight?

is it a co-operation
between sky-space & cloud-time?

what is it the clouds
are masquerading as?

or is the dance of Salome
to steady us,
        too frail to absorb
        the full spectrum
        of the sky-order.

we stand facing each
other, wordless &

        I am uncertain who
        is moving slower.

                                            Saturday July 05, 2015

I am writing about
clouds of the day before, the
day before.

memory-clouds.

clouds in retrospect

I took photographs imagining
I would write about them

but a cloud in retrospect

is not cloud at all
just an after-image.

                                            Sunday July 06, 2015

Today, I am in a state of rebellion against

myself, clouds, mostly

myself.

                                            Monday July 07, 2015

a shoaling miasma

of variform   apparitions

            scrolling like
                        ticker-tape
                  saying nothing.

ESSAY: JUST SAY NO

I am that kind of annoying poet who when asked to speak about my poetry will quite easily say: No. When asked to write an entire essay, my inclination is most definitely to say "No."

There are reasons for this – I am not just an ornery poet. I actually don't want my reader to hear what I have to say because (a) it won't be relevant in any way to you, reader, because what you get from the poetry will be completely different from what another reader and another and another get, and it will be TOTALLY different from what I "say" my poetry is "about." In fact, what ends up happening is that the reader says "Well I didn't get that from it at all," and this creates a kind of suspicion, a kind of question-mark . . . about oneself as a reader, about the poet et al. All of which are unnecessary.

(b) I actually don't know what to say. I really don't. I end up using words like hermetic, mystical and sound like a prat. However, I will never use the word avant-garde. When I was a younger poet, I did. To be fair, I did never knowing why I felt uneasy when I did. I know now. Nothing I say will be "true" about my work. The only other option is to use academia-speak, which I will leave to others who enjoy that.

The good news is in the case of the poems included in this illustrious anthology, it's really rather simple. Clouds. Every day. Write a poem. Now again, I don't want to say they are poems *about* clouds, because that would be that. I also don't want to say they're *not* about clouds at all, because surely they are . . . in some way. You reader need to read the poems and merge with the result that occurs as one embarks on such a method; poetic waxing on the same "object" every day, for a year.

The change of day being the *independent variable*, the clouds being the *constant* (lovely irony in that) and poetry itself being the *dependent variable* – in this field experiment.

SHARMILA COHEN

Travel Log 1: The Occupied Beds

We visited the leper colony,
but when we got there, everyone was dead.

Trying to make the best of it, we lay in the empty graves,
commenting on how shocking life could be.

All of the words that came out were foreign –
        we understood the language, but the tales
        were so different from those of our childhood.

(Our personalities change
                      based on the landscape.)

We inquired about everyone's relationship to sleep
                      and most people
said their beds were occupied
by strangers that would stop breathing
by morning. There were no questions of life and death –
        only of repetition and discomfort at the lack thereof.

(The methods of sleeping were varied and allowed us

                      to rob our neighbors.)

I wouldn't dare tell you there was anything romantic
about this picture, but
        when the skeletons hurdled onward in the distance
                we all went a little bit flush.

From *Stories in Which Everyone Dies in the End*

Having run all the errands
and done all the picking up,
there was nothing left
to do but await the end of days

***

She grew more and more obsessed
with genius. And then she slipped
on a banana peel and died.

***

My Sisyphean punishment:
I held my breath until I fainted.
I held my breath until I fainted.
I held my breath until I fainted.

***

"There are just too many gods to choose from," she said,
"how is one to decide?"
"I'll take them all," she said.
And then she died.

***

Travel Logs 2 & 3: The Sleep of Antiquity

2.
We ignored the ancient ruins
and took to the seas, refusing
to let fear get the best
of us. Or so we thought – until
  we were suffocated in the night
  by a dream of sinking ships
    and learned that drowning
    is always drowning,
even in your sleep.

3.
In Vienna, I went underground
And sought out the dead on my own.

  All of the bones were stacked
like firewood. I slept in the warmth
of ghostly flames and in sleeping
met a man who sang
a song of the plague.
  We waltzed and when it was over
  my skin was gone.

When the Dead are Dead

We left a trail of breadcrumbs
knowing they would be eaten by birds;

knowing we would likely never
find the artifacts of our former selves
at any point along the dried up riverbed.

There is a story we tell the children
in situations such as these –
      when the dead are dead
      and the living are feeling faint –

      it tells them everything
      is always the best it will ever be.

Travel Log 4: On Fieldwork

The archeological dig ended
in a release of fluids.

What we thought was a mummy
turned out to be the empty shell of a man,
filled with decaying scraps
of meat and literary detritus.

We confessed our sins
and found the world
far less relatable from that point on.

ESSAY

My work is preoccupied with the spaces between languages and cultures, the places where one thing can't necessarily be transposed into another context and still look the same—that is, for example, the idiomatic elements of language, cultural mores and traditions, mythology and folklore. This thinking was initially inspired and shaped by my work with translation and the notion that there is no one right way to translate a poem. As so many great thinkers from Borges to Benjamin have pointed out, it would be impossible to translate effectively without changing some things in the process. Those *things*, alongside the inventive nature of reconstructing them, are central to my thinking as a writer.

The poems included in this anthology come from a manuscript that investigates death as a cultural and literary trope. Death—as well as everything surrounding it—is a topic that so readily takes on a variety of mythologies; it exists for everyone, everywhere, but its treatment varies so greatly from culture to culture and individual to individual. This *treatment* is an inventive reconstruction and interpretation of death. As such, it can be seen within the same framework as translation and makes visible those things that are so seemingly impossible to transpose. For me, this exploration of death is a means of pointing them out and reconfiguring them within a new context; exploring the spaces between cultures; building something new with the existing blocks.

SHEIDA MOHAMADI

With *Don't Tell* Eyes

I want a man.
A *Sepeed river* man.
Body brighter than sand,
Voice flowing
Through these sea shells
and my white gull hands.

I want a man with summer eyes,
Ice cream eyes,
Eyes of *I won't tell.*

A man who wears mountain bells
and returns with the wind
to hold the moon's pale hands
and sing with the river
in the darkness of my rain.

I've heard he goes insane,
Races with death and wins,
Watches me from afar while I dance
Red on these lines.

Return from My Body's Black-and-Blue

Leeches, kindly leeches suck my blood
and the crane, heavy-handed crane
lifts my corpse up from the pit,
with my skull full of snowy days.

Leeches, kindly leeches
blacken my body
you return from my body blues
hitting your head against your hands!

Save your teardrops for me, love.
I have run head-on into myself, crashed into myself
and the road's searchlights have dumped me onto this lake's floor.
Look at how black I appear in your smoke-colored sunglasses!
And these women
look how they hide my breasts under their chadors.

Save your teardrops for me, love.
Why do you, so pale and fair, arrive so late?
And why has my son, so little
swelled so much inside me in the few months of my pregnancy?
And the leeches – kind leeches
Look how they suck my blood. . . .

I Look at Istanbul with Drunken Ears

This road has been intentionally brought here with the blue bus   with the strange crowd of pigeons
And the impatience of the shirt and the skirt and the boots
Something has happened in the mirror   what is the matter with you Istanbul?
You have put on somebody and this is the scent of the beloved from your shoulders   the scent of earth and geraniums
The evaporating colourful scent.

O, City with the eyes of the sea and colourful waves
Beyond the vapour in your back, walls of swear words and love letters
What is the matter with you Istanbul?
Where are we going with my feet of bronze in the middle of the night?
With these sweet smelling dead offering tea and cigarettes   why are we sitting here?
I want to make love to this stone man under the rain, o city
To sing barefoot to Bokhara, to listen to the body of the poplars
The air is an orchard of mint tonight
Do you hear?
– Your health   your health!

How sweet is being in love
These extravagant hands   these shops
The whirling Snow   pomegranate blossoms
Storks in water
And in shirts   shadow of a dark dance.

How did you find this room?
I turned into music with the scent of this bed and this quilt, did you know?
With the noise of these windows we laughed deeply . . . . With you.
O, city, I know the scratching of this line
These singing umbrellas
Something has happened to me with these clouds!
My eyes cannot say Istanbul
My hands cannot . . .

The sun moves slant

Too late now,
too late to undo your buttons
and let loose my liquid blue fingers
on your chest,
to turn the lock in my throat
and hear the *halla halla halla*
of your coming
from among apples and lemons.
Your shadow moves slant through mine.

Why is it that your kisses no longer leave
their mark on my purple dress?
Why is it that your body's tangerines
no longer swell from sucking my breasts?
Your voice no longer sends frogs
crrrrrrrrrrrroaking along my thighs.

Now, each time your voice grows cold-blue,
you snuff out your cigarette in my eyes
and half the clock's circle face
sinks to sleep in the ashes of my hair.

The violet wilderness of my body

Don't ask after me from the letters
From the white birds of your papers,
Which never flew.
From the violet wilderness of my body,
Whose wrinkled openings
Are filled with calm clouds

No!
Don't look for me
In any familiar place
When it rains,
Your shoes will slip on your remembrance of me
The hand of wind will close your umbrella
And the moon will kiss your cheek.

From...

You were standing there and
Clouds
were passing over your lovely moonlike face
passing
days
days
days
were passing over your lovely moonlike face
and I
here
left behind
and the
moon
from....

Lute-like Weather

Here
From the facing geraniums
Storm
Came and
Wind
Took away all the bougainvillea.

Oh my beloved
Today I was supposed to   listen to the sound of your eyes
To the sound of this warm earth
And these happy palms
You were supposed to tell me of poplars and domes
Of the irises and streets not winding into the future
Your hands were mean to smell of jasmine and saffron
My shoulder was to get drunk
My dress was weaving beautiful dreams
My body had a beautiful feeling
Oh! How I wanted to sleep deep in your eyes
But these dark smiles of yours   these dark smiles of yours   these dark smiles of yours

Beyond this vase
Nothing is serious
Not the Malibu fire
Nor the graffiti on the walls of Kandahar
Nor the putrid corpses of Baghdad

Oh, my beloved....

ESSAY

I'm looking for the right words to express myself. My feeling about poetry. Its place in life and its purpose. The power of poetry to illuminate, touch soul, work miracle.

Alas not possible. I can't extract the right sounds and images. Even me, with so strong a faith in words–their impact, potential to bond and make friends. Their power to liberate. Poetry is food to the soul, a nourishment I can't do without. For me, poetry is everything in a godless world. It's a prism through which I observe the world–the good and the bad, blessings as well as curses. Poetry gives horror a poetic touch. Pain tenderized, easy to swallow–if not digest. Poetry penetrates skin, allows a glimpse of the world under: the darkness, hidden miseries, unknown fears and collective tears. Black journeys I never fail to embark upon.

When woman speaks of her man, I'm totally with her. I feel I know her well: her longings, her hopes and fears.

And him too! I know the man, her husband. I feel his intrusion, his void, the futile wait standing out in rain with her, trembling with cold expectation, both overcome with doubts, ambivalence, self-loathing...

The man's still there with me... as densely as with woman... his elusive shadow... his featherweight... the sore of his unbearable void...

Oh there is more to say. Lots more. From here to eternity. But words are stuck in my throat... impossible to pry free and spurt... those evasive miracle words!

Oh I'm so furious with myself... the numbness... impotence... arrested shrieks...

A poet with a clutter of words... whirling, spinning, rumbling in my head... but to no purpose... no direction... no chance for release... just whirling and whirling... an endless ride in circles.

Strapped to a chair, utterly helpless... like my folks in *Kobane*... the ancient cradle now besieged by the beasts... Syria, Iraq, Afghanistan...I try to stir but my hands are tied... bare too like those of my people... the virgins fighting off monsters.

I am paralyzed, only my head rumbling with words... words... words.

SUN YUNG SHIN

Time Dilation: America, America

absolute shield of time...white husk of time
steal the blue sailors in the ransomed dark
black garden of the future, the coming sublime
utopia, utopia, your spendthrift disembark

lustre-high on the false sea; purchased sea, navy lace
burn the black-seed ocean into *the future, the future*
time-bridge spectacular and burnt-branded space
redeem the hole the torture, under this or that soldier

Spain beneath Spain, the empire beneath the empire
gold down throats; blinds-bright the last voice
body gilds a red-molten crown; figures a fire, makes us liars
blood-mint; forge a stutter, time's fragrant (empty) noise

all we want, a flaming house; nation's eternal arson
sentry, sentry, delivery devour, the past arrives, dial out to open

Autoclonography (for performance)

> "In 1998, scientists in South Korea claimed to have successfully cloned a human embryo, but said the experiment was interrupted very early when the clone was just a group of four cells. In 2002, Clonaid, part of a religious group that believes humans were created by extraterrestrials, held a news conference to announce the birth of what it claimed to be the first cloned human, a girl named Eve. However, despite repeated requests by the research community and the news media, Clonaid never provided any evidence to confirm the existence of this clone or the other 12 human clones it purportedly created."
>
> "Cloning Fact Sheet," National Human Genome Research Institute.

1.
the sonographic fetus is a *cyborg*—clonograph—dear future clones you are multiple—to use the letter s to *make more of someone*—to use the letter **s** to make a *very small silent black river*—into which many *babies have been borne away*—and under into the river under the river—the black ocean under the blue ocean—catacombs of bones of those *delivered unto the shore* beneath the shore—as men of God from Spain and *the Spain beneath Spain*—arrived with their ships of *death beneath death*—the world under this world that *outnumbers this world*

2.
dear future clones *I love you more*—than I love myself because there are *more of you*—than there are of me although I am your mother—and your sister and *your ancestor*—and look in the mirror at your young face—and look behind you at my olding face—and you can do something only prophets can do—which is to *see into the future*—Τειρεσίας / Tiresias killed two snakes with a stick—*Hera punished him and changed his sex*—he was *turned into a woman*—he served Hera as a priestess, he got married to a man and had children—when he came upon two snakes again he decided to leave them alone—it *broke the curse*—he was turned back into a man

3.
to love the word offspring—*to spring from a trap to spring from jail*—*sperkhesthai* "to hurry" hurry spring come rain shine—always spring in the wombs deployed for this purpose—ovaries are primed—the word *offspring* is really both singular and plural—the cell lines are cultured in the *singulary*—the word *single* will become a quaint idea *has become a quaint idea*—we won't need the letter *f* anymore in the middle of things—there will never be one knife or one self—*knives selves* doesn't that sound better *we are better together*—we won't need the word *I* anymore to love the word *we* more than *I*—we don't have to capitalize *we* even in the middle of a sentence—the *I* has been *sprung from its prison* no more stretcher for you letter *I*—who do you think you are letter *I* to be so tall to be like the Roman numeral one—*you don't stand for one anymore*—you don't stand up anymore *you are small again* a small *i* a short thing with a black dot for a face—we have always wanted a dot for a face—so much easier to look beautiful every day—if everyone's face is a dot than no one has to look beautiful every day—our dot is the same as your dot so why don't we exchange dots—no one will know the difference but *it might taste different behind the dot*—a little bit of different weather behind your dot yes—we have always wanted a manhole cover for a face—we have always wondered what is below the manhole—what keeps the city from

flooding?—what keeps the ark half built?—what keeps the animals from walking two by two by two by two?

4.
dear future clones we are *re-thinking* about you—*electrically we are electrifying* you in the plural you—*neuronally we are neuronifying* you in the spaces between our neurons in the salt sea—inside our skulls *skol* said those death metal Vikings for skull—when they drank from the skulls of their defeated—mead from honey *mead from a queen* and so many many baby bees everywhere—drunk on togetherness on doing being the same until they die—good bees they take out our bodies sweep them into the air the air—that is heaven *that is a good death* dropping at the same rate together—duty done *skol skol skol* we are picturing you in our mind as Athena born from her father's head—burst we like the word *burst*—and we want our head put back together—we want our head *not* split open like a watermelon—even if it meant we got to have *the daughter we always wanted*—even if we get the daughter without a mother—we don't need a mother we are father-mother—you only need one parent—and put the word *father* or the word *mother* on the shelves with the knives

5.
will we be taking *family photographs* together—we and you our future clones—how will we tell years later who is who is who is who is who—will we stand in the middle because we are the original—and you copies fan out around us in what kind of order—*who do we like the best today*—who does the photographer think has *the brightest twinkle* in their eye eye eye—do we all wear the same outfit where can we get so many of the same outfit—by then all the stores will sell so many of the same outfit—don't be ugly today or if you do don't go outside because we don't want anyone to see us—looking so ugly or shabby or old or female—*when you're looking so female older female just stay inside* nobody wants to see that—in such bright light at least bring some shade—or your shadow who isn't *the wrong color*—and your shadow no one can see our face our dot our aging dot not as dot-like as it used to be

6.
we have been making a documentary of these fetuses—sonograms just photographic slices now also 3-D imaging—*still all that blur* but no fetus is *the wrong color*—sometimes the wrong gender *the wrong gender in the dark*—sometimes the face the dot of the fetus is *facing away from us*—as if it doesn't want to see us doesn't want us to see them it *us ourselves their future our origins*

7.
in all the movies and television shows and books about clones—dear future clones they are always never actual clones—they are actors photographed again again again—but we are never fooled although *we love being fooled* all the time—we are afraid of the times we are not fooled—in our lives we don't actually own anything although *we pay* for things—we will pay for everything for you because you are our future—we didn't know we wanted to be *immortal*—but could you please not get yourselves into as much pain—we are worried about what all that pain will mean—*will it be our fault*—will it be our problem—will it be our future—my pain is your past but *you might forget me* I mean us we mean us

8.
to love the look of our own blood—*because it spelled things* it spells things for us—anything that was inside us recently *was* us—we know Freud would agree and Freud is *still inside* me meaning us—he might not want to be us—*he never dreamed about us*—Freud where are you in our body you must be *in the blood* because it comes from *the basement inside our bone*—and we think you like basements the way you like talking and we feel you—clinging in your three-piece suit to the underside an iceberg—*we will save you* from sea lions—there are things on the surface from *we cannot save*—we are loathe to *spill your blood* onto the blue-white milk ice floes—we are loathe to spill or spell a flotilla of ships approaches—all alike all alike *one might save us*—one might take you with us Freud please come with us—all these years into your future *you never dreamed about us* even once—but we dream about you Freud we dream about *the world beneath the world*

9.
future clones, we did not know that Freud *took his own life*—where did he take it *he took it into the future*—but before he could take it into the future he had to break it off *from the animal*—now he is *the animal beneath the animal*—you offspring we never knew we could make so many animals essentially an infinite number—we could repopulate the earth with ourselves with *the right machines* including ourselves—we could reproduce ourselves and *train ourselves* to reproduce ourselves to reproduce ourselves—this could go on until someone stops us or our death drive *thank you Freud*—allows us to return to *the room beneath the room*—the body beneath our body that is exhausted—that is mere breath that is leaning heavily on the airlock—with its *cool metal wheel* against our hot olding face

10.
we apologize we are less like us in *all the ways we are like us* like you like us we are so so sorry—we just knew that we would let ourselves down but *we didn't know what else to do*—*we didn't want to take our lives* because we thought it would be better—to give them away to all of you—it's true that someone always has to pay

ESSAY: THE POETRY UNDER POETRY

The radical equality of signs? My poetry is my ongoing attempt to understand and maybe reinscribe various terms of engagement underlying different kinds of violence and violations.

I think poets are interested in what poetic language can bear in terms of perception. Women poets living in countries other than their birth and writing in what may not be their mother-tongue may have a heightened relationship to what is considered "real" or "natural" by others.

> Poems are de- and re-familiarizing.
> New kinships of words and sounds and forms.
> Language is a stranger.
> Language is a hospitality.
> Poem is ritual.
> A poem is an occult thing. A thing that is spelled, a spelling, a cast spell. Magic. Summoning. A conjure.
> The poet travels, like Baba Yaga in a mortar and pestle.
> The poet curses by naming. The poet re-members.
> The poet is an anti-priest.
> The poet must destroy hierarchy through the field of language action.
> The poet is utopian.
> The poet creates a temporal and idiosyncratic grammar of feeling.
> Language is space.
> Language is time travel.
> The poet is an astronaut.
> The poet's currency is time and music.
> The poet bends the air.
> A poem is a machine, destroyer of dualism, a flamethrower on the false borders of this world.
> A poem is stitch-work.
> A poem is medicine.
> A poem is space.
> A poem is time.

TSITSI JAJI

Our Mother of Stone

Lichen covers over her cushion of flesh.
Where her breast once gave way she is rough
to the touch. Crowned

with a pot of water her eyes drop, dead
as the tail of the double-chinned lizard. Queen of
Heaven, she aches for nothing now.

Death's fugitive slips from her lap:
her chin quivers, her belly still knotted
since the strewing of its wild fruit.

Clouds of sulphur pass for seraphs. Heaven lights up,
turned green as the eye of a magnate tracking a tribe
of foolish children who flee from his coin.

Our Lady gathers up these runaways in her tender
choke-hold. The rich, she has sent fuming away, swindled
out of thread, and needles, and the nimblest fingers.

Our Embrace
    for Franklin D. Cason, Jr., after Brancusi

is monumental, a bloc representing
the phalanx that is us. Tending towards each,
other than the word our communal well utters,
we envision silence singly. This one sense is
our plenty, a sense of more than common sense.
G-d helped us, one might say, were misprision
not – in its own house – taken for language.
Our tongue in common remains unknown to
the greater world. We bind this region
true to our word, braced for the impact of
wind, dust, force, removal.
Schooled hard, we hold fast, and this
is the unrushed sense that speeds us
into each other, where we intend
to rest.   It's true, it gives us pause.
Metallicized, it presents us, *Eia!*,
with all we did not need to make in
order to be here all along. Sandstone
is not specified; boulder overstates this
plain monument to the two in one, now us.

Elections

That mustache, more visible after the razor.
That face. That wry old joke about the rooster
whose cockled crow sounds less like a croak,
and more like Sunday dinner, before dinner.

Like a dog barking at the sun.
Like a rally that felt like a party.
Like the pall before the storm.
Like carrying a load on your head,
while seated in the bus. Like this
if you thought Baba Jukwa was more
than hot air piping out of Facebook.

Like anyone would feel if their face were plastered
everywhere, smacked across mothers' buttocks wrapped in
cloth, posted in all post offices, all schools, all hospitals.
Change the dressing, sister, you would say. *Let it all air out.*

Like how one feels sometimes,
thinking about that selective
assemblage: history.
Like dawn, never new, never news.
Like when we…
Like when the When-We's whine:
See, we told you.

How a farm here and there, a car crash,
an enemy or two and a few mineshafts
account for haggard crimes against all humanity,
while mothers' mothers saw those When-We's
arriving with the gun, the bible,
and something short an inheritance.

Little lord fauntelroys,
how you loved your kitchen boys,
gardening,
and serving tea
and yes-madamming.

Toyi, toyi

And thus, the great leader's
bicameral brain is but the lonely
mind of one who has out-lived his heroes.
The ungentle goodnesses of night,
ah, the graceless airs of love.

                      The people
love the great leader, his excellency,
his honorable arch-comradeship.

The people love to see him thumb his nose
and toss great boogers at those buggers,
the bastard Brits. Admit it, then:

You love it, too.
You love it because
you do not need bread,

you do not need mealie meal,
you do not need sugar,
you do not need antiretrovirals,

you do not need a new wheelbarrow,
you do not need a prophet,
you do not need to change

your null and void Zimkwachas
into wads of golden USAs,
you do not need a green card,

you do not need a place to hide,
you do not live here.
You do not live here any more.

How I Write
          for Rachel Ellis Neyra, poet

Now, I see that
my wilderness
is our field,
and I call
my neighbor
to plough it
with me. Our
hoes dig deep.

Our harvest
amounts to something
an awful lot
like hope.

ESSAY: HOW I WRITE: PART 2

Writing poetry has often served me as a way to discover what I don't know. One of my favorite writers, Edouard Glissant, calls writing "a prophetic vision of the past" and another inspiration, Keorapetse Kgositsile, writes often of "future memory." Often I find writing poetry is road to revelation. It's sometimes disconcerting not to know until I write what the poem has to tell me, whether about highly personal histories or their intersections with what we consider the public. I grew up in Zimbabwe and although chiShona was technically my first language – the language I spoke to all except my mother in until I turned 4, English was, on an intimate level, my mother tongue. My mother moved to Zimbabwe in 1970, where she met my father. So I was raised in an intercultural home where rootedness was a complicated notion. I suppose I'm a second-generation migrant woman, having repeatedly crossed borders of language, geography, and idiom as my parents have. My writing is inevitably influenced by longing for what home might be, knowing I left Zimbabwe in 1993 to take up residence in the U.S. And it is haunted by the anxieties of my language troubles, manifest in the paradox that I am more at home with poetry in French, like Glissant's, than with the rich vernacular literature of Zimbabwe.

Elemental images of nature – stone, rooster, field – come easiest to me. But, whether explicitly, as in "Elections" or, more subtly, as in the celebration of obdurate resistance in the personal-political tangle of "Our Embrace," I am never not thinking politically. Like Fanon, who prays "O my body, make of me a man who always questions," I am, as a mixed race woman of Zimbabwean birth and American nationality, one whose public embodied identity in the U.S. is read as black, which is to say, always already called into a political condition of being under siege. Speaking, writing, reaching for the fullness of language is, for me, a ritual to make black life matter, not so much my own life, but the being, the existence, the survival of oppressed peoples (and particularly of Africans on the continent and in its diasporas). To borrow from Lucille Clifton, I write to invite my reader to celebrate with me "what I have shaped into a kind of life," even as I recognize that the self is always connected to collectivities. It seems, to me, that migrant and multiply-identified lives such as mine are not so common and yet, are the very Commons that define our contemporary global and inter-connected present.

YUKO OTOMO

from "A Stretch In Paradise"

Written after seeing the exhibition of "Louise Bourgeois - Moi, Eugenie Grandet, un processes d'identification" at the Maison de Balzac, Paris.

LOUISE

I am alone in a vast white room with two large mirrors facing each other on the walls, making a vision of "Infinity" actual. I sit, sinking into the deepening dusk. Unlike the other day, strangely, no streetlights leak in. Moment by moment, I delve further into the peaceful quietness of the day's end. "Aloneness" which has nothing to do with "loneliness" is so intense that I feel all the particles of my being dispersing into the air. I feel no shape; no weight; no identity, but my *soul*'s trembling. I usually never talk of something like "soul" or use the word too easily. But, now, in the quietness of a vast darkening room, all alone, for the first time, I feel something, something inside me clearly & definitely, something I can call "soul." After all my particles of "being here" dispersed in the air, what I am left with is my soul & its trembling.

Why do I let myself use a word such as "soul" to describe this tiny silent voice that is consistently aware of all the things in & out of my being in such clarity & modesty? Fortunately, the noise outside is minute & the day is passing its role to the approaching night in such a smooth monotonous but musical way, I am able to experience to see my "core." What fragile & helplessly faint, but ardently clear trembles this unseen unheard core of my consciousness keeps "ticking out!" Thoughts this trembling consciousness creates are completely beyond language of any sort. No grammars; no rules; no sentences; but the weight & the lightness of "thoughts" alone. Thoughts come & go, more like a pattern; rather than lines. Like waves, they come & recede in a condensed emotional clarity. There is no space for rational arguments here. It's all about the rock-bottom "essence" of one's consciousness.

As the clarity of the trembles of my soul gets more & more evident, my eyes witness the transition of a world of color to no color. The white wall changes into different hues/tones/shades of grey & shadows cast by window frames get darker & darker. Soon, I lose all the ability to differentiate colors of this world & realize, in dusk, that I too am colorless. "Infinity" created by 2 mirrors facing each other is now a door to the dark cosmos we live in. In the near total silence, devoid of voices of others or mine, I cry. I cry for Louise, for Eugénie, for my mother, for myself & for all of us: male or female who are born into "a human existence." I let my tears come out with no efforts to stop them, as if they are the voice of my trembling liquefied soul. We are born unconsciously & we die with so many thoughts packed within us. Where do all those thoughts go when we are gone?

***

When Balzac lived in this house on 47 Rue Raynouard, he must have had a great view of the city & the river. Now, his house is buried amongst a massive density of wealthy apartment buildings built in the early 20th Century. Like Sophie & Hans Arp's studio/house in Mendon, the original premise of the architecture & the geography of the location has been betrayed violently by the "progress" & "development" of the area.

I walk into his study; a modest small room with a modest wooden writing table & a rather bluntly large upholstered chair. There is a small fireplace & 2 windows in this room with a wooden floor. Through the side window by his writing table, the late afternoon sun beams through, hitting the surface of the table which has opened pages of "Modeste Mignon" 1844. In the glass bookcase, there is a black plaster cast of his hand. So contrasting to Chopin's delicate white light piano fingers, Balzac's fingers are like the ones of a butcher or a priest, bulky & heavy. I enjoy the idea of the tradition of their time: plaster cast hand portrait. Hands tell stories as much as faces.

***

"When I'm feeling pessimistic, I identify with her; I feel that my fate was in large part that of Eugénie Grandet." Louise says. & I mistake the words "my fate" as "my face". I face Louise's red portrait of Eugénie. The outline of her face & her hair, dissolving into somewhere=nowhere as if the whole particles of her existence are crying or liquefied. "Fate" & "Face", what's the difference? As we are born to live our lives, our "faces" become the peek holes to show our "fates". "Fates" are beyond us & they eventually make our "faces". Louise draw/paints Eugénie's face in red as if it were hers. Sadness & helpless pains look lost in the liquefying color "Red". Am I exaggerating my reaction when I say that I see your face in Eugénie's face, Louise?

"... I don't mean that this identification is total; I'm saying that it's partial and transitory. But it comes back all the time, because it's part of the fabric of my life..."

(L.B.)

Being misunderstood; wounded; pale and sad with suffering; remorse; regrets; sorrow and a few frail hopes... being prevented from functioning like a normal, happy person, years in her life passed without a single event to relieve the monotonous existence of hers. Such is the history of a woman who is in the world but not of it...

(condensed re-writing of Eugenie Grandet's life based on the excerpts by Balzac)

I walk among other women in the house from one room to another, being pulled into Louise's inner life. I suddenly stop in front of a humble fabric of used washcloth simply embroidered with 3 words. "Faith", "Hope" & "Charity." Being a captive of the weightless-feather like ephemeral clarity of these stitched 3 words, I tremble inside.

I have never grown up
I am standing near the window
I have spent my life making curtains
to hide the dinky glass

.

I have spent my life
listening to the chirping of the birds
the water dripping from the ceiling
and the traffic on 20th Street

.

I have spent my life making a trousseau
I who has never been trussed up
I give humor
not pity
I am not stupid I am only unhappy

.

.

(excerpts from *The Smell of Eucalyptus: Ode to Eugenie Grandet* by L.B.)

I see Louise & Eugénie woven into one tapestry of *someone* who was never given the chance to grow up. Buttons, needles & hooks, sparkling little rocks of transparency, dried roses & poppies, blue died twinkles of stars, a mist like a golden veil… years passing like nothing *"with the same actions performed daily with the same automatic regularity of clock work."*

(Balzac)

Is it not the noble destiny of women to be more moved by the dark solemnities of grief than by the splendors of fortune?

(Balzac)

I don't complain. I turn it into humor.

(L.B.)

***

More than 150 years ago, Eugénie stood by the window looking out at the world that she'd known nothing of. More than a century later, Louise stops complaining (crying), turning her pains into a humor as a revenge and gives us "Faith", "Hope" & "Charity" of our time. She says, *"It could be the story of my life. I feel for Eugénie Grandet…"* I feel for Louise, feeling for Eugénie. Then, I realize that I have never cried in this city, Paris. I've laughed; smiled; got angry; got sad; got frustrated, but, come to think of it, I have never shed tears in this city full of sad stories, the grey sky & a mist like drizzling rain in winter. Now, I cry for myself feeling for Louise feeling for Eugénie & I am almost transparent & non-existent in & out of my own soul. I lose myself more & more, sinking deeper & deeper into my tears, feeling for Louise & Eugénie, & my mother & me who all lost our chance to grow up normally one way or the other due to different circumstances. As darkness completely takes over the room, I finally stop crying & make a long sigh as if to trace & erase memory' paths. Then, I open my eyes & leave the room.

ESSAY

I draw/paint & write. In art, I stubbornly search for abstraction. In writing, I do many things. I write poems, haiku, essays, critical writing on art, art reviews, travelogues, anti-novels, novels & keep a journal. My mother tongue is Japanese of which I have not lost either in writing or in reading amazingly although I rarely use it. Now, for practical reasons, English is my main writing tool having lived in NYC for many years.

Influences on my poetic development come from many different angles, crossing cultures, genres & eras. Classical Japanese writers & poets: Sei-Sho-Nagon, Saigyo, Basho, Issa, Buson; Modern Japanese poets: Hagiwara Sakutaro, Takamura Kotaro, Yosano Akiko, Ishikawa Takuboku, Sato Haruo; Modern Japanese writers: Natsume Soseki, Nagai Kafu, Akutagawa Ryunosuke, Dazai Osamu, Kajii Motojiro; Modern haiku poets: Otomo Rikisei, Sakaguchi Gaishi, Kitahara Shimako, Kaneko Tohta; Western writers, poets & thinkers: Blake, D. H. Lawrence, Marquis de Sade, Baudelaire, Rimbaud, Dada/Surrealists poets, Rilke, Pessoa, Nietzsche, Walter Benjamin, Jack Kerouac, Frank O'Hara & poets I've encountered in life: Steve Dalachinsky, Ted Joans, Tuli Kupferberg, Herschel Silverman, Jayne Cortez, Ira Cohen, Amiri Baraka, Pedro Pietri, Jack Micheline, Jackson Mac Low & Robert Creeley. They have given me something vital & different to learn from.

My principle philosophy in poetry is "Essence" writing, the concept that I've created from the alchemically combined study of both haiku & (western) poetry. Instead of using poetic metaphors as devices to narrate & to describe the already existing poetic emotions per se, I wait for the essence of word/sentences to form *their own* poetic lives through a distillation process to show me *my own* unknown poetic thoughts & landscapes through theirs. I believe in "a universal language" as in Rimbaud's statement. I try to reach the realm of poems written by the universal soul. In order to do so, I strive to push my personal world to the maximum limit.

NOTES ON TRANSLATIONS

TRANSLATOR FOR CHRISTINA RIVERA GARZA: Herself (See page 311).

TRANSLATOR FOR ZHANG ER: Joseph Donahue is an American poet, critic, and editor. Donahue was born in Dallas, Texas, and grew up in Lowell, Massachusetts. He attended Dartmouth College for his undergraduate degree, went on to Columbia University, and lived for many years in New York City. He now resides in Durham, North Carolina, where he is a senior lecturing fellow at Duke University. The third volume in Joseph Donahue's ongoing poem "Terra Lucida," entitled "Dark Church," is from *Verge*. Other recent titles include *Dissolves* and *Red Flash on a Black Field*.

TRANSLATOR FOR LEA GOLDBERG: Rachel Tzvia Back (See page 319).

TRANSLATOR FOR RULA JURDI: Michelle Hartman was born in the USA, but she is currently living in Montreal, Canada. She is Associate Professor of Arabic literature, McGill University. Her interests cover Francophone literature of the Arab World; Arabic literature and the politics of translation; women's literatures; language use and literature. She was the second runner up for the Banipal Translation Prize 2009 for her translation of Iman Humaydan's novel *Wild Mulberries*. Her recent book *Native Tongue, Stranger Talk* is an anti-colonial reading of how women writers from Lebanon who write in French use Arabic words to advance messages about gender, nation, ethno-religious belonging, and class in their novels.

TRANSLATORS FOR SAFAA FATHY: Poet, editor, and translator **Pierre Joris** was born in Strasbourg, France, and raised in the town of Ettelbruck, Luxembourg. Joris is the author of numerous collections of poetry, including *Poasis: Selected Poems 1986-1999* (Wesleyan University Press, 2001), *Aljibar* (Editions PHI, 2007), *Aljibar II* (Editions PHI, 2008), *Meditations on the Stations of Mansur Al-Hallaj* (Chax Press, 2013), and *Barzakh: Poems 2000-2012* (Black Widow Press, 2014) as well as two volumes of essays, *A Nomad Poetics* (Wesleyan University Press, 2003) and *Justifying the Margins: Essays 1990-2006* (Salt Publishing, 2009).

Ken Kincaid is an editor, writer and translator who lives and works in Paris.

TRANSLATORS FOR SHEIDA MOHAMADI: Soleh Wolpé is a poet, playwright, and literary translator. She was born in Iran and now lives in Los Angeles, California. Wolpé is the author of three collections of poetry and three books of translations, and she is the editor of three anthologies.

Dr. Ahmad Karimi Hakkak was born in Iran and now lives in Los Angeles. He was professor and director of the Roshan Centre for Persian studies at the University of Maryland. Karimi-Hakkak has written nineteen books and over one hundred major scholarly articles.

Dr. Farideh Pourgive was born in Shiraz, Iran, where she now lives. A scholar and translator, she is the author of six books and professor of English at University of Hiraz, Iran.

Poet, writer, and translator **Dr. Freshteh Vaziri Nasab** was born in 1959 in Kerman, Iran. She received her PhD in English literature from Goethe University of Frankfurt and lives in Germany. She has translated three plays and a collection of poems from German and various other poems from German and English.

CONTRIBUTOR BIODATA

Born in Canada, of Russian Jewish heritage, **ADEENA KARASICK** is a New York based poet, performer, cultural theorist and media artist and the author of seven books of poetry and poetics. Writing at the intersection of post-Language Conceptualism and neo-Fluxus performatics, her urban, Jewish feminist mashups have been described as "electricity in language" (Nicole Brossard) and noted for their "cross-fertilization of punning and knowing, theatre and theory" (Charles Bernstein), "a twined virtuosity of mind and ear which leaves the reader deliciously lost in Karasick's signature 'syllabic labyrinth'" (Craig Dworkin). Most recently is *This Poem* (Talonbooks, 2012) and *The Medium is the* Muse: *Channeling Marshall McLuhan* (NeoPoiesis Press, 2014). She teaches Literature, Critical Theory at Pratt Institute at St. John's University in New York and she is co-founding Director of KlezKanada Poetry Festival and Retreat. The "Adeena Karasick Archive" has just been established at Special Collections, Simon Fraser University.

AMANDA NGOHO REAVEY was born in Manila, Philippines, and currently lives in Milwaukee, Wisconsin. She has also lived in England, France, Italy, and Greece. Her work appears in *Construction Magazine, Galatea Resurrects* #23, and *The Volta*, among others. *Marilyn* (The Operating System, 2015) is her first book.

ANDREA BRADY's books of poetry include *Vacation of a Lifetime* (Salt, 2001), *Wildfire: A Verse Essay on Obscurity and Illumination* (Krupskaya, 2010), *Mutability: scripts for infancy* (Seagull, 2012), *Cut from the Rushes* (Reality Street, 2013) and *Dompteuse* (Bookthug, 2014). She was born in Philadelphia and moved to the UK in 1998. She is Professor of Poetry at Queen Mary University of London, where she runs the Centre for Poetry. She is director of the Archive of the Now (www.archiveofthenow.org), a digital repository of recordings of poets performing their own work, and co-publisher of Barque Press (www.barquepress.com). She lives in Hackney with her partner and three small children.

Born in Montréal, now living in New York City, **ANGELA CARR** is the author of three books of poetry, most recently *Here in There* (BookThug, 2014), and two books of poetry in translation, most recently *Ardour* by Nicole Brossard (Coach House Books, 2015).

ANIA WALWICZ was born in 1951 in Swidnica, Poland (pre-WWII Schweidnitz, West Prussia), and migrated to Australia in 1963, where she teaches creative writing and currently lives. She has published the books *Writing, Boat, Red Roses, Elegant,* and *Palace of Culture*. She is currently completing her sixth book, *horse*.

French-born American poet **ANNE TARDOS** has been living and working in New York most of her adult life. Among her recent books are *NINE* (BlazeVOX], 2015); *Both Poems* (Roof Books, 2011); *I Am You* (Salt, 2008); *The Dik-dik's Solitude* (Granary, 2003). She is the editor of three posthumous volumes by Jackson Mac Low: *Thing of Beauty: New and Selected Works* (California, 2008); *154 Forties* (Counterpath, 2012); and *The Complete Light Poems* [with co-editor Michael O'Driscoll] (Chax, 2015). Tardos is a Fellow in Poetry from the New York Foundation for the Arts.

BARBARA BECK is a poet and translator. She was born in Berlin, raised in Minnesota, USA; she currently lives in Paris, France. Her poems have appeared in such journals as *Ekleksographia, Van Gogh's Ear,* and *The Café Review* and the anthology *Strangers in Paris* (Tightrope Books, Toronto, 2011). Translations include a selection from French poet Jérôme Game's *Flip-Book*, forthcoming in an anthology from Enitharmon Press, London, in 2016; poems by Vannina Maestri in *Aufgabe*; poems by Dominique Quélen in *ParisLitUp*; and Cid Corman's *Livingdying* (translated in collaboration with Dominique Quélen), published in French as *Vivremourir* (L'Act Mem, 2008). Since 2002, she has been editor of *Upstairs at Duroc*, the English-language literary journal published in Paris.

Born in northeastern China, now living in Melbourne, **BELLA LI** is a writer, editor and PhD candidate, and a managing co-editor at Five Islands Press. Her poems have been published in a range of journals and anthologies, including *Meanjin, The Kenyon Review* and *Best Australian Poems*. Her chapbook *Maps, Cargo* (Vagabond Press, 2013) was shortlisted for the Wesley Michel Wright Prize. *Argosy* (Vagabond Press, 2017)—a book of poetry, photography and collage—is her first full-length collection.

Born in Illinois, educated in southern California, and now living in Bath, England, **CARRIE ETTER** is the author of three collections: *The Tethers* (Seren, 2009), winner of the London New Poetry Prize; *Divining for Starters* (Shearsman, 2011); and *Imagined Sons* (Seren, 2014), shortlisted for the Ted Hughes Award for New Work in Poetry by The Poetry Society. She also edited *Infinite Difference: Other Poetries by UK Women Poets* (Shearsman, 2010) and Linda

Lamus's posthumous collection, *A Crater the Size of Calcutta* (Mulfran, 2015). She is a Reader in Creative Writing at Bath Spa University.

CECILIA VICUÑA is a poet and multimedia artist born in Santiago de Chile. Exiled since the military coup in Chile in 1973, she now lives in New York. Before that she lived in London, Bogotá, and Buenos Aires. She is the author of twenty-two poetry books, most recently *Spit Temple, The Performances of Cecilia Vicuña* (Ugly Duckling Presse, 2012) and *Cecilia Vicuña: The Selected Poems 1966-2015* (Kelsey Street Press, 2016).

Poet and playwright **CHRIS TYSH** is the author of several collections of poetry and drama. Her latest publications are *Our Lady of the Flowers, Echoic* (Les Figues, 2013); *Molloy: The Flip Side* (BlazeVox, 2012), and *Night Scales: A Fable for Klara K* (United Artists, 2010). She is on the creative writing faculty at Wayne State University. Her play *Night Scales, a Fable for Klara K* was produced at the Studio Theatre in Detroit under the direction of Aku Kadogo in 2010. She holds fellowships from The National Endowment for the Arts and the Kresge Foundation. Her latest project, *Hotel des Archives*, features verse "transcreations" from the French novels of Beckett, Genet, and Duras.

CIA RINNE, born in Gothenburg, grown up in Germany and having lived in Helsinki, Athens/Greece, as well as Copenhagen, and now living in Berlin, is the author of *zaroum* (Helsinki 2001) and *notes for soloists* (OEI Editör, Stockholm 2009), both published as a single volume in France (Le clou dans le fer 2011), *should we blind ourselves and leave thebes* (H//O//F 2013), the online Joakim Eskildsen (e.g., *The Roma Journeys*, Steidl 2007). Her latest books *Skal vi blinde os selv og forlade Theben* (Virkelig, Copenhagen) and *l'usage du mot* (kookbooks/Berlin, Gyldendal/Copenhagen), and *L'Ours Blanc*, (Éditions Héros-Limite/Geneva) were published in 2017 collection *archives zaroum* (Afsnit P 2008), and the sound work *sounds for soloists*, as well as documentary books, in collaboration with Sebastian Eskildsen, 2012.

CRISTINA RIVERA GARZA is the award-winning author of six novels, three collections of short stories, five collections of poetry, and three non-fiction books. Originally written in Spanish, these works have been translated into multiple languages, including English, French, Italian, Portuguese, and Korean. The recipient of the Roger Caillois Award for Latin American Literature (Paris, 2013), as well as the Anna Seghers (Berlin, 2005), she is the only author who has won the International Sor Juana Inés de la Cruz Prize twice, in 2001 for her novel *Nadie me verá llorar* (translated into English by Andrew Hurley as *No One Will See Me Cry*) and again in 2009 for her novel *La muerte me da*. She has translated, from English into Spanish, *Notes on Conceptualisms* by Vanessa Place and Robert Fitterman; and, from Spanish into English, "Nine Mexican Poets," edited by Cristina Rivera Garza, in *New American Writing 31*. She was the Breeden Eminent Scholar at Auburn University and a fellow at the UCSD Center for Humanities, Fall 2015. She received a Senate Grant from UCSD and the prestigious three-year Sistema Nacional de Creadores grant from Mexico. Born in Mexico, she is currently the director of the MFA Program in Creative Writing at UCSD.

Born in Seattle, now living in Berlin, **DONNA STONECIPHER** is the author of four books of poetry, most recently *Model City* (Shearsman Books, 2015). She has also lived in Iran, France, and the Czech Republic.

ÉIREANN LORSUNG was born in Minneapolis and lived there until 2006. Since then, she has lived in rural France, the midlands of England, and rural Belgium, where she now runs a tiny residency center for writers and artists, Dickinson House. A 2016 NEA fellow in prose, her prior publications include two collections of poetry (*Music For Landing Planes By* and *Her book*) published by Milkweed Editions (US).

Born in Beijing, **ZHANG ER** lived in New York City for 17 years before moving to the Pacific Northwest. She is the author of five collections of poetry in Chinese, most recently *Morning Not Yet* (Showwe, Taipei 2015). She has seven chapbooks in English translation, among them, *The Disappearance of Little Fang Family Lane* (Belladonna, 2015). Her selected poems in two bilingual collections, *So Translating Rivers and Cities* and *Verses on Bird* are from Zephyr Press. She co-edited and participated in the translation of the bilingual volume *Another Kind of Nation: an Anthology of Contemporary Chinese Poetry* (Talisman House Publishers). She also wrote opera libretti in English for American composers. One of them, *Moon in the Mirror,* was recently performed in NYC in 2015. She teaches at The Evergreen State College in Washington.

Born in Lahore, now living in Ossining, **FAWZIA AFZAL-KHAN** is the author of two books of scholarly criticism, two edited anthologies, one of which focuses on multi-genre writings by Muslim women; she has published two plays and several poems, most recently in *Language for a New Century: Contemporary Poetry from the Middle East, Asia, and Beyond* (W.W. Norton, 2008).

HAZEL SMITH is a poet, performer, and new media artist and her website is at www.australysis.com. Hazel was born in Leeds, England, lived in London for many years, and now lives in Sydney, Australia. She has published four volumes of poetry: *Abstractly Represented: Poems and Performance Texts 1982-1990* (Butterfly Books, Sydney, 1991); *Keys Round Her Tongue: short prose, poetry and performance texts* (Soma Publications, Sydney, 2000); *The Erotics of Geography: poetry, performance texts, new media works*, with accompanying CD Rom (Tinfish Press, Kāne'ohe, HI, 2008) and *Word Migrants* (Giramondo Publishing, Sydney, 2016). She has produced three CDs of poetry and performance work, *Poet Without Language, Nuraghic Echoes* and *Returning the Angles*, and numerous collaborative multimedia works, including *motions*, with Will Luers and Roger Dean, which features in the Electronic Literature Collection, Volume 3, 2016. She is a member of austraLYSIS, the sound and intermedia arts group, she has performed and presented her work extensively internationally, and she has been commissioned by the Australian Broadcasting Corporation to write several works for radio. Hazel is a Research Professor in the Writing and Society Research Centre at Western Sydney University, and is the author of several academic and pedagogical books including *Hyperscapes in the Poetry of Frank O'Hara: difference, homosexuality, topography*, Liverpool University Press, Liverpool, 2000; *The Writing Experiment: strategies for innovative creative writing*, Allen and Unwin, Sydney, 2005 and *The Contemporary Literature-Music Relationship: intermedia, voice, technology, cross-cultural exchange*, Routledge, New York, 2016. She is co-author with Roger Dean of *Improvisation, Hypermedia and the Arts since 1945*, Routledge, London, 1997, and co-editor with Roger Dean of *Practice-led Research, Research-led Practice in the Creative Arts*. She is co-editor of *soundsRite*, a creative arts journal of online sound and writing based at Western Sydney University.

IVY ALVAREZ is the author of several chapbooks — her latest being *Hollywood Starlet* (Chicago: dancing girl press, 2015) — and two full-length collections: *Mortal* (Red Morning Press, 2006), and *Disturbance* (Seren Books, 2013). Born in the Philippines and raised in Australia, she lived in Scotland, Ireland and Wales before arriving in Auckland, NZ in 2014.

JANE JORITZ-NAKAGAWA's ninth poetry book titled <<*Terrain Grammar*>> is forthcoming in 2017 with theenk Books. Recent books include *FLUX* (BlazeVOX, 2013), *Distant Landscapes* (theenk Books, 2015) and the chapbook *diurnal* (Grey Book Press, 2016). She is also an essayist who occasionally writes in addition to poetry both fiction and crossgenre works. Born in Harvey, Illinois, Jane is now a permanent resident of Japan. Many of her interviews with poets have been published online.

JANE LEWTY is the author of *In One Form To Find Another*, winner of the 2016 Cleveland State University Poetry Center Open Book Competition.

She has published one previous poetry collection, *Bravura Cool* (1913 Press: 2013), winner of the 1913 First Book Prize in 2011, and she has co-edited two essay anthologies, *Broadcasting Modernism* (University of Florida Press: 2010) and *Pornotopias: Image, Apocalypse, Desire* (Litteraria Pragensia: 2009). A graduate of the Iowa Writers' Workshop, she has held faculty positions at University College London, the University of Northern Iowa, and the University of Amsterdam. She currently lives in Amsterdam, the Netherlands, and Baltimore, USA.

Originally from Iowa, now residing in France, **JENNIFER K. DICK** is the author of *Circuits* (Corrupt, 2013), *Enclosures* (BlazeVox eBook, 2007), *Fluorescence* (University of GA Press, 2004), and 5 chapbooks: *No Title* (Estepa editions, Paris, 2015), *Conversion* (Estepa editions, Paris, 2013, including art by Kate Van Houten), *Betwixt* (Corrupt, 2012), *Tracery* (Dusie, 2012), and *Retina/Rétine* (Estepa, 2005, including art by Kate Van Houten and a translation into French by Rémi Bouthonnier). She is currently at work on a large prose poem project about the CERN while awaiting responses from presses for her manuscripts *Lilith: A Novel in Fragments* and the book length prose poem collaboration *Orphery*. Jennifer also translates French poets (a selection of Jean-Michel Espitallier poems is in the June 2016 issue of *READ* and her book translation of *What to see* by Christophe Lamiot Enos is forthcoming in fall 2016 (Presses Universitaires de Rouen et du Havre), and she has edited two books on translation theory in the social sciences. While working as a Maître de Conférences (Associate Professor) of American Literature and Civilization at the Université de Haute Alsace, Mulhouse, Jennifer curates the *Ivy Writers Paris* reading series in Paris and the *Ecrire l'Art* mini-residency for French authors at La Kunsthalle Mulhouse. She is a poetry editor for *VERSAL* out of Amsterdam, writes book reviews for *Jacket2, Drunken Boat,* and other journals and a poetics column called *Of Tradition and Experiment* for *Tears in the Fence* (UK). She has also lived in England and spent extensive time in Italy, Spain, and the Czech Republic.

JENNIFER KRONOVET is the author of two poetry collections: *The Wug Test* (Ecco, 2016) and *Awayward* (BOA Editions, 2009). She co-translated *The Acrobat*, the selected poems of experimental Yiddish writer Celia Dropkin. Under the name Jennifer Stern, she co-translated *Empty Chairs*, a book of poems by Chinese poet Liu Xia. A native New Yorker, she lives in Guangzhou, China, and is planning a move to Berlin, Germany.

JI YOON LEE is a poet and translator whose most recent publication is a book of translation, *Cheer Up, Femme Fatale* (Action Books, 2015). She is the author of *Foreigner's Folly* (Coconut Books, 2014), *Funsize/Bitesize* (Birds of Lace, 2013), and *IMMA* (Radioactive Moat, 2012). She is the winner of the Joanna Cargill prize (2014), and her manuscript was a finalist for the 1913 First Book Prize (2012). Her poems and translations have appeared in Asymptote, Eleveneleven, The Volta, PANK, Bambi Muse, Seven Corners, The YOLO Pages, The Animated Reader, and & Now Awards 3. She was born in South Korea, spent a few years in the United States as an infant, moved back to South Korea, and emmigrated to the United States as a teen. She received her MFA in Creative Writing from the University of Notre Dame.

Born in Atlanta, Georgia, **JODY POU** is presently living in the south of France. She has previously lived several years in Paris, Rome, and New York City. She is the author of two books of poetry, *Will* (Les Petits Matins, 2009) and *I thought j'irais en bloom* (Le Bleu du Ciel, 2014).

LARESSA DICKEY is a poet, movement artist, and somatic worker. Born in Tennessee, Dickey received her MFA in 2005 from the University of Minnesota. She's the author of several chapbooks including *A Piece of Information About His Invisibility* (MIEL), *apparatus for manufacturing sunset* (dancing girl press), and *Little Voice Box*, a microseries chapbook also from MIEL. Her collection *Bottomland* was published in 2014 by Shearsman, and a second book from Shearsman entitled *[Roam]* is forthcoming in late 2016. The Backwaters Press will publish *Twang* in 2017. She currently lives in Berlin.

Hebrew poet **LEA GOLDBERG** was born in 1911 in Koeningsberg, East Prussia, and spent her early years in Kovno (now Kaunas), Lithuania. Her mother tongue was Russian and though her first poems, written when she was still a young girl, were in Russian, already in her teens Goldberg adopted Hebrew as her language of poetic composition. After completing her doctoral studies at the University of Bonn, Goldberg emigrated to British Mandate Palestine in 1935 and lived the remainder of her life in Israel, first in Tel-Aviv and later in Jerusalem. She passed away in 1970. Goldberg was a versatile and prolific writer, with published works that include poetry (ten collections), plays, literary criticism, verse and stories for children, novels, and volumes of translations of European classics into Hebrew that she translated from seven different languages. The Goldberg poems included in this anthology are from *On the Surface of Silence: The Last Poems of Lea Goldberg* (Hebrew Union College Press and University of Pittsburgh Press, 2017).

Born in Iruma, Saitama-ken, Japan, raised in North Carolina and now living in New York City, **LEE ANN BROWN** is the author of five books of poetry, most recently *Other Archer* (Presses Universitaires de Rouen et du Havre, 2014), and founding editor of Tender Buttons Press.

LISA SAMUELS was born in the United States and now lives in Aotearoa/New Zealand. She has also lived in Sweden, Israel/Palestine, Yemen, Malaysia, and Spain. The author of thirteen books of poetry and experimental prose – recently *Anti M* (Chax 2013) and *Tender Girl* (Dusie 2015) – Lisa has also published non-fiction books, critical essays, and soundwork.

M. NOURBESE PHILIP is a poet, essayist, novelist and playwright who lives in the space-time of the City of Toronto. She practised law in the City of Toronto for seven years before leaving to write. She has published five books of poetry, including the seminal *She Tries Her Tongue; Her Silence Softly Breaks*, one novel, and three collections of essays. Her most recent work of poetry, *Zong!*, is a genre-breaking exploration of memory, history, and the transatlantic slave trade. Among her awards are the Pushcart Prize (USA), the Casa de las Americas Prize (Cuba), the Tradewinds Collective Prize (Trinidad and Tobago), the Lawrence Foundation Prize for short fiction (USA), as well as the Arts Foundation of Toronto Writing and Publishing Award. Her play, Coups and Calypsos, was a Dora Award (Canada) finalist. She is a Guggenheim Fellow in Poetry (USA), a McDowell Fellow, and a Rockefeller Foundation (Bellagio) Fellow.

MAIRÉAD BYRNE emigrated from Ireland to the United States in 1994, for poetry. In Ireland she worked as a journalist, hospital domestic, arts centre director, playwright, and teacher. Her books include twelve collections of poetry and five collaborations with visual artists, most recently *Famosa na sua cabeça (Famous in Your Head)*, selected and translated by Dirceu Villa (São Paulo: Dobra Editorial 2015). She earned a PhD in Theory and Cultural Studies (Purdue University 2001) and works as a Professor of Poetry + Poetics at Rhode Island School of Design in Providence.

MARCELA SULAK was born in Texas and now lives in Tel Aviv. She is the author of three books of poetry, most recently *Decency* (Black Lawrence Press, 2015), four book-length translations, most recently T*wenty Girls to Envy Me. New and Selected Works of Orit Gidali* (University of Texas Press), which was nominated for the 2016 PEN Award for Poetry in Translation. She co-edited the 2015 Rose-Metal Press title *Family Resemblance. An Anthology and Exploration of 8 Hybrid Literary Genres*. She is an associate professor of English at Bar-Ilan University.

MEGAN M. GARR is the author of *Terrane* (MIEL, 2015) and *The Preser-*

vationist Documents (Pilot Books, 2012). She edits the literary & arts journal *Versal*, which she founded in 2002. Originally from Nashville, Tennessee, USA, Megan now lives in Amsterdam, the Netherlands. Her website is www.meganmgarr.com.

Born in Tokyo, Japan, **MICHELLE NAKA PIERCE** is the author of nine titles of cross-genre work, including *Continuous Frieze Bordering Red* (Fordham University Press, 2012), awarded the Poets Out Loud Editor's Prize. Pierce served as dean of the Jack Kerouac School of Disembodied Poetics from 2011–2015. She is Professor of Creative Writing & Poetics at Naropa University and directs the Writing Center and Core Writing Seminars. Currently, she lives in Boulder, CO; she lived previously in London, Yokohama, and Albuquerque.

Born in Saigon, Vietnam, **MỘNG-LAN**, multi-artist, poet, writer, painter, photographer, composer, multi-instrumentalist, singer, dancer, and teacher of Argentine tango, left Vietnam on the last day of the evacuation of Saigon. Having received a Stegner Fellow in poetry for two years at Stanford University and a Master of Fine Arts from the University of Arizona, she lived 5-6 years of her adult life in Tokyo, Japan, teaching with the Univ. of Maryland; returned to Vietnam on a Fulbright Grant; lived in Bangkok, Thailand; and has lived many years in Argentina. Now she divides her time between the United States and Argentina, and travels to Asia and Europe. Winner of a Pushcart Prize, the Juniper Prize, the Great Lakes Colleges Association's New Writers Awards for Poetry, and other awards, Mộng-Lan's poetry has been nationally and internationally anthologized to include being in *Best American Poetry* and *The Pushcart Book of Poetry: Best Poems from 30 Years of the Pushcart Prize*. She is the author of eight books and chapbooks, which contain her poetry and artwork and include *Song of the Cicadas* (UMASS Press, Juniper Prize); *Why is the Edge Always Windy?* (Tupelo Press); *Tango, Tangoing: Poems & Art*; the bilingual Spanish/English edition, *Tango, Tangueando: Poemas & Dibujos* (Valiant Press); *One Thousand Minds Brimming: poems & art* (Valiant Press). Visit: www.monglan.com

NANCY GAFFIELD is a senior lecturer in Creative Writing at the University of Kent and an award-winning poet. She was born and brought up in Illinois and Colorado. Before moving to England in 1990, Nancy lived in Japan and Egypt. Her collection *Tokaido Road* (CB editions 2011) relates to the woodblock print series "53 Stations of the Tokaido Road," by the Japanese artist Hiroshige. The collection was nominated for the Forward First Collection Prize and won the Aldeburgh First Collection Prize (2011). It has been described as "a fascinating fusion of Western and Eastern art by someone who is respectful of both." Her second collection, *Continental Drift*, was published by Shearsman in 2014. Nancy was commissioned by Okeanos Ensemble to write the libretto for *Tokaido Road: A Journey After Hiroshige* (Shearsman 2014) based on her poetry collection. The chamber opera, composed by Nicola LeFanu, premiered at the Cheltenham Music Festival in July 2014 before touring to other high-profile venues throughout the UK. Nancy has also published three pamphlets: *Owhere* (Templar 2012), *Zyxt* (Oystercatcher 2015), and *Meridian* (Oystercatcher 2016).

NATHANAËL* is the (self-)translating author of a score and five books written in English or in French, including *Feder, a scenario* (2016), *Asclepias: The Milkweeds* (2015) and *Sotto l'immagine* (2014). Extrinsic translations include works by Édouard Glissant, Hilda Hilst, and Danielle Collobert. Nathanaël's translation of *The Mausoleum of Lovers* by Hervé Guibert was recognized by fellowships from the PEN American Center and the Centre National du Livre de France. Nathanaël's works are published in the United States, France, and Québec. She lives in Chicago. (*All references to a prior name are obsolete.)

Born in Toronto, Canada, **NORMA COLE** has been living in San Francisco, California, since 1977. Some of her books of poetry are *Spinoza in Her Youth, Natural Light, Where Shadows Will, Win These Posters and Other Unrelated Prizes Inside* and most recently *Actualities*, a collaboration with the painter Marina Adams. A translator of French poetry, she has translated Danielle Collobert's *It Then*, Fouad Gabriel Naffah's *The Spirit God and the Properties of Nitrogen*, Jean Daive's *A Woman With Several Lives* and his first book, *White Decimal*. Cole is also a visual artist.

PATRICIA DEBNEY was born in Texas and moved to the UK in 1988, soon after graduating from Oberlin College. Her first collection, *How to Be a Dragonfly* (Smith Doorstop Books, 2005), won the 2004 Poetry Business Book & Pamphlet Competition. Her second collection, *Littoral* (Shearsman Books, 2013) was written in a beach hut, and her chapbook (*Gestation*, Shearsman Books, 2014) and full collection *Baby* (Liquorice Fish Books, 2016) address ageing, dementia and mental illness. Her work has appeared in Forward anthologies, the Sunday Times, *Tears in the Fence*, and most recently the Best British Poetry of 2015. A former Canterbury Laureate, she is Reader in Creative Writing at the University of Kent.

WANG PING was born in Shanghai and came to the USA in 1986. Her publications include *Flying: Life of Miracles along the Yangtze and Mississippi*, memoir (forthcoming from Calumet Press), *Ten Thousand Waves*, poetry book from

Wings Press, 2014, *American Visa* (short stories, 1994), *Foreign Devil* (novel, 1996), *Of Flesh and Spirit* (poetry, 1998), *The Magic Whip* (poetry, 2003), *The Last Communist Virgin* (stories, 2007), all from Coffee House, *New Generation: Poetry from China Today*, 1999 from Hanging Loose Press, *Flash Cards: Poems by Yu Jian*, co-translation with Ron Padgett, 2010 from Zephyr Press. *Aching for Beauty: Footbinding in China* (2000, University of Minnesota Press, 2002 paperback by Random House) won the Eugene Kayden Award for the Best Book in Humanities. *The Last Communist Virgin* won the 2008 Minnesota Book Award and Asian American Studies Award.

RACHEL TZVIA BACK – poet, translator and literary scholar – was born in Buffalo, NY. After a childhood of moving back and forth between the US and Israel, she returned to Israel to stay in 1982. Since 2000, she has been living in the Galilee, where her paternal great great great grandfather settled in the early 1800s. Back's full length poetry collections include *Azimuth, On Ruins & Returns* and *A Messenger Comes (Elegies)*. Her translations of pre-eminent Hebrew poets include *Lea Goldberg: Selected Poetry & Drama; Night, Morning: Selected Poems of Hamutal Bar Yosef; With an Iron Pen: Twenty Years of Hebrew Protest Poetry;* and *In the Illuminated Dark: Selected Poems of Tuvia Ruebner*. She has been the recipient of various awards and grants, including the Dora Maar Brown Fellowship and a PEN Translation grant.

ROSMARIE WALDROP was born in Kitzingen am Main, Germany, in 1935 and attended the Universities of Würzburg, Freiburg, Aix-en-Provence, and Michigan (Ph.D. 1966). She lives in Providence, RI, where she co-edits Burning Deck Press with Keith Waldrop. Her books of poetry include *Driven to Abstraction, A Key Into the Language of America, Split Infinites, Blindsight, Love Like Pronouns,* the trilogy *Curves to the Apple (The Reproduction of Profiles, Lawn of Excluded Middle, Reluctant Gravities),* and *Gap Gardening: Selected Poems*. She has also published two novels *(The Hanky of Pippin's Daughter* and *A Form/of Taking/It All)* and 2 books of essays *(Dissonance (If You Are Interested)* and *Lavish Absence: Recalling and Rereading Edmond Jabès)*. She translates from French (Edmond Jabès, Jacques Roubaud, Emmanuel Hocquard) and German (Friederike Mayröcker, Elke Erb, Ernst Jandl, Oskar Pastior, Ulf Stolterfoht, et al.).

RULA JURDI was born in Venezuela, grew up in Lebanon, and moved to the US at the age of 23. She has been living in Montreal, Canada, during the last ten years and she teaches Islamic History at McGill University. She writes poetry primarily in Arabic, but has written a few poems in English. Several of her poems appeared in Arab journals such as *al-Tariq* and *al-Adab*. Her two poetry collections were warmly received by critics. A number of her poems have been translated into English by Michelle Hartman and into French by poet Nadine Ltaif, and they have appeared in *Les carnets d'Ishtar, Jadaliyya,* and *ArabLit.*

SAFAA FATHY was born in Egypt but now lives in France. She obtained her PhD from the Sorbonne in 1993. She was a program director at the International College of Philosophy. She is a poet, filmmaker and essayist. Her most recent films are *Mohammad saved from the waters* and *Derrida's elsewhere.* She also makes film poems, such as *Nom à la mer* and *Hidden Valley.* Jacques Derrida, with whom she co-authored a book, *Tourner les mots au bord d'un film,* also prefaced her plays *Terror* and *Ordeal.* Her latest published collections of poems are *A name in a bottle at the sea* and *Revolution goes through walls* (English translation is forthcoming). Her most recent essays are *Scream, see and believe,* and *The secret in the image.*

SASCHA AURORA AKHTAR is a trans-race, multi-dimensional, sub rosa poeto-bot. She was patented in Pakistan. Had upgrades in pre- 9/11 U.S.A. Was released onto shelves in the U.K. Her roboto-poetics have been widely anthologized and translated into Armenian, Portuguese, Galician, Russian, Dutch, and Polish. Anthologies include *Cathecism: Poems for Pussy Riot* (English Pen, 2012) and *Out of Everywhere* (Reality Street, 2015). She has also been part of poetry protests – *Against Rape* (Peony Moon, 2014), *Solidarity Park Poetry – Poems for the Turkish resistance* (Ed. 2013). Her most recent collection is *199 Japanese Names for Japanese Trees* (Shearsman, 2016).

SHARMILA COHEN is originally from New York and currently lives in Berlin. She initially moved on Fulbright Scholarship to complete project involving poetry in translation and now works as a freelance writer, translator, and editor. Along with Paul Legault, she founded and still co-runs the translation press Telephone Books. Her poetry and translations can be found in *Harper's Magazine, Circumference: Poetry in Translation,* and *Epiphany,* among other places.

SHEIDA MOHAMADI, poet, fiction writer, and journalist, was born in Tehran, Iran, and now lives in Irvine, California. She was the first Poet in Residence at the Jordan Center for Persian Studies at the University of California, Irvine, for the 2015-2016 academic year and Poet in Residence at University of Maryland in 2010. Sheida has been a member of Pen Center USA since 2010. She published four books. Her first book, a work of lyrical prose titled *Mahtab Delash ra Goshud, Banu!* (The Moonlight Opened its Heart, Lady!), came out in Tehran in 2001 and her second, a novel titled *Afsaneh-ye Baba Leila* (The Legend of Baba Leila), was published in Tehran in 2005. Her third book, *Aks-e Fowri-ye Eshqbazi* (The Snapshot of Lovemaking), is a collection of poems published underground in Tehran, 2007, and republished 2012. Sheida's next collection of poems, *Yavashhaye Ghermez* (Crimson whispers) was published in Paris in 2015. Her Poems have been translated into English, French, Arabic, Czech, Germany, Turkish, Kurdish, and Swedish.

Born in Seoul, Korea, now living in Minneapolis, **SUN YUNG SHIN** is the author of a book of prose *Unbearable Splendour* (Coffee House Press, 2016) and two books of poetry *Rough, and Savage,* and *Skirt Full of Black* (Coffee House Press, 2007, 2012); editor of two anthologies of essays on race *A Good Time for the Truth: Race in Minnesota* (Minnesota Historical Society Press, 2016) and *Outsiders Within: Writing on Transracial Adoption* (South End Press, 2006); and author of a bilingual Korean/English fiction book for children, *Cooper's Lesson* (Lee and Low Books, 2004).

TSITSI JAJI was born on a small mission station in Zimbabwe and spent most of her childhood in Harare before attending college in the U.S., where she currently resides. She has published a chapbook, *Carnaval,* which appears in the set of *Seven New Generation African Poets* (Slapering Hol, 2014). Her first full-length collection, *Beating the Graves,* was named runner up for the Sillerman First Prize and will be published by University of Nebraska Press in 2017. She is also an associate professor of English at Duke University and has published a scholarly book entitled *Africa in Stereo: Modernism, Music and Pan-African Solidarity* (Oxford University Press). She has lived briefly in France, South Africa, and Senegal in the course of her academic research.

YUKO OTOMO is a visual artist & a bilingual (Japanese & English) poet/writer. She was born in Sasebo, Nagasaki, Japan, 1950. She moved to NYC in 1979 where she still lives. She has read in various venues, such as the Poetry Project @ St. Mark's, Tribes Gallery, Bowery Poetry Club, Issue Project Room, The Stone, ABC No Rio, PS1, The Queens Museum, CUNY Graduate Ctr, The Shed Space, Smack Mellon in NYC, as well as in France, Germany, and Japan. Her publications include "Garden: Selected Haiku" (Beehive Press, reissued by Sisyphus Press), "Sunday Afternoon on the Isle of Museum" (Sisyphus Press, reissued by Propaganda Press), "PINK" (Sisyphus Press), "Small Poems" (Ugly Duckling Presse), "The Hand of The Poet" (UDP), "STUDY & other poems on art" (UDP), and "Elements" (the Feral Press). Her work also appeared in journals such as *Tribes Magazine, 6x6, Big Bridge, Long Shot, Maintenant, H.O.W. Journal, Boog City, The Unbearables Assemblage Magazine, Zen Monster* and others.

ACKNOWLEDGMENTS

ADEENA KARASICK: Earlier versions of part of this work were published as a broadside, *The Shed Space Editions*, in Spring, 2015, and as an online "Stir-Fry" vispo text constructed by Jim Andrews (http://vispo.com/StirFryTexts/adeena/index.html).

AMANDA NGOHO REAVEY: This work is an excerpt from *Marilyn*, which was published in 2015 by The Operating System, an imprint of Brooklyn Arts Press.

ANGELA CARR: This selection of poetry is reprinted from *Here in There* (BookThug 2014).

ANNE TARDOS: "Efnogla 1-3" appeared in the book *Uxudo* (Tuumba Press / O Books, 1999). "Ami Minden" appeared in the book *Cat Licked the Garlic* (Tsunami Editions, 1992). "Some of Them" appeared in the book *The Dik-dik's Solitude* (Granary, 2003). "Itt Pedig Hunting: Nine 122" and "Ziglio While: Nine 126" appeared in the book *NINE* (BlazeVox, 2015).

BARBARA BECK: "Heat Island" appeared in Issue 15 of *Upstairs at Duroc* in 2014.

BELLA LI: "La ténébreuse" appeared in the book *Land Before Lines*, Nicholas Walton-Healey (photographer), Melbourne: Hunter Publishers, 2014. "io sono l'amore" and "The Memory Machine Elena Obieta" appeared in *Argosy*, Sydney: Vagabond Press, 2017.

CECILIA VICUÑA: "Justice" is an excerpt altered from *Instan*, Kelsey Street Press, 2002. The "Word & Thread (Variation)" is loosely based on the book of the same title, translated by Rosa Alcalá, Morning Star Publications, Edinburgh, 1996, and fragments of *QUIPOem*, Wesleyan University Press, 1997.

CRISTINA RIVERA GARZA: "Conjuring" was published in SpiralOrb.net; "Be not terrified" was published in *New American Writing 31*.

DONNA STONECIPHER: This poetry was previously published in *Model City* by Shearsman in 2015.

ÉIREANN LORSUNG: "When I say fathers..." was first published in *The Atlas Review*. "An archaeology [W]" was first published in *Precipitat*.

FAWZIA AFZAL-KHAN: "Kiss" was published in the online journal *Sugar Mule*, 2013; "M/Other" appeared in *Asiatic* vol 3 in 2009 and "For My Daughter's Muslim Past, Cordoba" in *Tiferet*, 2006.

HAZEL SMITH: *Metaphorics* (in three parts) was published by Sydney-based publisher Giramondo as part of *Word Migrants* in March 2016.

JANE JORITZ-NAKAGAWA: Thanks to *FourW* and *Tokyo Poetry Journal* for featuring my poetry in their anthology and journal.

JENNIFER KRONOVET: A version of the essay *Fighting and Writing* appeared in the *Ottawa Poetry Newsletter* in August 2015.

LARESSA DICKEY: The poem "Sequence" appeared in issue number 43 of *Verse* in winter 2015.

LEA GOLDBERG: These poems appeared in *Lea Goldberg: Selected Poetry and Drama* (The Toby Press, 2005) and in the bilingual edition *On the Surface of Silence: The Last Poems of Lea Goldberg*, translated by Rachel Tzvia Back (Hebrew Union College Press and University of Pittsburgh Press, Spring 2017).

LISA SAMUELS: The three opening poems are from *Symphony for Human Transport*, forthcoming in 2017 with Shearsman Books (UK).

MAIRÉAD BYRNE: "Thinking of You" was published in *Decals of Desire* (October 2016). "Water" is a development of an earlier poem, "Soup," published in the *Ocean State Review* (Summer 2013). "Toronto to Boston" was published in *Throg Sludge* (September 2014).

MARCELA SULAK: "La Malinche's Love Letters to Hernando Cortes" was previously published in *Decency*, with Black Lawrence Press, 2015.

NATHANAËL: *Augustment* was previously published as a limited-edition Belladonna chapbook in December 2015.

ROSMARIE WALDROP: The 5 poems are taken from *Splitting Image* (La Laguna, Tenerife: Zasterle Press, 2005).

SAFAA FATHY: The poems are translated from: Safaa Fathy, *Revolution goes through walls*, Sharkayet, Cairo, Egypt, 2014 (English translation is forthcoming).

SHEIDA MOHAMADI: "Return from My Body's Black-and-Blue" appeared in *Atlanta Review*: Poetry from Iran, Spring-Summer 2010. "I Look at Istanbul with Drunken Ears" appeared in *City Escape*, Vol. II, 2014.

TSITSI JAJI: An earlier version of "Elections" was published in *Illuminations*, 2015.

NOTES

BELLA LI: "io sono l'amore": title and section titles are from the film *Io sono l'amore*, dir. Luca Guadagnino, 2009.

"The Memory Machine Elena Obieta": epigraph, section titles, and some phrases are from the novel *The Absent City*, Richard Piglia, trans. Sergio Waisman, London: Duke University Press, 2000.

"La ténébreuse" was written in response to a photograph taken of the author, appearing in the book *Land Before Lines*, Nicholas Walton-Healey, Melbourne: Hunter Publishers, 2014.

HAZEL SMITH: Notes: *Metaphorics*
Metaphorics is in three parts. The first section was written by cutting and pasting, with some modification, comments about metaphor from the Internet. The sources were as follows:

Against Metaphor. Undated. *State of Emergency*. http://gauchesinister.wordpress.com/2010/10/12/against-metaphor/.

AMD Pronunciation Studio. Undated. The 56 Worst Analogies from High School Papers. http://www.angmohdan.com/56-worst-analogies-high-school-papers/.

Donald Campbell and Henrik Enckell. 2005. "Metaphor and the Violent." *The International Journal of Psychoanalysis* 86 (3): 802-23.

Richard A. Fumerton.1995. *Metaepistemology and Skepticism*, Lanham: Rowman and Littlefield.

"Metaphors". Undated. 2014. *The Economist*. http://www.economist.com/style-guide/metaphors.

What Is a Metaphor? Undated. *About Education*. http://grammar.about.com/od/qaaboutrhetoric/f/faqmetaphor07.htm.

Judy Rees. Undated. The Mind Reader's Guide To Metaphor. https://www.udemy.com/the-mind-readers-guide-to-metaphor/.

Ekaterina Shutova and Tony Veale. 2014. Tutorial: Computational Modelling of Metaphor. *Conference of the European Chapter of the Association for Computational Linguistics*, University of Gothenburg, Gothenburg. http://eacl2014.org/tutorial-metaphor.

Al Vernacchio. 2012. Sex Needs a New Metaphor: Here's one. https://www.ted.com/talks/al_vernacchio_sex_needs_a_new_metaphor_here_s_one.

Mark Frank Warren. 2008. "Music as Metaphor: a Powerful Tool in Management Development". *National Farm Management Conference*, Oxford. http://www.researchgate.net/publication/235954865_Music_as_metaphor_a_powerful_tool_in_management_development.

JANE JORITZ-NAKAGAWA: I'd like to note the influence of some paintings by Japanese artist Nakamura Hiroshi on part of this work.

JENNIFER KRONOVET: All italics in the poems are from *Tao of Jeet Kune Do* by Bruce Lee.

M. NOURBESE PHILIP: Partially sourced from Wikipedia.

NORMA COLE: Partially sourced from Wikipedia. Acknowledgments – Hardie Philip-Chamberlain.

These poems are from *Local Action*, a manuscript in progress.

"Nowhere do artists and writers have power, but nowhere in the world do they have less power than in the United States." Raúl Zurita (Email correspondence, May 8, 2007, from Santiago, Chile, to Valerie Mejer.) And in "Zurita and Cormac: The Story of Our American Sentimental Education." (At *Harriet: a poetry blog*).

RULA JURDI: Ghassan Kanafani is an iconic Palestinian figure. He was a novelist and political activist assassinated with his niece by Israeli Intelligence, Mossad.

SUN YUNG SHIN: Source of epigraph: https://www.genome.gov/25020028#al-12.

WANG PING: These two lines are taken from Qu Yuan's *Zhao Hun* (Summoning of Souls) with slight moderations.

www.ingramcontent.com/pod-product-compliance
Lightning Source LLC
Chambersburg PA
CBHW020639300426
44112CB00007B/166